Global Migration and Social Change

Series Editor: **Nando Sigona**, University of Birmingham, UK and **Alexandra Délano Alonso**, The New School, US

The *Global Migration and Social Change* series showcases original research that looks at the nexus between migration, citizenship and social change.

Forthcoming in the series

Migration, Crisis and Temporality at the Zimbabwe–South Africa Border: Governing Immobilities
Kudakwashe Vanyoro

Out now in the series

Social Networks and Migration: Relocations, Relationships and Resources
Louise Ryan

Mediated Emotions of Migration: Reclaiming Affect for Agency
Sukhmani Khorana

The EU Migrant Generation in Asia: Middle-Class Aspirations in Asian Global Cities
Helena Hof

Migration, Health, and Inequalities: Critical Activist Research across Ecuadorean Borders
Roberta Villalón

Find out more at
bristoluniversitypress.co.uk/global-migration-and-social-change

Global Migration and Social Change

Series Editor: **Nando Sigona**,
University of Birmingham, UK and **Alexandra Délano Alonso**, The New School, US

Find out more at
bristoluniversitypress.co.uk/global-migration-and-social-change

THE GERMAN MIGRATION INTEGRATION REGIME

Syrian Refugees, Bureaucracy, and Inclusion

Morgan Etzel

BRISTOL
UNIVERSITY
PRESS

First published in Great Britain in 2023 by

Bristol University Press
University of Bristol
1–9 Old Park Hill
Bristol
BS2 8BB
UK
t: +44 (0)117 374 6645
e: bup-info@bristol.ac.uk

Details of international sales and distribution partners are available at bristoluniversitypress.co.uk

© Bristol University Press 2023

British Library Cataloguing in Publication Data
A catalogue record for this book is available from the British Library

ISBN 978-1-5292-3123-6 hardcover
ISBN 978-1-5292-3127-4 ePub
ISBN 978-1-5292-3128-1 ePdf

Cover design: Andrew Corbett
Front cover image: Abdulazez Dukhan/azyeux.com
Bristol University Press use environmentally responsible print partners.
Printed and bound in Great Britain by CPI Group (UK) Ltd, Croydon, CR0 4YY

FSC
www.fsc.org
MIX
Paper | Supporting
responsible forestry
FSC® C013604

For Marli

Contents

Glossary of German Terms

Anerkannte Flüchtlinge	Recognized refugees according to asylum law § 60 Abs. 1 Aufenth G.
Asylberechtigte	The original law for granting asylum in Germany based on Article 16a of the German Basic Law
Asylbewerber	A person applying for asylum
Aufenthaltstitel	Residency permit
Ausländerbehörde	German Foreigner's Office
Aussiedler	Former German repatriates
Duldung	Tolerated foreigner with limited legal status, designated for deportation
Fehlbeleger	Registered German refugee still living in Emergency housing
Immobilienmaklermakler (Makler)	Real estate agent
Kommunen	Cities, towns and unincorporated areas
Länder	German Federal State
Leitkultur	'Leading Culture', the concept of cultural model based on German and European Enlightenment values

Migrationshintergrund	Migrant background: German residents and citizens with at least one parent not born in Germany
Niederlassungserlaubnis	Permanent residence permit
Parallelgesellschaft	Parallel societies
Subsidiär Schutzberechtigte/ Subsidiären Schutz	Subsidiary protected refugees with fewer rights than officially recognized refugees
Widerrufsverfahren	Removal procedure: encompassing several bureaucratic layers of deportation and loss of status

Acknowledgements

Writing this book has been a journey along which I have encountered many individuals and institutions to whom and which I will be forever grateful and indebted, beginning with my many Syrian collaborators. Anas in particular has become a great friend since we met at the beginning of this project. He was always patient and open with me, allowing me to get to know his family and friends over the years. The names of the participants in my research are anonymized throughout this book, so I cannot name them here, but I am so thankful to them for allowing me into their homes, and for the many meals and pots of tea shared.

My research would also not have been possible without the support of many institutions that allowed me through their doors. First, thanks to the Jobcenter München, Zentraleinheit Flüchtlinge (ZEF) and the Jobcenter Kassel, Flucht und Migration 477 for transparency and allowing me to spend so much time with the employees there. The asylum office at Ausländerbehörde München (the Foreigner's Office, Munich) and the Munich branch of the German Employment Agency were also very generous in allowing me to conduct interviews with their employees. The offices of the aid agency Caritas in Munich and Saarbrücken were also generous with their time.

The research for this book was made possible through my doctoral grant from the Hans-Böckler Foundation, which not only provided generous funding for my research project but is also one of the most important social and economic research centres in Germany, which I was proud to be a part of over the years. I am also thankful for the Böckler Foundation's additional funding that allowed me to fund small work group with a focus on forced migration alongside my colleagues Kim Viktoria Bräuer-Zeltner and Stephanie Warkentin. Thank you for all your feedback and insight. I was lucky enough to be mentored by Eberhard Raithelhuber, who was also supportive and informative to my work throughout my stipend period and remained a mentor afterwards.

I was based at the Department of Social and Cultural Anthropology, Ludwig Maximilian University of Munich for the duration of my research and am indebted to the supervisors of my research, Professor Magnus Treiber and Professor Martin Sökefeld. When I had almost given up trying to find a supervisor in Germany to support my project, Magnus took it on and was there challenging me, but also giving me the freedom to find the right path and supporting me when I found it.

I also spent time as a Visiting Fellow at the Refugee Studies Centre at the University of Oxford for a term and benefited from the particular insight of Ruben Andersson, Naohiko Omata, Nando Sigona and Derya Ozkul. I am thankful for the well-organized programme that Mathew J. Gibney, Tom Scott-Smith and Alexander Betts made an enriching environment to work in. My cohort Diego Caballero Vélez, Daniel Howden and Kate Ogg made a great group to be there with: thank you for your support.

I am also thankful I was able join the PhD Summer School of the International Migration, Integration and Social Cohesion in Europe (IMISCOE) in 2018, at which I benefited from the mentorship of many colleagues and experts, particularly Anastasia Christou and Eleonore Kofman, who became valued mentors to me. I presented the research found in this book at several conferences and am particularly thankful for the feedback during those organized by the European Association of Social Anthropologists (EASA) and Netzwerk Fluchtforschung.

When I went to Turkey in 2015, I was finishing my master's in Peace, Conflict and Development at the Jaime | University I, which was supported through a Rotary Global Scholars Grant. I am grateful to have met my friend Hassan Almossa who hosted us there and still operates the Kids Paradise charity aiding people in Syria.

There are those who have been both great friends and essential colleagues, including Daniel Kunzelmann, Michael Mögele, Andreas Hackl and especially my close friend Vivian Schönbächler. I also would not have been able to begin my research in Turkey without the generous support of the Rotary Foundation of Downtown Los Angeles during my master's study in Spain, from which I was still getting support during my initial visit to Turkey in 2015.

I am endlessly thankful for the support of my family. Marli, Jan, Pedro and Pam have been there from start to finish in this endeavour.

This book is the edited version of my PhD dissertation that was defended in 2020 at Ludwig-Maximilians-Universität in Munich. I am thankful for the support given to me by the university during my research.

Introduction

Transnational refugee research in crisis

This was not the image I knew of refugees of a civil war. Refugees of a war brutally fought over the last four years living in Turkey should be living in camps, receiving some kind of aid from internationally organized bodies like the UN Refugee Agency (UNHCR) or the International Red Cross (IRC). This was my naïve thought when I arrived in Reyhanli in 2015.

Unlike the bustling tourist cities and modern metropolises, Reyhanli resembled a dusty backwater, a city expanding for all the wrong reasons. The city had gone from a small town of tens of thousands with a Turkish majority before 2011 to a bustling city with apartments being constructed at an exponential rate and a growing Syrian majority population by the time I arrived there. This was the summer of 2015 and Turkey was hosting over a million Syrian refugees. Like those in Reyhanli, the vast majority lived in urban centres and could only survive in Turkey earning income through backbreaking labour or savings they brought with them from Syria. Meanwhile, on the borders of Europe, a 'crisis' was being forged both internally and externally.

I had spent the summer working on a farm in southern Italy while writing my master's thesis and wanted to go over land to Turkey, where I would meet four other student colleagues from the university. There, we conducted a workshop during August to teach refugees of the Syrian conflict photojournalism and documentary filmmaking with an emphasis on peace building. In July, I took the ferry from Bari to Albania and spent a few weeks travelling up the idyllic Adriatic coast. The atmosphere across the Adriatic region was relaxed, with little public acknowledgement or discourse about the rising daily count of refugee deaths in the eastern Mediterranean. The deaths of migrants were nothing new in recent history (UNHCR 2019).

I realized that I would not have the time needed to go by land the rest of the way as planned, so I took a flight from Tirana to Istanbul. At Istanbul Airport I was stopped by the plain-clothes Turkish security forces, who asked where I would be travelling to. In ignorance I replied that I would be travelling to Hatay. I was immediately taken to an interrogation room and questioned about my journey. 'There are many young Europeans going there to join ISIS right now. You want to join ISIS?',[1] one of the officers asked. They did not believe my response and interrogated me in the makeshift security room for the next few hours before finally letting me take my flight to Hatay. They explained that because of my beard and long hair, I looked like a foreign radical heading off to join a civil war. I only convinced them I was not by showing them my Facebook messages and some of my work as a photographer and filmmaker. I finally arrived in the capital of the Hatay region, Antakya, and met my colleagues, the host organization and our driver. We travelled in the dead of night overland with the Syrian border in view of the small village of Reyhanli.

Over the course of the next month, we carried out the workshop project and several other small projects that came up with aid organizations. As the days passed, two things became more apparent after spending time with aid agencies, many young men and several families broken apart by war. First, life in Turkey was unsustainable for Syrians at that time. And, second, there was nothing I could say, either morally or rationally, to convince the young men not to travel to Europe as the number of Mediterranean boat crossings and deaths soared.

In the last part of our workshop, the participants were assigned to find a subject around which to develop a documentary or photo story. One group decided to film a story about their friend who lost his arm filming the war in Syria when a rocket hit the car he was filming in; they wanted to tell a story about his road to recovery and building a life after the injury. There were several other stories about families that suffered serious injuries from the war and needed medical care. The last short documentary was about how Syrians' access to higher education in Turkey excluded refugees. This was before legal changes in 2016,[2] which increased the rights of Syrians. Nonetheless, Turkey's asylum policy is not part of the general 1951 Refugee Convention and therefore did not officially recognize or give wider rights to refugees coming from outside of Europe (Ihlamur-Öner 2013). Because of this, there was a deep sense of uncertainty and temporality in Reyhanli.

The city of Reyhanli, which is only a few kilometres from the Syrian border, is part of the larger province of Hatay, which up until 1938 was part of Syria and has lasting emotional and symbolic ties to Syrians who were aware of the history in the region (Chatty 2017). However, there was a regional differentiation in the reaction to the flows of Syrian refugees since 2011, who were called 'guests' by the Turkish government. In Antakya there were rumours of a deep resentment towards Syrians – it is known as a more nationalistic city, but in Reyhanli there was a sense of a new city evolving, albeit a new city that was steeped in the exploitation of the most vulnerable. My university colleague Vivian, who organized the workshop with me, had been there the summer before. 'There are so many new flats here!', she told me. 'And of course, they take advantage of the desperation and make the price really high for Syrians, plus sometimes they are forced to pay up to six months' rent in advance just to get a flat.' Even at the closest point of flight from Syria, just a short drive from Idlib in Syria, the resources required to survive were enormous, and families were increasingly separated by borders and cities.

One smouldering afternoon, the temperatures reached 45°C and I stood outside with all the men under the shade of the workshop building during our break. We took our cigarette breaks after the morning session, but the two women in the workshop, one wearing a niqab, of course could not join us. So, it was our trainers, Vivian, Edgard, Angela and Irene with all the men – it was a time for us all to talk more freely.

One of the Syrians from Aleppo, Hussain, lit a new cigarette with the old one. 'Before the revolution, I never smoked before', he said. 'Me too', said Hassan from Idlib. Hassan had come from Syria after the border with Turkey closed and was shot at by Turkish border police as he crossed. 'They just shoot at you directly?', I asked. 'No, they make a kind of warning shot in the air, then if you still run, they will try to shoot at you', he explained. I felt terrible that he had literally risked his life to come to this little workshop, suddenly feeling inadequate in my presentations. 'But you should come back with me. Come to Idlib, you will be my guest', Hassan said. At the time, Idlib was controlled by the Islamist, al-Qaeda-like group al-Nusra Front (later Jabhat Fatah al-Sham). 'Don't worry, them and the FSA [Free Syrian Army] will give us protection if we say we are journalists', he said. When asked about the barrel bombs from the Assad regime, he shrugged and said that there was nothing he could do to protect me from that. The other men changed the conversation to potential travel to Europe. Some wanted to cross over to Greece and go to Sweden. No one wanted to stay in Southern Europe or France. But maybe Germany?

I hesitantly asked if they would be worried about crossing the sea and cautioned that they would face other problems, discrimination, anti-immigrant violence or difficulty finding work, but then I remembered the previous night.

We had been invited to Anas' house for tea. His second-youngest brother served us tea, his oldest brother was there to visit from Istanbul, and his other five sisters and two brothers were still in Syria – his father was killed early in the war by ISIL. He would always joke to me: 'We are less like siblings and more like a football team.' While I sat and drank endless amounts of extremely sweet and dark tea, I looked at Anas, at the time 20 years old, his brother, 18 years old, and the three other young men who were part of our workshop, and I thought about their fractured families and their lack of opportunity here. What could I, in such a privileged position, advise them to do? To not take a gamble on the journey to Europe in the face of hopelessness?

Although I have begun here with a reflection on a time of 'crisis' and war, this book is about what happens after refugees have made it somewhere 'safe'. But I introduced this through my early experience with Syrians on the Turkish border because this book is also about what is perceived as a linear journey from refugee in transit to refugee settled and then refugee 'integrated'. However, it is not a linear journey. It is cyclical, something that returns continually to its point of origin and at various stages of its process. Migration is more often than not a transnational process – at times both or either physically and existentially. After now having spent years with some of the participants, I see that it is the struggle of the modern anthropologist to capture these processes of multiple locations in a physical and existential sense (Hannerz 2003; Jackson 2005; Andersson 2014; Cabot 2019), and even more so to create an explanatory framework that outlines something that could be referred to as 'culture' (Hage 2005). So, it is at the point of origin that I begin; a point of disjointed connections, of traumatic loss both physically and emotionally, and of hope for an imagined future. For several of the people I met in Reyhanli, that imaginary became reality a few weeks after I left and they joined the hundreds of thousands who paid smugglers to arrive in Europe, many settling in Germany by choice, a few stopping at the Greek border by force and others arriving in Germany by chance.

This book is mostly a positive account of new arrivals making their way. However, the critical focus is what occurs under the surface: how the mechanisms of the state may have failed refugees or how the discrete functions of German social fields are exclusionary to the refugee, no matter what level of requirements they fulfil. Finally, it is critical of the forced nature of this hegemonic relationship between asylum seekers and the administrative state. Nonetheless, at the forefront of all of these themes is the modern European policy on migration – particularly one in the wake of the broader rejection of multiculturalism in favour of the more tangible term of integration. Integration became the cornerstone of migration policy based in the post-9/11 world in which those perceived to be (by choice) living on the peripheries of society must be integrated to the whole of a unified national society. And thus, beginning in 2000,

Germany reflected the sentiment of other European nations by adopting a migration policy based on rewards for 'good integration' and becoming a 'good immigrant'. The policy was unfortunately built on two lies: first, that there could be an imaginary society into which immigrants could integrate (Schinkel 2017); and, second, that idea that migrants of colour do not face forms of discrimination, racism and structural exclusion. I see integration as a placeholder for a neoliberal immigration policy that is based on welfare chauvinist notions, which instead of developing a positive relationship between newcomers and the bureaucratic state drives distrust in the plurality of modern democratic values and principals. In the end, it is a story I hope to tell. One framed a crisis of individuals but in the end proved how even those in the most ideal situation to succeed in such state interventions succeeded because of factors that were only marginally influenced by state-mandated integration.

This is if anything a story of the enormity of challenges, emotional 'bending' and morphing refugees must face and undertake to retain their core identity through all the reconstitution necessary to inevitably escape the constructed person and become born anew as a participating member of 'society'. The performance that refugees undertake in attempting to construct and reconfigure their *identities*, a subject discussed in terms of *governmentality* (Brettell and Sargent 2006) and more recently in terms of *cultural citizenship* (Tuckett 2018), I consider to be a step beyond an approach that encompasses both legal constraints and social imaginaries. As Gullestad (2006) noted, in what may seem to be an obvious observation, nations use language and symbolic gestures to reassert the image of a White majority, which in turn enforces the exclusionary nature of the *nation*. This was against the backdrop of the collective decision of European governments to move away from *multiculturalism* to address immigrant populations in the early 2000s, and adopt a policy of *integration* that remains the ideological framework for nations to consider foreigners. Among critical perspectives that continue to analyse the way in which Western countries institutionalized who belongs and who does not, the work of Bridget Anderson (2013) and Étienne Balibar (2009) may best articulate the interplay between *the state, the people* and *the social imaginary*. The debate about how powerful European nations have redefined inclusiveness based on the conditionality of integration policy has continued to be a divisive issue among scholars, which has made addressing integration policy the focus of extensive research (Joppke 2007; Paulle and Kalir 2014; Abadi et al 2016; Schinkel 2017; Favell 2019). Some scholars have taken up these challenges and have focused on the experience of precarious migrants from an anthropological perspective, yet have avoided a focus on integration itself (Cabot 2017; Tuckett 2018). Alternatively, this book is centred on the critical view of integration, one that acknowledges that the very idea that migrants need to be integrated is an 'ahistorical' vision of 'imagined societies' (Goldberg 2015; Schinkel 2017). Yet, integration remains a central focus of the book without debating the dubious validity of the prospect of an individual *integrating* into a *society*. Instead, this book will outline what impact these 'philosophies of integration' and integration policies have on refugees in Germany.

Finally, the word *integration* is included in the title of this book, I would like to make the point clear from the outset that the term 'integration', which is often associated with other words like *assimilation* or *incorporation* in academic discourse, describes the German government integration programme and the a reification of this idea among refugees and state bureaucracies. This is not an attempt to sidestep the ongoing and convoluted discourse on integration, but rather to flip it on its head, making the experience of refugees the centre of the study.

What is an integration regime?

So, if I am not interested, as so many have been, in measuring (Crul, Schneider and Frans 2012; Heckmann 2015; Degler and Liebig 2017; SVR 2019) or critically analysing *integration* as a policy or social framework (Favell 2013; Hadj Abdou 2014; Joppke 2017; Hinger and Schweitzer 2020), why add it into the central framework of the book? In researching European migration today, integration becomes impossible to avoid, not least because it is the foundation upon which refugees maintain and improve their legal status in European countries. Nonetheless, the more I attempted to avoid focusing on the state's integration policies and turn the focus on the refugee, the more the attention was returned to a state-framed discourse.

In 2019, during several presentations of the results of my research at European academic institutions, I found that members of the audience continued to press the issue of integration despite my positioning of the term. 'But how do refugees themselves define integration?', one prominent migration professor of forced migration asked me. It became clear how entrenched and entangled integration was to the nexus of the academic, the legal and the social discourses. Through this entrenchment and discourses that have centred on the absurdity or 'neocolonialist' (Schinkel 2018) assumption that there is a unified society that migrant *must choose* to integrate into, the glaringly obvious point is that even if these frameworks were true, migrants of colour face discrimination at all levels of access to 'society', from asylum applications to private housing (Ehret 2002; Riedel and Schneider 2017a; Schnuck and Schöffel 2017; Dean 2020). It is precisely this casual assumption that integration is a real, tangible thing that migrants can strive towards in a meritocracy-based society that David Theo Goldberg concisely criticizes:

By contrast, integration seeks to open up to contestation norms, rules of engagement, and values of assessment. If the aim is to engage as equals, the terms of engagement must be structured to conjure confidence in their fairness. Integration gestures at the ground rules for such a negotiation. It assumes, somewhat naïvely, that if the procedures are fair, the outcomes must be just (think here of Rawls), no matter that deep existing imbalances in power and possibility will materially affect inputs and outputs in the negotiable exchange. As with assimilation, integration is more at ease with what I would call, enigmatically, racial nonracialism than with anti-racism. Racial nonracialism seeks to sidestep historical legacies of racial arrangement and injustice. (Goldberg 2015, 20)

Nonetheless, it was on this basis that Germany and other European countries formulated their integration laws, and leaders resoundingly agreed that multiculturalism had utterly failed (Weaver 2010). Here, I agree with Schinkel's (2017) critique of integration as policy, which questions whether refugees or migrants can or should integrate into a 'host society' in an idealistic sense, and furthermore wholeheartedly rejects the notion that homogeneous society exists within a nation state that would preclude the integration of a particular ethnic or national group. Nonetheless, the formulations and implications of policy are critical, whether researchers agree with them or not. The categories that researchers reproduce and are often in danger of essentializing (Dahinden, Fischer and Menet 2020) remain necessary for a critical comparison. 'This paradigm of normalized difference' (Dahinden 2016, 2210) is essential to migration research. As Hadj Abdou notes: 'Migration research is constituted by this politically constructed logic of migration as anomaly. Without it, there would be nothing such as migration and immigrant integration studies' (Hadj Abdou 2019, 3).

I understand integration to denote the German government's prioritization of language learning, formal education and secure employment as the hallmarks of the 'good' refugee (Etzel 2021). Such critiques are necessary to make clear a position on the issue, but do little to operationalize the problem. Foucault helps to clarify the discourse by explaining that to be radically critical is not to point out what is wrong with the current situation, but rather to get to the root of normative realities and 'flush out' where such thought is rooted, which is essential for the transformation of such thought (Foucault 1988, 154). Syrian refugees arrived in Germany unaware that a regime of government-mandated integration programmes would in many ways shape their experience. Since the primary interest of this book is that of the refugee experience, I focus on the question of how refugees navigate this German integration regime, not necessarily the experience of street-level bureaucrats implementing such policy. Furthermore, both the German refugee integration regime and the refugees themselves are not static; they are influenced by their environments and are dynamically changing. So, how do both negotiate their realities in practice, influencing each other over time? In the case of refugees, how do their transnational lives shape the way in which they navigate German bureaucracies?

First, there are two concepts to highlight here in relation to navigation. One is the use of the term 'navigation'. *Social navigation* is a concept developed by Henrik Vigh, using his analysis of youth in a post-war context navigate 'through attentiveness to the way in which agents seek to draw and actualise their life trajectories in order to increase their social possibilities and life chances in a shifting and volatile social environment' (Vigh 2006, 11). Vigh (2010) goes on to describe the process of navigation as something that is not done over or around, but *through* volatile environments. The extremes of youth in war do not apply particularly to my research; rather, Syrian refugees socially navigate the *immediate* and the *imagined*, which is to say they use a sense of dual temporality to imagine a future in order to navigate the uneven accountability of the German administrative state. Similarly, Tuckett (2015) uses the concept of navigation to address the way in which migrants navigate the Italian *documentation regime* to formulate modes of rule bending and informal approaches in order to gain a more secure legal status. From an existential perspective, some of these notions can also be found in Michael Jackson's explanation of control of one's self-determination – a 'governance and adjustment between the self and other' (Jackson 1998, 18): 'Should self and other become so polarized and estranged that there is a complete breakdown of dialog between them ... the existential loser has recourse to extreme counteractive measures to break the deadlock, to make good his or her loss, and revitalize the social system' (Jackson 1998, 19).

In other words, when faced with a feeling that both physical and symbolic actions are irrelevant because of unequal power positioning, the alternative is to act informally to circumvent unequal systems of power. As Treiber (2014) notes, this is a tool for those who may have exhausted all other options in a state of crisis. Alternatively, I argue in this book that this kind of navigation does not always produce positive results in the context that some authors present. Many of the informal ways in which refugees navigate the integration regime highlight the failures of the state rather than refugee ingenuity.

Finally, the use of the term 'regime' is too often applied as an *a priori* concept in many disciplines relating to refugee and migration studies. I distinguish my use of the term and narrow its application by applying a governmentality approach to regimes (Horvath, Amelina and Peters 2017). In a similar manner to the way in which Neilson and Mezzadra (2013) have used 'regime' as a framework for understanding borders and global inequalities, I use the term 'integration regime' to explain the way in which integration law is contested by both the refugee and the local administrative state. In other words, the state cannot be rarefied into a powerful single entity, but is rather negotiated at the local level with influences shaped by norms developed from an overlapping and intertwined mix of social and legal entanglements, as well as national and transnational elements. Furthermore, the regime is *supranational* because it negotiates the tensions between EU, international, German and local law.[3] Alternatively, the integration regime, like the migration regimes or *regimes of mobility* (Glick Schiller and Salazar 2013), is a way to consider integration both as a policy *and* an act viewed by bureaucrats and other actors as something that people *do*. However, it is also something that develops over time in the refugee imaginary as a way to evaluate their peers and incorporate their own principles of integration imaginaries. By using a *regimes* approach to integration, I reveal that integration is a policy that has various tools required to operationalize and reify it into action, and at the same time integration is something reconceptualized by those essentialized as the *outsider*, the *migrant* or the *refugee*. In short, it takes many forms and exists in and beyond governance and governmentality.

Conflicts and crisis

In the opening section I rather casually framed the so-called refugee crisis as something created by European states. The crisis from a European perspective emerged out of many factors, but also two events that overlapped in 2015: the violent conflict in Syria, and a European border and migration regime that had in recent years become an *industry*. The research presented in this book is about what happens after a crisis. However, integration is only one aspect of the European migration control system that was developed over the previous decades to keep people out. When a civil war erupted in Syrian in 2011 following the 'Arab Spring', millions of refugees flowed into neighbouring Lebanon, Turkey, and Jordan. Only when migrants began crossing the Mediterranean did the 'unprecedented' situation become a crisis from the European perspective (Crawley et al 2018). The politicization and media debates of who was a refugee and who was a migrant would have lasting implications for Syrians seeking to build a new life in Germany (Crawley and Skleparis 2018; Sigona 2018). The real crisis was indeed the Syrians and other nationals who were so desperate that they were willing to risk their lives and give large sums of money to smugglers in order to arrive in Europe.

   In one of the most comprehensive accounts and explanations of the repercussions of both the militarization and industrialization of European border protections, Andersson (2014) outlines the 'illegality industry' of the relationship between European states and North African countries, exposing a network of governments, aid agencies, activists and academics that are complicit in this industry. Along the same lines, I will not attempt to retread lines of inquiry into global inequality-driven migration, based on colonial legacies in which rich countries have long been attempting to exclude those they have previously and/or presently and directly and/or indirectly exploited (Balibar, Mezzadra and Samaddar 2012; Harding 2012; Mezzadra and Neilson 2013; Carr 2016; Tazzioli 2018). Nor do I wish to rehash the complexities of migrant routes, in which informality (Treiber 2014) and arbitrariness of controls (Fassin 2011; Tsianos and Karakayali 2010) supersede imagined legal barriers. After all, this story is about the fortunate who arrived safely in Europe, not at its periphery. However, how refugees arrived and their first experiences with the German state played a critical part in their interpretation of the social welfare state and their ability to navigate integration policy. What it means to attempt to integrate was conceived well before the so-called refugee crisis and was part of a long-term social project that helped to solidify the divided 'German identity' at the expense of the *other*.

A German migration policy in crisis

For the last two decades, and well before the long summer of migration in 2015, Germany had been attempting to reform immigration framed in a neoliberal approach to global governance.[4] Although these reforms began officially with the change in citizenship law in 1999 (Bauböck 2006), the legal changes that took place in 2005 resulted in a massive welfare state reform. These included the so-called Hartz IV reforms (that drastically reduced unemployment benefits) and the first German immigration law (*Zuwanderungsgesetz*) that altered the treatment of migrants, both of which are now intrinsically tied to the integration regime (Geddes and Scholten 2016). Critical to both was the concept of *fördern und fordern*, which translates as something like 'support and challenge'. Historical legacies of racism also shaped the legal approach to migration, where alongside every liberal step towards the inclusion of migrants, a reactive response based in anti-immigrant sentiment was also used to tighten migration controls and develop more conditions for migrant inclusion (Faist 1995; Aybek 2012). For instance, after a long debate on citizenship policy, legislators passed a reform in 2000 that outlawed dual citizenship, particularly aimed to force Turkish citizens to choose between German or Turkish to avoid 'divided loyalties' (Partridge 2012). This compromise between liberal and conservative governing parties that continued for the following years followed a post-war notion that *wir sind kein Einwanderungsland* (we are not a country of immigration) and moved towards an acceptance that Germany not only was a country of immigration, but that it also needed migrants for economic gains and competition (Geddes and Scholten 2016; Danielak 2019).

In many ways, the German government's early migration policy institutionalized racism in the 1960s by recruiting labour under the so-called 'guest worker' programme for only the lowest areas of the labour market for foreigners from Greece, Italy, Turkey, Morocco and Tunisia, freeing up high-paid work for German citizens (Lewicki 2018). The *policy narratives* (Boswell, Geddes and Scholten 2011) were framed for generations in radicalized language that in more recent years assumed a more discreet tone, using language that often emerged from university scholars as critical analysis and manipulated by right-wing populists and neo-Nazis to spread xenophobic rhetoric. Key to these policy narratives was the notion of 'parallel societies' (*Parallelgesellschaften*) coined by German sociologist Wilhelm Heitmeyer in 1996 (Bock 2018) to describe Turkish communities – framed in fears of rising youth Islamic extremism – that have chosen to isolate themselves, albeit on the basis of discrimination, which is causing a so-called 'disintegrating society'. Later came the term *Leitkultur* (leading culture) from another sociologist who drew upon the mythical Eurocentric Enlightenment thinking, calling for culture that can guide foreigners (Abadi et al 2016). But as Sökefeld points out, the conservative Christian Democratic Union (CDU) party sought in 2000 to form a 'Leitkulturkonzept' modelled on the notion that along with learning the German language and accepting democratic values, foreigners should accept 'Western democratic values' (Sökefeld 2004, 10). This indicates that early on in the integration debate, conservatives directly excluded Turkish Muslims from ever possibly integrating under their terms. The last neologism that has been hijacked by public figures is a 20-year-old census designation that has only recently been used to return to the notion that Germanness is something that one inherits through blood and thus true citizens of Germany are only truly German by birth (*jus sanguinis*) (Will 2019). The term *Migrationshintergrund* (migrant background) originally emerged from the 2005 German census, indicating the descendent of at least one non-German parent, but has since been applied as convolution of the ethnic blanket term used in the US: 'people of color', which in public discourse has – especially in the context of 'the Sarrazin debate' – further tied together these neologisms by both reasserting the 'post-racial' aspects of German law and making them biopolitical at the same time (Bojadžijev 2016; Will and Nowicka 2021). All of these neologisms are rooted in the German post-war public development that intrinsically tied national identity and discrimination. Since Germany was until only recently conceived of as a country of immigration, it became rather engrained that Germanness was something people were born with and thus, if discrimination occurred, it was rooted in xenophobia (*Ausländerfeindlichkeit*), not racism or other forms of discrimination. This helped to perpetuate the feeling from later generations that they were foreigners, although they were born and raised in Germany (Sadeghi 2018), which after German unification joined a rather global tradition of cultural racism (Lewicki 2018; Moffitt, Juang and Syed 2018). What is key to consider here are the foundations of integration indivisible from discrimination.

The preceding discussion outlining the historical framework of asylum and migrant rights is not intended to imply when or how asylum should be considered just or deserved. This debate can be found extensively elsewhere (Gibney 2004; 2018), along with similar debates on migrant rights, citizenship and exclusion (Castles 2000; Schierup, Hansen and Castles 2006; Mezzadra and Neilson 2013; Carr 2016; Brown 2017). Instead, I aim to present a notion that blank 'othering' for integration politics is an ahistorical approach to understanding the roots of both policy and the way in which policy can be interpreted by asylum seekers. The book will show how these shifts in social moods, or *Stimmungswechsel* (Borneman and Ghassem-Fachandi 2017; Cabot 2017), are rooted in historical treatment of migrants and shape how refugees and bureaucrats conceive of these forms of inclusion.

Legal frameworks and German Sozialpolitik

One of the key arguments of this book is against the reification of the state as a centre of power in the Foucauldian sense. In order to understand the mechanisms of bureaucracy and thus the means by which refugees navigate them, I look critically at the function of the law and its interpretation across locations; in order to address this, two approaches are necessary. First, Germany is a federal republic in which there is much room for legal interpretation at the local level, especially in the areas of culture and education; thus, there is a significant degree of regional difference when it comes to policy implementation. Second, the function of the welfare state plays a significant role in the integration regime.

On the ideological front, the introduction of integration legislation was precluded by local initiatives on integration, but after a national plan emerged, nearly every Länder (Federal State) and Kommune (Municipality) had a different integration roadmap for migrant integration (Friedrich and Waibel 2012). Additionally, regional differences in the interpretation of the law have lasting implications for refugees. This can be found as a historical issue that continues today, as noted by other research:

> Prior to 1990, most of those who met the formal requirements for naturalization could still be rejected at the discretion of bureaucrats (*Ermessen*) as 'not in the best interest of the German culture'. Further discretionary criteria imposed by local or state authorities explained enfranchisement gaps from one Bezirk [neighbourhood] to another. (Mushaben 2017, 143)

The 'discretion' of street-level bureaucrats (Lipsky 2010) at local administrations will have significant implications for the three levels of refugee experience with the bureaucratic state: asylum, integration programmes, and access to permanent residency or citizenship. I will show how the governmentality of the integration regime is visible in and outside the administrative offices of the state.

In relation to the second point, it was noted earlier that the development of a federal plan for immigration, the National Action Plan for Integration (in some official contexts called the National Integration Plan), coincided with deep cuts in welfare unemployment reforms, Hartz IV, but the slow rollback of the function of the European welfare state had already been in decline since the 1990s. Schierup, Hansen and Castles frame this issue using the term 'social exclusion', meaning that the foundations of the liberal welfare state were not attainable for a large portion of the population – a 'negation of citizenship' (Schierup, Hansen and Castles 2006, 1). Addressing the German *Sozialpolitik* (social policy),[5] which is the top-down state policy for the administrative side of the welfare state, the writers argue that the model developed from the 1950s relies on 'full employment', without which the costs of extensive social programs become unsustainable (Schierup, Hansen and Castles 2006, 143). Graeber's (2011) argument that social welfare is about debt not employment, certainly alongside the events of the so-called global financial crisis dating back to 2008 and other events in recent decades, provides good ground to reject this notion. Work by the leading labour research group in Germany, the Institute for Employment Research (IAB), shows a clearer corollary between immigration, unemployment and vacancies (Klinger and Weber 2018). In other words, the welfare state has been tied to integration law in Germany, and regular immigration and the generosity of the benefits relating to health, education and unemployment are actually a biopolitical aspect of immigration regulation: they do not create the social burden that is embedded in welfare chauvinism. Arguments made to the economic end of the spectrum involving the question of 'who pays the burden?' (Bauböck 2006) serve more of a narrative discourse than a practical interrogation of situations emerging for the impact of refugees on the stability of the welfare state. Finally, the broader framework of welfare reform can be considered in a Europe-wide conceptualization that is aimed at promoting the idea that German *Sozialpolitik* should prevent 'poverty and social exclusion' (Reis and Siebenhaar 2015, 11). This book will outline why the notion of a federally unison and equal integration programme, and the policy philosophy that refugees entering the labour market contribute to *good integration* both produce 'arbitrary outcomes' (Gupta 2012).

Constructing the field: across space and time

I must now make a rather abrupt transition from historical and theoretical perspectives to the more practical contexts of this study. When considering the constellation of bureaucracies, agents, actors and clients in the integration regime on the one side and the asylum seekers, refugees and residents on the other side, the following question emerges: how to reconcile these groups and how to access them appropriately?

As the preceding paragraph notes, researching diverse subjects using ethnographic methodologies can be rather elusive. For migration researchers, especially those focused on a similar subject matter as in this book – namely, the lives of those settling in Europe – more conventional research has benefited from fixity in fieldwork: using a centre, a government office (Eule 2018) or an aid organization (Cabot 2014; Tuckett 2018) to access its interlocutors. However, my early access to collaborators serendipitously developed in Turkey and my work traced them through their journey to Germany. My fieldwork did not emerge out of any kind of fixed location; rather, I continued to follow my collaborators as they moved to new locations in order for the work to evolve. In many ways, a more progressive approach to fieldwork, expanding beyond the fixity and the othering that led to the so-called turn in anthropology, is what Ulf Hannerz describes in a critique of 20th-century anthropological fieldwork:

> That field was also usually a rather fixed entity to worry about, a 'tribe', a village, some place you could get to know by covering it on foot and engaging with its people face to face. And it was self-evidently a matter of 'being there' – away, rather than 'here'. Now we do not seem to be so sure what the field is, or where it should be, if it is real or perhaps virtual, and even if there has to be one at all. (Hannerz 2010a, 59)

In addition to addressing the field differently, I was also interested in accessing the bureaucracy directly, so the fieldwork also included several bureaucratic institutions, which allowed me varying levels of access.

Several fields emerged throughout this process. On the one hand, the term *field* itself has a double meaning. First, following the work of Pierre Bourdieu, the word 'field' has several meanings that are found in my work; the first, *fields*, denotes spaces where various forms of *capital* are negotiated, exchanged and accumulated. According to Bourdieu, the state can be considered an 'administrative field' or 'field of public office' – the sector that we particularly have in mind when we speak of 'state' without further precision – which is defined by the possession of the 'monopoly of legitimate physical and symbolic violence' (Bourdieu 2014, 4). At the administrative level, the bureaucratic actors are indeed part of this field, but also, within this administrative field, a transnational social field of Syrian refugees can be found, in which street-level bureaucrats are also a part. Second, there a more the practical notion of the field, relating to the field where the empirical work is located; these are the locations, actors and collaborators that will be outlined in the following.

Accessing the field

Taking cues from Amit's (2000) notions of *constructing the field* and contemporary approaches to grounded theory (Morse 2009; Charmaz 2014), my fieldwork began in the period which I partly discussed in the Introduction of this book when reflecting on my time in Turkey in 2015. For several reasons, I moved to Germany in early 2016, which meant the refugees I knew had already gone through the asylum application process, which started towards the end of 2015; they lived in temporary housing and some had already begun to attend integration courses. In order to retrace some of the gaps in which I was not present, I applied discourse analysis[6] and narrative interviews.

When my project began, the Syrian Civil War was still being intensely fought and was increasingly complicated by various aggressors entering the conflict. ISIL militants had swept across the eastern portion of Syria, and in doing so had increased their foothold in a large oil-rich territory they had already claimed in Iraq (Al-Baalbaky and Mhidi 2018). The al-Nusra Front, an al-Qaeda associated, and what my collaborators considered a 'moderate', Islamic militant group, had also claimed territory in the region surrounding and within Idlib in the west of Syria, where several collaborators had family. Additionally, the Russian military had increased its presence along with the US as the main financial actors along with regional contrary interests, including nearly every Arab state and neighbouring Turkey (Munif 2020). The main conflict between the various factions of Syrian revolutionary fighters, the most dominant being the FSA, was soon overshadowed by the brutality and extremist ideology of ISIL. In the months before I arrived in Turkey, the last two border crossings between Syria and Turkey had been closed to civilians. Turkey already housed an estimated two million Syrian refugees, although they were designated 'guests' rather than refugees and were thus denied many of the rights outlined by the 1951 UN Refugee Convention (also known as the 1951 Convention Relating to the Status of Refugees and the 1967 Protocol). Those wishing to join family members in Turkey or make their way onwards to Europe were forced to either risk being shot by Turkish soldiers or to pay smugglers thousands of euros (Associated Press 2014).

The conditions described earlier contextualize my introduction to the collaborators I met in Reyhanli in 2015. This was also a period in which the mafia of smugglers along the Turkish coast going into the Greek islands were ineffectively contested by the EU border control apparatus Frontex, leading to an increase of thousands of deaths between 2013 and 2016 (Mandic 2017). As I observed the situation in Turkey, while teaching courses to 70 Syrian refugees, it became clear that the war in Syria would become more brutal in the future and the prospects of a continued existence in Turkey was untenable for most Syrians. Therefore, those with the financial and psycho-physical ability shared their plans with me about how they would travel to Europe in the following months, despite my attempts to forewarn them of the dangers and obstacles they would face upon arrival.

Within months of leaving Turkey, a few of my collaborators began their journey to Europe and over the following year we maintained contact until I arrived in Germany and was able to visit them. From this point, it took another year for me to gain funding for a research project and begin my fieldwork.

By beginning with Syrians who I had met and developed a relationship with previously, my research started with a deeper connection to collaborators, allowing me research inside households of traditionally modest migrant families – something normally achieved through trusted connections. Additionally, these relationships allowed me to navigate the relatively challenging aspects of working with research collaborators in urban settings. The contested multisited ethnographic approach has been adopted by migration scholars to avoid 'methodological nationalism' and as a reaction to globalization in migration research (Marcus 1995; Amelina and Faist 2012; Boccagni 2016). If transnationalism is the concept that heavily guides this work, then multisited ethnography is a good method to deploy in the field. Boccagni further elaborates on the theme: the overlap of transnationalism and multisited ethnography as a complement to each other, but also supporting Marcus' critique of the 'Malinowskian complex' in its placement of ethnographic research as one of remote exoticism, and at the same time the critique of methodological nationalism stating that: 'Both critiques highlight the implausibility of the traditional over-reliance on a bounded, territorially based, and supposedly homogeneous entity – whether a culture or a society – as a field or even as a unit of analysis' (Boccagni 2016, 4).

Boccagni further highlights that multisited research in general should not be the methodological object, but rather to investigate the multitude of relationships interacting between the *spaces* of research locations (I would also add the element of *time*).

In the case of limiting factors, subjects and sites are based on the slow development of further collaborators and access to institutions. I began where my collaborators lived and where I lived. I was guided by the work of other ethnographers of bureaucracy and migration, which was perhaps best articulated by Andersson in *Illegality Inc.* (Andersson 2014) and by

Gupta in *Red Tape* (Gupta 2012), the *traditional* ethnographic research that is conducted at *sites* does not accurately capture the diversity and challenges of current social anthropological inquiry (Amit 2003; Hannerz 2010). However, I position my fieldwork based on Andersson's notion of the 'extended field site', which on the one hand brings together diverse groups of interlocutors and on the other hand 'takes this focus on agonistic social interfaces and repeats it across diverse locales' – in other words, 'one site, many locales' (Andersson 2014, 284). This allows me to bring together Syrian refugees, German administrative bureaucrats, volunteer workers, aid workers, the German media, political actors and local public sentiment into one research frame. However, unlike work in contested areas of conflict, such as borders, researching the integration regime is as slow-moving as bureaucracy itself. There are punctuated events presented throughout the book, but it was not feasible to anticipate them and be present at all of them due to geographical and bureaucratic restrictions. Certainly, I would have enjoyed being present during the integration courses, at every important appointment for new residency or asylum, or at more meetings that refugees had with job agents. However, I was often denied access to locations in some cases and in others found that the locations were not relevant to my research questions.

For this reason, my approach of Amit's understanding of *constructing the field* applies to a great extent to my fieldwork. Although I was not immersed in my collaborators' daily lives in an extreme sense, I was reflexively immersed in the field because it is lived every day in the political, public and social reality of my personal experience as a privileged immigrant in Germany. I would also add that the work situates itself apart from current ethnographic migration research in Germany by allowing fluid sites to emerge through the movement of collaborators.

The majority of available research on German migration benefits from access to refugees or asylum seekers by using institutions to 'snowball' collaborators. The merits of this approach are demonstrated by a diversity of collaborators and consistent access to these networks (Bhimji 2016a). However, long-period ethnographic studies of Syrians in Germany since 2015, especially those with a critical ethnographic approach, are found among research within bureaucracies and framed within communal politics or local aid organizations (Hinger, Schäfer and Pott 2016; Etzold 2017; Schittenhelm and Schneider 2017; Eule et al 2019). The limited research that attempts to capture a holistic perspective (Bhimji 2016b) reveals the opportunity to present this particular period from a novel perspective. This will serve as the only completed study that traces the lives of collaborators from Turkey to Germany and through their entire experience with the German integration regime. Because I shared or had insight into their lives before migrating to Europe, I had a connection with collaborators that was returned to, in a way compressing time through experiences. We developed imaginaries of the past, future and present that would evolve throughout my project. In other words, having lived part of the migration process with collaborators, we are able to view some of the shifting existential landscapes from the same angle.

Although research may be multisited and transnational, it must consider the nation state implication on research regimes and policy, as well as the interplay between the two (Fassin et al 2015). The approach to the subject of Syrian refugees in Germany as a politically engaged issue is to commiserate with the consideration of my positioning as a researcher and the reflexive applicability of the subject.

In these terms, I acknowledge that not only do I attempt to take the perspective of Syrian collaborators, but that I also engage in the politically and socially active issues associated with controversial measures in Germany. These range from public protest to volunteer work not directly associated with but nonetheless significant to what can be considered fieldwork. It is a great resource to be able to engage in a subject with such depth, but in acknowledging this aspect, I also acknowledge my position within the integration regime.

Finally, interviews were carried out in English and German and were recorded when possible or necessary. From an anthropological purist perspective, not conducting interviews in the native language (Arabic) may be methodologically called into question. However, I would counter this with the notion that communication can be an expression of a constellation of moods, contexts and power relations. The dynamic that several collaborators began speaking English with me and later, as we together struggled to learn German and take on the nuances, inflections and regional differences in the language, produced unique outcomes to our relationship. What could be more ethnographic than being a migrant with collaborators and, over the course of years, learning to live and speak in a foreign place simultaneously?

Conclusion

Here I have presented some of the broader contexts of what will follow in this book. My approach to the field, the historical perspective of conflicts, and the development of policy alongside a theoretical understanding provide a strong foundation to the conclusions I draw from my empirical work. Since this book has followed refugees on a journey in many ways, confined to the perceived limitations of the state, I have constructed the book in a way that is in part linear and in part existentially rooted in the integration regime itself. For this reason, the book is divided into three parts.

While Part I narrates the arrival of refugees into Germany, it uses a form of discourse analysis and narrative interviews to trace Syrians' experience arriving in Germany, as well as their experiences before arriving, and how and why they decided to make such an arduous and unpredictable journey. It consists of two chapters: 'The Path to Asylum' and 'Asylum Decisions and Thereafter'. Chapter 1 addresses how the 'crisis' developed on the side of the Germans and attempts to retrace the journey of refugees arriving in a time of bureaucratic chaos and arbitrariness. In doing so, it uses many of the narrative interviews from refugees to present the context of the 'long summer of migration', as well as exploring the beginning of how obscure policy would come to shape many parts of the refugee experience in Germany. Chapter 2 outlines the bureaucratic elements of asylum and how refugees were perceived publicly on shifting ground over the course of one year. It follows a period after refugees received an asylum decision and began experiencing some of the challenges presented by the integration regime. It is framed by the prelude to officially being part of the integration regime and contextualizes how these early experiences shaped how collaborators became disillusioned with the imagined state. It also introduces aspects of localized differences in bureaucracies and refugee experience.

Part II begins from the perspective of refugees as they enter the integration regime. In the two chapters – 'Young Refugee Men: Saarbrücken' and 'Families: Osnabrück and Hameln' – the focus is on how two distinct strands of Syrians, families and young men, have access to different forms of social capital and are uniquely situated to navigate bureaucracy and social constructions. Chapter 3 is framed in the fieldwork from Saarbrücken and the particular conditions that the networks of young Syrian men faced while navigating the integration regime. The themes of housing, access to German language courses and work are explored in relation to locality. This is where collaborators began to have a feel for navigating bureaucracy and experienced difficulties as a result of previous and current conditions in the context of trauma. They navigated through their obligations for conditional inclusion, but what remained were structural problems that were overcome through the particular application of capital. Chapter 4 focuses on the lives of families living mostly in rural settings, the particular characteristics and circumstances of this group, and the key factors that help them navigate the regime. Families faced a more complicated set of institutional and family-oriented obstacles that influenced their decisions and also their relationship with the state, but the obstacles also informed the way in which they experienced discrimination in Germany.

Part III follows the potential and reality of outcomes. It deals with how the regime produced refugees that may or may not one day become 'good' citizens. Similar to the notion of 'from good refugee to good citizen', the chapter approaches the social and legal construction of the 'good refugee' in juxtaposition to the limitations imposed by both imaginaries. It includes two, briefer chapters: 'Institutionalized Integration: Munich and Kassel' and 'Pathways Forward and Pathways Uncertain'. Chapter 5 serves as a bridge between the transition from state-managed integration to independence, which means it focuses on the inner workings of agents that attempt to 'manage' and regulate refugee integration. In this chapter there is a thematic and practical shift because the empirical work is drawn from the field in the Job Centre and other German bureaucracies. The chapter also deals with the power of certain administrative centres over others, and the mismatched expectations that develop between bureaucrats and clients. Additionally, it highlights the regional differences produced through political influences in Kommune and local resources versus the contradictions of a federal vision for integration. Often, these agents are the gatekeepers whose actions influence the following chapter, exploring the outcomes that collaborators now experience. Chapter 6 is about the tensions that have emerged as refugees gain independence from the state, yet they remain excluded from many aspects of social citizenship. The second half of Chapter 6 serves as a counter to the previous chapter insofar as the collaborators featured are often fundamentally and existentially excluded from social and political life, as well as grappling with the elements of learned discrimination and institutional limitations. These final chapters are about how the premise of integration based on ideologies of meritocracy are limited in scope. The nuances of even the most 'qualified' refugees reveal institutional shortcomings and experiential traumas that have little to do with the power of state intervention on migration and integration policy.

Finally, the book closes with a look forward to the potential that this work provides in terms of envisioning a theoretical approach that bridges the two strands of reality construction and interaction between the state and groups through an ephemeral experience. It considers how a particularly large number of Syrian refugees who entered Germany in 2015 were mostly young men and the policies that developed alongside this group in order to steer the situation towards an economically beneficial outcome. It also looks forward by looking back: contextualizing the events of the COVID-19 pandemic and police violence within the current immigration policy in Germany and the experience of collaborators with this policy.

The word *integration* is now a cornerstone of political and social action – perhaps even a call to action. It is one that demands foreigners who enter a European nation conform to a certain standard of living, imagined or otherwise. It simultaneously demands that the citizenry qualify and patrol this integration of foreigners, but does not predicate a demand upon the citizenry to accommodate a foreign population. The social sciences, with a notably reluctant contribution from social anthropologists, have long debated how to conceive of the incorporation of 'migrants' into a 'foreign' nation state. In the 1980s and 1990s, multiculturalist approaches to migration management emerged as a dominant theoretical framework, which was met with both celebration and call for recognition of the marginalization of certain foreign nationals. This approach has been continually championed, critiqued and adapted by Canadian researcher Will Kymlicka (2018). Other prominent social scientists in the burgeoning field of migration studies have struggled against the progressive concept of transnationalism, often falling back on reactionary calls for a return to assimilationist theories (Brubaker 1994; 2001; Crul 2016; Alba 2017; Kivisto 2017). Nonetheless, the prevailing policy orientation has incorporated much of the *othering* (Anderson 2013) approach to migration that positions migrants in an ahistorical postracial context (Bojadžijev 2016). As will be outlined in the following sections, much of this research was done in parallel with the ongoing development of integration ideology that shifted the European legal framework from multiculturalist to integration-oriented migration policies (Heckmann 2015), yet from these adoptions, relevant criticism emerged from detractors of both assimilationist theories and multiculturalism by way of Favell (2016) and not surprisingly more variations of the same concepts that rather missed the mark by developing a term called 'superdiversity' (Vertovec 2007; Grzymala-Kazlowska and Phillimore 2018; Meissner 2018), which have been roundly critiqued from a postcolonial perspective (Ndhlovu 2016). Superdiversity, originally associated with the work of Steven Vertovec (2007), has been taken up by many European scholars, who argue that it moves beyond some of the issues addressed by intersectionality and has been used as an exploratory framework to describe modern cosmopolitan cities. In terms of migration research, the theory adds little in terms of critical analysis and serves merely as a descriptor for researchers subscribing to notions of *static societies*. As if the multitude of labels one can place on an individual inhabiting cities in the 'Global North' may provide an explanatory framework to help them understand the experience of migrants, it is difficult to envision how one can find a way to operationalize this approach in light of postcolonial and race theory, as well as practise theory in a way that has not already been done more accurately. However, the most comprehensive work addressing these attempts to justify such approaches to migrant integration, assimilation and superdiversity can be found in Schinkel's work, which has not only recognized the neocolonialist aspects of integration mandates and subsequent research to 'measure' integration, but also presents a well-founded critique of what he calls 'immigrant integration imaginaries' (Schinkel 2013, 1143; 2017, 3). Schinkel reduces research analysis of *imaginaries of integration* to analyse how populations use 'moral monitoring' to measure foreign populations' integration, which calls into question research frames that only focus on how well immigrants fit into the imagined society constructed by what is perceived to be Europeanness. He further notes that 'the difference at stake is *not the difference between well-integrated persons and not well-integrated ones*, but *between those for whom integration is not an issue at all and those for whom it is*' (Schinkel 2017, 3, original emphasis). In other words, Schinkel makes an argument similar to Anderson's (2013) contention that states have envisioned themselves as organized by 'values' instead of groups that are arbitrarily grouped in an area based on national borders. The antithetical side of this notion is the one produced in the imaginary of Syrian refugees about European democratic values (Chakrabarty 2007).

However, the aim of this part of the Introduction, although it continues to address the social construction of the refugee in both social imaginary and related social fields of refugees and of the German population (including the media, symbolic political action, activism and volunteerism), is the analysis of the construction of the bureaucratic state as a mechanism to form refugees into good residents – naturalization prospects are discussed in Part III. To consider this point, I return to the notion of parallel experiences; on the one side of this work are fields of Syrian refugees in Germany as conceived through Bourdieu's understanding of social fields (Bourdieu 1985), and on the other is the German integration regime.

Syrians who gained asylum status between 2015 and 2016 entered the German integration regime. They soon began to be evaluated by public perception and measured in terms of those who were or who were not 'well-integrated' migrants. This period, beginning in 2015, serves as a window to examine how the state acted and remained accountable to integration policy, and how the perception of those experiencing these actions changed over time. Instead of reifying the state, I observe local bureaucracies, and how refugees interact and react to those bureaucracies. As Gupta notes: 'Paying attentions to the everyday practices of specific bureaucracies and to the dissemination and circulation of reified representations of the state is critical to comprehending the nature of bureaucratic interventions in the lives of the poor and effects of such policies and programs' (Gupta 2012, 33). I am intrinsically interested in the situation of the poor rather than those who are immediately dependent on the lowest rung of the German social welfare state benefits system, which provides an interesting contrast to Gupta's notion, but more precisely serves as a foundation to study bureaucracies regardless of conditionalities like national wealth or corruption.

Another helpful frame to be considered is Vigh's (2006) concept of *social navigation*, which he uses to describe the navigation through periods of volatile insecurity. However, I reframe this discourse to unpack a concept I call *orientation stasis*, which arises from the constant legal changes and inconsistencies that have developed since the so-called refugee crisis. This notion is alluded to when Vigh invokes Hage's (2003) concept within the most desperate situations of isolation and dissolution – what he calls *social death* (Vigh 2006, 104). Vigh describes a type of navigation that one must travel through rather than over or around 'social environments' (Vigh 2006, 12), but more interestingly applies a number of theoretical frames that require existential thinking to imagine an outcome once one has navigated through a period of violability (Vigh 2010). Syrian collaborators are often in positions where their means to navigate bureaucracy become unclear or invalidated and, in an attempt to regain agency, they orientate towards a particular decision in some way in order to continue to be active and assert control. With these considerations in mind, the following discussion often 'zooms in' and invokes *the individual* within networks and fields of refugees; as such, I should clarify what I mean by the *individual*.

I separate the individuals concerned here – Syrian refugees with protected status in Germany – into two groups: networks of young men and networks of families, which I will outline in detail in what follows. Sökefeld (2015) interestingly turns to the work of Norbert Elias by using the term *figuration* to describe the experience of individuals as social actors. This concept can be seen as a precursor to practice theory, which allows for a conceptual bypass the structure/agency impasse. Sökefeld writes:

> He refused to privilege or reify 'society' or 'the social' – or 'structure' … to separate it from the individual human being; rather he emphasized the necessity to think about both the individual human being/actor embedded social relationships and the social composed of individual human beings, and resulting from their interaction. (Sökefeld 2015, 11)

On a similar basis, I consider the individuals whom I have come to know since 2015 to be part of two distinct networks of refugees. What will emerge in the following chapters is how the two groups have uniquely characterized networks, although they are part of the larger *social field* of Syrian refugees, and have access and the ability to accumulate distinct forms of capital, and use their capital within these transnational social fields in ways that are distinguishable from one another (Bourdieu 2009). However, there is indeed much overlap between the two groups. The greatest shared experience is the kind of *illusio* in which they both invest, albeit in differing ways (Bourdieu 1998). In other words, following the conception of the term *illusio* as Bourdieu describes it, or the way one has a 'feel for the game', young Syrian refugee men and families arrive with similar expectations and imaginaries for the future, and the ideas in which they conceptualize how they may navigate towards a secure future in Germany are similar to other migrant histories (Jackson 2005), but I consider this from a conjunctional analysis.

Finally, the forms of *capital* that emerge from the *symbolic power* derived from these two social fields must move beyond the original methodological nationalist limitation of cultural capital. Within the understanding of symbolic power, a university degree is a universal qualification and can be considered a form of capital, however it must also be *performed* within the limitations of what is governed by norms (Bourdieu 1993; 2009). The forms of capital must not only be creatively spent within bureaucratic structures, but must also contend with the *arbitrary outcomes* (Gupta 2012) of the governmentality within local administrations of the state. Skills that need to be officially recognized by the German state in order to gain employment are at the mercy of the scrutiny of local bureaucrats. Officials who dismiss previous experience may disenfranchise some refugees who are dependent on perceived authority for their orientation. The reproduction of the legitimacy of state agents is an application of authority that may support access to labour markets or education, but will impact how collaborators strategically use their social and cultural capital within the social field of Syrian refugees.

PART I

Arrival, Processing, Status

1

The Path to Asylum

This chapter is primarily about arrival. However, in order to understand how and why asylum seekers arrived in Germany, it is necessary to examine the historical development of migration policy in Germany as well as the circumstances of the so-called refugee crisis. I will first outline how the public imaginary anticipated and framed the events leading up to the summer of 2015, and then I will draw from my fieldwork to show how these circumstances were perceived by refugees arriving to apply for asylum.

The bureaucratic hurdles of staying

The imaginary is a particular kind of existential world building before and during migratory paths. The desire to move – and in the case of displaced peoples, the necessity to move – comes with an existential feeling of needing to go somewhere during this trajectory of migration. As this imagined trajectory builds through waiting times, conflict, uncertainty and small successes, imaginaries of both a future with new life between *space* and *place* emerge. By 2015, many of the interlocutors in my ethnographic fieldwork had already solidified a strong image of life in Germany through existing ties to the country or images in the news media. This chapter explores how these imaginaries of order and democracy before leaving for Europe influenced the reaction to the chaos and disorder of arriving in Germany during a time of crisis. These early interactions with German residents and the bureaucratic state would have lasting implications on the choices they would later make navigating the integration regime. The chapter will also frame this experience from the perspective of the refugees themselves and show how migration and refugee research can apply the entirety of the often circular and ongoing aspect of moving across national boundaries to create a holistic analysis a migration experience.

First, what may be considered 'settled' in one line of thought in migration research is continually unaccounted for in others. The very nature of migration studies or refugee studies is framed in location and movement, which creates an embedded tension between the tendency to study a single site and the challenge of considering several areas as one unified experience. In other words, does the empirical work centre around experience or geographies and conditionalities? Second, if, as I attempt to argue in the following discussion, research can be grounded in *both* experience and locality, then the pursuit of this unification requires a situation-specific applied framework.

Although 'sedentarist' notions of refugees have long been refuted and have been analysed through the 'national order of things' (Malkki 1995), studies in migration research continue to apply methods and theories that grapple with attempts to solidify 'sites' through which refugees travel (Hage 2005; Xiang 2013). There are zones of flight from conflict: internally displaced persons (IDPs) and refugees; zones of transit: migrants and refugees (both illegal and legal); and, finally, zones of 'settlement' (relocation, removal and root building). As the long summer of migration in 2015 made newspaper headlines with citizens holding 'refugees welcome!' banners, there were major legal decisions being made in Germany that would have significant implications in the coming years, both socially and politically. Not unlike subaltern analysis of an imagined Europe (Chakrabarty 2007), Osseiran (2020) applies empirical work from Istanbul to show how imaginaries of Europe and the EU allow Syrian refugees to differentiate countries as 'transit' (Tuckett 2018) and 'destination' zones to be navigated through.

Germany, in the minds of many refugees, was the last 'zone' on this trajectory. However, as Treiber reminds us, along the journey there is a specific 'acquisition and transformation of knowledge' that is not governed by a simple formulation of structure and agency; instead, it is 'a … learning process, involving risks and danger, but also permitting the acquisition of knowledge in new situations and environments' (Treiber 2013, 189). In other words, the 'journey' has huge implications for the collection of knowledge that will be applied to more chaotic environments later on. Contrary to the notion that the stages are only relevant throughout the journey, the punctuated events along the journey are key to understanding the way in which refugees react to their new environment. Another key difference between the journey and place of 'settlement' is the social imaginary that is at play and in constant renegotiation between those previously residing in a location *about* new arrivals and a separate social imaginary constructed by refugees themselves.

I presented the concept of social imaginary in the Introduction. Additionally, Charles Taylor's understanding of the social imaginary adds some depth that is relevant here. He defines the social imaginary as 'the ways people imagine their social existence, how they fit together with others, how things go on between them and their fellows, the expectations that are normally met, and the deeper normative and images that underlie these expectations' (Taylor 2004, 23). This incorporates a complex and shifting web that connects experience and public narratives to groups that in turn add their outward subjectification into their realities. It is how they manage expectations in order to navigate new environments.

The stage of asylum should be part of the 'settlement' phase of migration, but this too is contested; even within the borders of Germany, asylum seekers and legally recognized refugees[1] negotiate movement. Upon arrival in a territory, there are some refugee movements *forward* to other European countries. Alternatively, there are also at times existential (sometimes physical) *return* movements back to transit countries or to countries of origin. In other words, the journey is circular, either physically, emotionally or existentially. In the most practical sense, the notion that refugees have settled upon entering an asylum-granting European country cannot be linked to any form of longevity or security.

From this perspective, the integration regime also reaches into the asylum phase of refugee movements. Asylum seekers from selected countries of origin, based on legislation in Germany that occurred during the so-called refugee crisis of 2015, are afforded many of the legal rights associated with access to work and language courses enjoyed by refugees with legal protection. In German law, these are asylum seekers from countries with 'good staying prospects' (*gute Bleibeperspektive*). Again, in the most practical sense, the lines of inquiry that I have set out in this book between 'migrant', 'asylum seeker' and 'refugee' overlap, blur and join completely. Indeed, the following chapters will detail with more clarity some of the nuances in the complicated migration, integration and asylum laws in the EU and Germany. However, here I am interested in highlighting the ways in which imaginaries cross space and time through periods of travel and settlement, and then sometimes more travel and more settlement. The subsequent interpretation of the summer and autumn of 2015 in Europe and particularly Germany is based on narrative interviews and media analysis, which begins with the movement of refugees from 2014 onwards and incorporates social changes in the milieu of media, public discourse, activism, volunteerism and political policy in Germany when the reaction to such movements peaked. The narrative then follows refugees through the chaotic and bureaucratic scramble of the government to process asylum applications, house refugees and distribute them across the country. For Syrian refugees, these periods were punctuated by short, intense periods followed by slowed periods of waiting.

This section will depart from the rest of this book in two ways: first, it uses biographic, narrative interviews to develop its empirical claims instead of the more participant observation-dominated sections of the rest of this book; and, second, it focuses on arrival, asylum and the short period thereafter, which 'sets the table' for the implications of how Syrians navigate bureaucracy. In other words, the experiences and knowledge accumulated along the way as well as imaginaries of what could or should be awaiting them in a longitudinal sense influence the way in which they interact with the administrative state. This is a theme influenced by Bourdieu's notion of *habitus* and *illusio* that will be examined in greater detail throughout the following chapters. However, for the purposes of this chapter, the expectations of refugees as they arrived in Germany are underscored by the basic principle that they were fleeing a completely undemocratic country and entering one with deeper sets of values and organization. Interwoven are various points of media analysis of the so-called refuge crisis that have been studied in depth elsewhere (Sökefeld 2017; Bojadžijev 2018; Karakayali 2018), but are nonetheless necessary in order to understand how the refugee identity is shaped both from within and externally by the nonrefugee populace.

However, one of the aims of this book is to present the experience of interlocutors by way of German integration programmes, which means experience with the so-called *integration* programmes. Thus, the process should actually begin after a positive asylum claim. Yet, as noted earlier, and applicable to those who I call 'privileged refugees'[2] – who are legally 'asylum seekers' at this point in my narrative – they *may* gain favoured *access* to integration programmes earlier than other asylum seekers, with the caveat that it is unclear if asylum seekers can actually access and use these 'benefits'. Therefore, this chapter revisits the asylum process, and the so-called refugee crisis of 2015, to both map the complete story of refugee arrival and state integration experiences, and express exactly how their early arrival will later shape the ongoing challenges faced by collaborators navigating bureaucracy.

Finally, the timeframe outlined is from the initial journey to Germany and an asylum application until receipt of a residency card. Once within German borders, the path to positive asylum is inundated with a range of bureaucratic actors, as Ilgit and Klotz explain:

> Among these various bureaucracies (translated into English, with corresponding German acronyms) are the following: the Federal Ministry of the Interior (BMI); the Federal Office for Migration and Refugees (BAMF); the Federal Statistical Office (DSTATİS); the Federal Institute for Population Research (BiB); the Federal Government Commissioner for Migration, Refugees and Integration; the Federal Government Commissioner for Matters related to Repatriates and National Minorities in Germany; the Federal Police (BPol); the Federal BA (BAA); and the Federal Office for the Protection of the Constitution (BfV). (Ilgit and Klotz 2018, 5)

It is not the intention here to outline the exactness of the asylum accounts,[3] but rather the evolution of asylum since the events of 2015 and what that meant for the asylum seekers before and after that period due to rapid legal and local policy changes, and how they were able to use their capital and the precarity of the situation. Overall, this existential journey is framed in the social process of Syrians that moves from performance to precarity. Within that journey is a need for a *regimes of mobility* approach to the complex interactions between state agencies and migrants (Glick Schiller and Salazar 2013; Eule, Loher and Wyss 2018). Similarly, Eule describes these tensions as 'a constantly evolving field of contested control in which state authorities and migrants engage in a reciprocal cycle of discipline and resistance, law enforcement and avoidance, exclusion from the right of transnational mobility, and its appropriation against the state' (Eule, Loher and Wyss 2018, 2817). Unlike other accounts that highlight refugees' successful strategies to overcome the asymmetrical relationship they have with the state (Tuckett 2015), many of the learned behaviour and lack of viable information from the administrative state pushes refugees into decision making that works against their interests. In a desire to maintain mobility among chaos, refugees sought to assert agency through decisions that would in some cases drive greater tensions in terms of securing livelihoods in Germany.

Crisis in context

The 'refugee crisis' that politicians and media used to describe the wave of migrants crossing into Europe, mainly over the Mediterranean, began in 2013, but peaked in absolute numbers and produced visually striking images of human suffering in 2015 during the 'long summer of migration' (Bojadžijev 2018). How refugees were perceived before they arrived and what they experienced during the journey would come to embody much of their early life in Germany. The double existence of migrants both in the media – images of hundreds crowded into small boats and the dead washing up on European shores – and in the social imaginary can be found in the narratives of the interlocutors represented here, who arrived in the window between 2014 and 2016.

Syrians who fled Turkey and other countries experienced firsthand the vast movement of humans crossing borders, often with the help of smugglers, which was driven by a single focus towards a destination at all costs. Alternatively, from the position of the German public and politicians, this was a slow-moving crawl of humans carrying their lives on their backs, bypassing countries of potential asylum that would be more hostile to foreigners. In other words, two different narratives emerged: one drawn from experience, a self-narrative, and another that was constructed from afar, turning individuals into a homogenized group of refugees.

In the end, there were over one million asylum applications across Europe, with 40 per cent of them in Germany – a fact that would later be conflated by the media with headlines claiming: 'Germany on Course to Accept One Million Refugees in 2015' (AFP 2015; Bojadžijev 2018). The new reality at the German border emerged out of changes in the EU border and refugee regime over the last few decades and the protracted intensity of the revolution in Syria (Tsianos and Karakayali 2010; Tazzioli 2018). The starting point of the mobility regimes should be to note how Germany's asylum policy has increasingly limited the ability of refugee settlement and the legal complications of joining family members once refugees have been granted asylum, which often drives migration through informal means (Fassin 2011), bypassing the legal structures. In other words, the European refugee regime has in many ways produced a class and gender divide that allows those with enough youth, enough money and, more often than not, the safety of the male gender to simply pay to arrive at the border of the most democratically favourable European country to apply for asylum instead of waiting in Turkey for an agency like the UNHCR to support an asylum claim.

Germany has in fact taken in over 20,000 resettled Syrian refugees since 2013 (Chemin et al 2018, 36), but, as noted earlier, the bureaucratic hurdles, waiting times and complicated processes influence the alternative of using smugglers to reach Europe. These alternative routes unsurprisingly increased alongside a peak period for migrant deaths at sea. In 2015, the UNHCR recorded 3,771 migrant deaths at sea and in 2016 another 5,096 (UNHCR 2019). Migrant routes over sea are divided into three areas, which in essence follow a western route from Morocco to Spain, a central route from various North African countries to Italy, and an eastern route from mostly Turkey to the Greek islands. With regard to the last of these migratory routes, the UNHCR recorded 856,700 migrants crossing the Mediterranean in 2015, a number which can be assumed to be greater in relation to the number of asylum applications that summer (UNHCR 2019).

However, the reaction from EU Member States during the summer of 2015 varied from affable to hysterical. Although Angela Merkel will be remembered for her phrase 'Wir Schaffen das!' (quite literally: 'We can manage it') in September 2015 (Mushaben 2017), in July that year she was highly criticized for her apathetic response to the insecurity of a young Palestinian girl, patting her back and telling the audience that Germany could not handle all refugees (BBC 2015). But by September, Southern and Eastern European countries like Greece, Hungary and Austria, as well as other countries on the so-called Balkan route, had begun blocking border crossings and attempting to stop the flow of asylum seekers (Hinger, Schäfer and Pott 2016). When Merkel uttered those now famous words, referring to the decision not to block border crossings with Austria and suspend the Dublin Regulation (Karakayali 2018), she was attempting to come to terms with the foundations of the German Basic Law and the historical context of refugees in Germany, which motivated a broader humanitarian approach to EU law (Sökefeld 2017). The Dublin Regulation is an EU agreement and is part of the overall modern vision of uniform asylum outlined by the Common European Asylum System (CEAS), which was established to prevent refugees from applying for asylum in multiple countries and, more importantly, to return those who apply for asylum to safe third countries (Bhimji 2016b). However, even before 2015, research had already revealed flaws in the system, but this became protracted due to the burden placed on Southern European countries receiving the bulk of asylum applications, along with a fingerprint system that would later reveal discord between German government agencies (Brekke and Brochmann 2015). This decision to suspend the Dublin Regulation would become a symbolic split between the development of *Willkommenskultur* (welcome culture) and the growth of a public debate on Germanness, as well as the rise in right-wing extremist movements (Bojadžijev 2018).

In the broader European context, during and shortly after the so-called refugee crisis, social engagement was increasingly motivated by the public images of migrant flight and life in Europe. In Spain earlier that year, I joined colleagues and some activists associated with the Catholic Church in our town in preparing for the arrival of refugees. The Spanish government announced that it would join other European states in a form of burden sharing to resettle refugees. It organized housing, prepared free Arabic courses for volunteers and developed a network between my local university, the Catholic Church in the city and local municipal governments. However, no resettled refugees ever arrived. Governments complained about quotas and policy, but little action was taken and the focus was removed by the direct movement of people by that summer.

Along with images of overcrowded boats and a young child lying face down dead on the beach,[4] in Germany the print and news media delivered the public images of abandoned schools, underoccupied villages, football stadiums and military barracks[5] overwhelmed by the number of refugees (Hagen and Maxwill 2015; Tegeler 2016); however, the term '*Willkommenskultur*' not only changed the discourse about refugees, but also spawned a wide range of research interests (Bittner et al 2015; Hinger, Schäfer and Pott 2016; Fleischmann and Steinhilper 2017; Karakayali 2018; Liebe et al 2018). Germans looked at their neighbours' closed borders and xenophobic political rhetoric, and instead began volunteering in record numbers: taking part in organizing emergency shelters and community language assistance, and acting as a bridge to state–operated asylum measures (Safouane 2017; Sökefeld 2017). Ethnographic fieldwork conducted by Braun (2017, 39) presents an interesting perspective of volunteering culture inside emergency shelters by highlighting the fact that the majority of volunteers were 'elderly, female volunteers with a bourgeois background'. Other researchers (Liebe et al 2018) note that the jubilation over *Willkommenskultur* 'peaked' in November

2015. This gave way to conservative political attitudes towards mass migration and the rise of not only more violence against asylum seekers, but also an increase in the popularity of the political party Alternative for Germany (Alternativ für Deutschland [AfD]), which encapsulated and amplified anxieties to hysterical levels (Benček and Strasheim 2016). Additionally, the celebration of *Willkommenskultur* stands in stark contrast to the violence against refugees that increased over the following months (Hinger, Schäfer and Pott 2016). Studies also show that over 70 per cent of respondents had not previously been involved in volunteer work with refugees (Karakayali and Kleist 2016). The shift in refugee law was in part motivated by the sheer volume of asylum applicants, but it was carried out and adjusted as a result of previously outlined developments.

The equal distribution of asylum seekers to German Länder was based on a decades-old burden-sharing format, the so-called Königsteiner Schlüssel (Königsteiner Key), which distributes asylum seekers to cities and German Länder based on the number of residents and taxes paid in each state. The Königsteiner Schlüssel was applied in conjunction with a Wohnsitzauflage (Residency Obligation) beginning in 2016, which mandated refugees to continue living in the city they originally settled in for at least three years or until they no longer received social benefits (Etzold 2017; Hörisch 2018; Bogumil, Kuhlmann and Proeller 2019). However, in the chaos that unfolded in 2015, many of these formalities were enforced and certainly no national approach that controlled the distribution of asylum seekers across the country could be found with consistency. Contrarily, border police often supported their onward journeys to other European countries (Eule et al 2019). The impact of where and when Syrians applied for asylum would have lasting implications on their experience with the integration law-mandated language courses, access to social networks and practical matters like finding affordable housing. The distribution of refugees based on time and place had arbitrary outcomes as a policy standpoint and created bureaucratic tensions within the system of administration itself.

From the perspective outlined in the previous sections, the early experience of Syrians was shaped by the social imaginary that would transition from *Willkommenskultur* and 'Wir schaffen das!' to the volatile political changes, which would have lasting impacts on the 'integration goals' set out by policy makers (Safouane 2017). The cases are nuanced based on time of arrival; some collaborators benefited from early arrival, and others were negatively impacted by their time of arrival because of slow access to language courses, despite the policy insistence that language was a key indicator for good integration. Furthermore, the legal changes that would come in 2016, which limited movement but gave the right to those with a 'good prospect of being allowed to stay' – more specifically, '[a]sylum seekers in this group come from countries with previous protection rates of over 50 percent (currently Syria, Eritrea, Iraq, Iran and Somalia)' (Konle-Seidl 2018, 31) – impacted refugees' immediate access to language courses and labour markets (Bröse, Faas and Stauber 2018).

Finally, the volatile legal landscape further shifted the political and public imaginary that would reframe asylum based on a nation-state approach to granting protection. The changes in asylum law beginning in 2016 were also intended to curb asylum applicants by directly rejecting those with nationalities from so-called 'safe return countries' that included all applicants from Balkan states, which were in large part historically granted asylum as a result of North Atlantic Treaty Organization (NATO) intervention in Kosovo (Bauböck 2006; Schittenhelm and Schneider 2017; Chemin et al 2018). From a policy standpoint, the German government essentially removed the individual decision making and divided countries into those with a *good perspective* for asylum, asylum applicants whose cases would be fully reviewed under asylum law, and 'safe return' countries, who should be directly rejected and deported (Hinger, Schäfer and Pott 2016). The refugee advocacy organization Pro Asyl (2018a; 2018b) provides a clear picture of who 'benefits' from policy based on country of origin instead of individual cases, indicating that Syrians not only face the shortest times for processing asylum claims but also receive the highest rate of positive asylum claims. Work by Schittenhelm and Schneider (2017) provides a necessary view into the microcosm of the daily work of BAMF employees, showing how workers' decision making was under pressure to be efficient and influenced by the pragmatics of deciding on a Syrian asylum claim to process over a Serbian asylum claim because it would be a more indisputible decision: 'The applicant's country of origin is the preeminent classification for knowing whether the official will reject or accept the application' (Schittenhelm and Schneider 2017, 1706).

If it is at all possible to consider a group of refugees to be 'privileged' within the integration regime, then Syrians certainly fit within a potential category. In 2015, 99 per cent of Syrians were granted recognition as refugees (*Anerkannte Flüchtlinge*), but by 2016, this had shifted and only 57.6 per cent were given recognized refugee status, while 42 per cent were given subsidiary protection. One of the employees at the German Foreigner's Office (Ausländerbehörde) in Munich explained how Syrians specifically experienced this change:

'In the past and also now, the Syrian people here say "we cannot go to the embassy" ... Then when the war started and they changed a little at the *Bundesamt* in 2015 and 2016, they said, "okay if you can prove your identity you get a decision earlier than the others because we know you are Syrian, and we know about the war, and so we can decide easily" ... Then there was this refugee who said he's Syrian but he was German or French[6] and then they stopped this procedure again and looked closer at the people.' (Anja, Munich 2019)

In other words, in order to receive full recognition as a refugee, Syrians would have to have a passport from Syria as the only way to prove their identity after this false case in 2015. Before this case, they could use other means to prove their identity, which produced a conflict from Syrians who did not want to travel to the Syrian embassy and give money or information to the Assad regime in Syria for a number of reasons. The administrative shift also served as a way to impose a limit on more refugees entering the country; Syrian refugees without passports would only be granted subsidiary protection – a status with limited rights and, most importantly, no right to family reunification. Although the political aspect of developing an immigration policy may appear to reify the state and a coherent law, the actual practice of legal implementation has an arbitrary temporal factor that favours location and time over fairness and justice.

Applying for asylum: how to choose where to settle ... if you can?

The date is 13 September 2015. The excitement has been building since you got on the crowded train in Austria. You can't believe that you will arrive in Munich in a few hours. You get off the train along with what seems like thousands of other migrants. Volunteers are waiting at the Hauptbahnhof exit holding signs reading 'Refugees welcome!' and waving, while others are offering clothing or food. A large police presence makes you nervous. You approach the police, but others avoid them and move on. After a long line, you indicate that you are a Syrian national and wish to apply for asylum. You are given a short medical examination and are fingerprinted, and are now part of the EASY (Erstverteilung der Asylbegehrenden) database that records all asylum seekers entering Germany. You are safe. No more violence in Hungary at the border, no more threats from smugglers for more money, no more risk of drowning at sea on the way to Greece; you can breathe a sigh of relief at last. But what now? Maybe you know someone already in Germany – a family member or a friend – or maybe you have a plan where to go next.

Through endless news coverage, political posturing, documentary films and public discourse allowed onlookers to have a rather visceral experience, with the entirety of what transpired in the summer of 2015 – there was even a film released in 2020 by German public television channel ARD called *Die Getriebenen*, which dramatized these events. However, and since the events were framed in crisis, there was little room left for the question following the crisis: *but what will happen now?* The majority of research and public debate then returns to the more practical question of how systems manage the capacity of the enormous number of refugees, the engagement of volunteer, or, in the case of integration, what mechanisms are in place to support them and what are the capacities of refugees to contribute to German society. This section will explore the individual context of several collaborators who arrived in 2015 and their early interaction with the state. However, I do not engage with the bureaucracy of asylum decisions, the subsequent court decisions or the nuance of asylum law. I want to present a case based on my ethnographic work from the perspective of the Syrians who experienced it, and the work that focuses in depth in other areas tends to overshadow these experiences with bureaucracy itself, not what bureaucracy does to the people affected by it. Lastly, there are a number of significant studies on asylum decision making in Spain (Jubany 2011), arbitrary bureaucracies in Austria (Dahlvik 2018), legal asylum loopholes and failures across Europe (Gill and Good 2019) and, like this book, a Bourdieuian capital approach (Joormann 2020), all of which provide distinctive insights, but do not particularly relate to the way in which the refugee integration regime produced racialized notions of refugeeness and narrowed the margin of what is an acceptably well-integrated refugee.

Arrival

Nazir arrived on 10 October 2015 in Munich and used his social network of other Syrians to help him decide on the best place to apply for asylum. The first officials he came into contact with said that they could choose where to go. He explained: "We could go to another city, we could stay in Munich. [But] there was a relative that said this city [near Saarbrücken] was good and also fast enough to get the identification card, so we went to Saarland." After applying for asylum, he began his stay in a small town not far from Saarbrücken.

Anas was applying for asylum near the city of Lebach. He wrote to me on Facebook in September 2015: 'Even if the situation was easy to cross. It's a matter of luck. Death does not make mistakes with anyone.' A few minutes later, he wrote 'I will see you in Europe'. He wrote that he was in Europe on 14 October 2015. His trip took 30 hours, four of which were at sea, where he feared for his life. In November, he was in St Ingbert waiting for the asylum decision. I was living in Spain at the time and we wrote to each other every few weeks, sometimes months, on Facebook.

When I talked to him about his time two years later, Anas reflected on the journey with a strange duality. Unlike other discussions I had with him back in 2017 when we met again in person, or those with agents at the city administrative level in Germany, there was a pronounced difference between the periods he experienced control, the periods where he felt a complete loss of control and a more nuanced manoeuvring through the chaos, which I found to be the case with most of the Syrians I spoke with about their arrival.

Like the others, Anas had a clear idea in mind when he crossed the German border in early September 2015; he would go to Saarbrücken, where his good friend Osama had already settled and had offered him a place to sleep. But when they arrived by train in Passau, he revealed he was at the complete mercy of arbitrary bureaucratic mechanisms. He explained how he was taken off the train there arriving with thousands of other refugees:

> 'So, we were on the train. I had the ticket to Frankfurt; I was planning to go to Saarbrücken. But in Passau, on the border, the police came and they said "Everyone who don't have a European passport please go out" … They took us. All of us. Everyone from Syria, everyone who didn't have a passport. Because there were more trains coming. So, they were only collecting us on the train and they are waiting until they have a train full of refugees before leaving. Then it was 2 am or 1 am and the train started the trip and I had no idea where. There were a team from the Red Cross, I asked them, "where are we going?" They said, "we are not allowed to tell you where you are going, but it's okay, don't be afraid". So, after few hours maybe six or seven, and we were near one village. It was twenty minutes or thirty minutes from Hannover.' (Anas, Saarbrücken 2019)

In other cases, the police or border guards and agents inside Germany were attempting to manage the chaotic situation by directing refugees to travel on their own, but Anas was simply taken on a train somewhere beyond his control, only to arrive outside Hannover and be offered a 'menu' of asylum locations:

> 'There was a lot of refugees there, they told us, "If any wants to go to Norway? Denmark? Or another country he can let us know because they don't have to make a fingerprint. Anyone who wants to stay in Germany, please come here". I said, "I want to stay in Germany but I don't want to stay in Hannover". They said, "Then you need to order a taxi and go to the train station". So, just like that, I asked someone who was in the camp, I want a taxi. We left with three or four other friends. We all wanted to go the direction south.' (Anas, Saarbrücken 2019)

From there, they took a train southwest to Saarbrücken. Anas stayed one night with Osama, but Osama advised him that he should go and apply for asylum now; if he waited, it would not look good for his asylum application and it could take longer. He moved on to the region's main asylum processing area, which at the time in Saarland was the city of Lebach. The region of Saarland shares a border with France, which meant it was crowded with asylum seekers from arrivals in Germany and France. Anas observed that asylum claims were being processed for nationals from Tunisia, Algeria and other countries. From his perspective, there was also no coordinated control of where refugees were being sent to ease the overcrowding in Lebach; they just took a picture of him and said he could stay there, but sent other people to the city of Trier in the north. "It was only employees there, they looked at you, they make a picture and someone said, 'you stay, you go, you stay, you go'. There was no data which they based their decision on if you are to stay here or not, it depends on the employer", he said. Then finally, after a doctor checked him to be sure he had no contagious diseases and given any necessary vaccinations, he was allowed to make his official plea for asylum, something he and other collaborators called 'court'.

However, this reveals an underlying misunderstanding that is a product of knowledge gained through other refugees and not official sources. They were never before 'court', the procedure was first done when they actually presented their case to the Federal Office for Migration and Refugees (Bundesamt für Migration und Flüchtlinge, BAMF). BAMF makes all first asylum decisions and the decisions from BAMF may be challenged in the local court within two weeks of the initial decision (Schittenhelm and Schneider 2017).

Shortly afterwards, Anas was relocated two more times because there were too many refugees to provide with temporary housing in Lebach and the second city to which he was transferred. Refugees normally have to remain near where their claim is made, so he was lodged in an unused school for several months. This was when he wrote me online back in 2015: 'I live now in a mass housing. It's a little difficult. I have to wait for a residence permit here'. 'How long will you wait?', I responded. A few minutes later, he wrote back: 'Between 2 and 3 months. It's routine. And I mostly wait.'

Later, when I visited him in Saarbrücken, Anas showed me the document that a woman from a language school asked him to sign when he arrived there. It ended up being a contract to stay and study German at that location even after he received his Aufenthaltstitel (residency card). At the time, he wanted to move back to Saarbrücken and live near his friends, but he was forced to stay there and live in shared housing provided by the language school, with several other men, for a number of months. This was in November 2015, but he would not begin his official integration course until February 2017. Yet, two important relationships were developed while he stayed at the school, which will be discussed later on.

In another case, Mohammad crossed into Austria and was told by the police that those with money must go to Vienna and those without must take a train to Germany. Towards the end of 2015, Mohammad arrived in the city of Horst in the north of Germany and applied for asylum. Those who arrived there spent one night in a massive tent that sheltered around 150 other male asylum applicants – women were housed in a separate tent. During his wait for an asylum decision and his residency card, he would go on to Rostock – the site of violent attacks against migrants in the 1990s – for six months and was hosted by the local authority in a vacant hotel with six other asylum seekers. He explained how he thought this area was full of racist people because when he and a group of other refugees were walking on the street, someone yelled from a car window: "Go back to your country!"

Rasha arrived in Germany with her three daughters after her husband, Hakim. He had been in Lebanon when the civil war spread across Syria. Then he and several other men set out on foot, walking nearly 1,000 kilometres from Lebanon through areas to avoid the fighting and finally crossed illegally into Turkey. He was also in our workshop in Reyhanli and, like Anas, arrived in Germany almost directly after I left them in Turkey in the summer of 2015. Once Hakim received his asylum in Germany, he was able to sponsor Rasha and his daughters to come to Germany via a family reunification visa (*Familiennachzug*). This process involved a series of trips to the German embassy in Turkey and many bureaucratic hurdles, as well as time and money spent in Turkey. It was not an option for Rasha to bring her four daughters by informal means. They arrived in a suburb of the city of Osnabrück, and stayed in a container for the next nine months.

Hassan arrived in Germany by accident. He and his brother were on their way to Sweden and had to pass through Germany on the way there. He had already spent months in jail in Damascus for participating in student protests against the Assad regime and later spent several months working in Egypt before finally travelling informally to Europe. As he and his brother tried to change trains in Germany, they were separated when the police stopped them and asked for their documents. Hassan was questioned while his brother looked on from a distance. They made the kind of silent communication that perhaps is reserved for those as close as brothers, and Hassan signalled that his brother should go on without him. He knew that once the police asked him for his passport, he would be fingerprinted, processed and forced to make an asylum claim in Germany, not Sweden. This was in 2014 and before the 'crisis', when the police at the border were handling asylum seekers with stricter adherence to the law.

Adel and Abdul were attempting to reach Central (Germany) or Northern Europe from Turkey, but were stopped once the borders in Greece were closed and, like Abdulazez, were forced to live in the camps there until they were granted asylum in Germany.

These 'vignettes' of narrative accounts have retraced some of the experiences that collaborators had as they crossed borders from 2014 to 2015, and have shown how timing, space and pace factor into this experience. To a greater extent, these narratives relate to the first encounter that the Syrians experienced with both the administrative state and with the German public. Even in earlier cases, relationships with other Syrians were key to where they chose to settle, which indeed had to do with contacts, but was also strategic. They made clear attempts to get their asylum processed quickly in some cases, but in others they experienced a sudden reaction to their new reality, which would be slow-moving. The factor of temporality will be explored in more depth in Chapter 2. However, the early impressions in Germany signalled a new form of negotiation that collaborators would have to navigate, one that, as shown earlier, was heavily dependent on arbitrary practices and various attempts to reassert control in a chaotic environment.

Perception verses reality

Although at times in the previous situations, Syrians were able to manage their narrative and perform refugeeness, in most cases, once they were confronted with the power of agencies, there was no option to navigate a bureaucracy or perform part of the imaginary of refugeeness in order to maintain agency. Refugees who crossed borders were – to apply another seafaring analogy – more like a small ship in a storm, moving in the direction that the sea carried them and only clinging on for survival. But these time periods of chaos arrived at critical moments that would shift into continued movement or extended periods of immobility. Alternatively, politicians like the Green Party's Katrin Goering-Eckardt seized on the opportunity to portray Germany as a welcoming country, claiming they could create a *Septembermrchen* (September fairy tale), while industrial leaders were considering refugees as an economic opportunity (Hinte, Rinne and Zimmermann 2015; Karakayali 2018). Bojadžijev's analysis of discourse during this time captured the neoliberal approach noted earlier, most notably highlighting the political shift away from the humanitarian side of migration and the political questions that emerged: *how do we keep those unwanted out and once migrants are in, how are they going to contribute?* (Bojadžijev 2018). This approach took a critical look at the way in which social imaginaries and the administrative state shaped perceptions of the 'other', but did not necessarily address *how* these constructions shaped the experience of refugees, in other words how public discourse in and about the so-called refugee crisis and periods of so-called integration influenced the way that refugees constructed their own identities. Additionally, public discourse created a subjectification of refugees that reduced the complexity of their incredibly diverse experiences. One point is clear: the time of arrival was a prelude to what was to come, namely, insecurity, distrust in institutions and punctuated periods of agency.

Academic accounts and studies attempting to capture the nature of this period (Ostrand 2015; Woltin, Sassenberg and Albayrak 2018) tend to essentialize new Syrian arrivals in Germany as one homogeneous group with somewhat equal resources and similar problems, or at times confuse the legal status of refugees with other country nationals seeking asylum in Germany, failing to take note of the particularity of the various stages of the integration regime (Pearlman 2017). Arrivals who became my main early interlocutors chose the location of settlement for very different reasons and in the following sections I will detail the repercussions for these decisions. Nevertheless, I have used this chapter to contextualize this experience in the broader social and political atmosphere in Germany. The through line I attempt to present here is one of arrival, networks and capital, and how these were used in subsequent months by collaborators. Where they settled and how they settled was important and was not always based on capital, but sometimes circumstance. However, in the period following the initial asylum application, one that was characterized by months of waiting in discomfort, networks became more important and slowly became more localized and specialized. Broader categories began to emerge, like young men and families, in addition to being differentiated like Syrian nationals compared to other-country nationals, which provided a range of benefits. In other words, whether they arrived or received asylum before or after the crisis had drastic social and legal implications on the capacity for collaborators to access social capital and other resources to help navigate the integration regime. The next chapter 'zooms in' a bit more on the area-specific, locality-based consequences of where collaborators settled and less on the broader migration movements.

2

Asylum Decisions and What Followed Thereafter

While Chapter 1 addressed the social imaginaries that were at play during the long summer of migration in 2015, this chapter will reframe some of those events to spotlight the power imbalance between refugees and the *local administrative state*. In a very unique dynamic, the construction of social realities on both the side of Syrian refugees and the side of German residents, as well as the bureaucratic state, dictated the way in which relationships between the two would develop over the following years. This chapter focuses less on the individual narratives and more on public narratives about refugees. It will look at how public narratives influenced both policy and its implementation. More specifically, it frames key events that shifted the public imaginary and produced a reaction from the refugees, insofar as their subjectification as 'the refugee' led them to lose control of their own narratives. Chapter 1 moved quickly through the processes of asylum and the role of the local administration. This chapter will return to some of those periods to show how the bureaucratic formulations of policy and the arbitrary implementation of integration policy were seen at the local level, defying the portrayal of a unitary national integration process.

By reframing the events in terms of both shifting public discourse and power, I will draw on the large body of literature on *waiting* to describe the particular case of Syrians in Germany using what I call *orientation stasis*. This orientation stasis occurs in times of insecurity and inability to rely on previously learned (and embodied) behaviours – or, to use Bourdieu's concept, their habitus becomes something that disorients them rather than guides them. This chapter builds on previous theoretical work from Jackson (2005), who applies Bourdieu's concepts of *illusio* (feel for the game) to the situation of refugees arriving in new and unknown circumstances.

Refugees arriving in 2015 began to question the stability of their everyday ability to successfully navigate regimes of asylum and apply accumulated capital, which was compounded by the desire to continue (existentially) moving forward. This drove refugees to attempt to *move*, but the outcomes were often undesirable, so they remain existentially immobile – in other words, in stasis. Social capital is particularly of interest because it is the most visible form of capital that migrants accumulate and exchange in different social fields. Along the way, they use their networks to try to accumulate social capital that will benefit them, but, as noted earlier, they are in a highly volatile and unpredictable environment where they apply unreliable information in order to keep moving.

Regional and national asylum

At this point in the asylum process, two rather interesting trends emerged: at one end of the spectrum, the inner workings of the complex distribution of administration authority between Länder and Federal (Bund) reveal bureaucratic hurdles, and at the other end, these processes evolved uniquely through space and time. In principle, this federal and local structure, which is actually dictated by the terms of Germany's Basic Law (Grundgesetz), should present a unified federal structure of distribution of authority handling asylum claims. However, the German federal government is administered locally, which often supersedes notions of uniformity, or notions of the state in general (Gupta 2012).

The work of Bogumil, Hafner and Kastilan definitively outlines the asylum procedure as it plays out in cities and small towns. This work shows the tensions that emerge between federal law and also the flexibility of state interpretation and application of asylum laws, including the difficulties in implementing the sweeping changes in asylum laws in 2016. A complex network of government agencies and nongovernmental organisation (NGO) actors were allocated responsibility by the federal and regional governments. The agency's work covers the scope of both asylum periods for citizenship applications. Although complex, government agencies structurally and legally appear to be well organized and without bias. However, in practice, studies have shown inconsistencies in the legal interpretation of asylum procedures (Schittenhelm and Schneider 2017, 31–33; Glorius and Doomernik 2020; Joormann 2020) and regional variation in asylum and residency law (Eule 2014; Hinger, Schäfer and Pott 2016; Riedel and Schneider 2017b). Furthermore, asylum cannot be considered 'deracialized'. The racialization of asylum seekers has been argued elsewhere (Gowayed 2020), and class in the context of intersectionality plays a role in asylum court appeals (Joormann 2020). Furthermore, the roadblocks against fair integration begin at the neocolonial externalization of Europe as an idea and region (Gutiérrez Rodríguez 2018). In other words, the inequalities that German federalism contributes to the unfairness in asylum are only compounded by racist aspects of migration control and integration ideologies.

What emerges is a problem of administrative coherence and policy fluctuations, which make the implementation of the law produce arbitrary outcomes. The local BAMF offices make asylum decisions, but Schittenhelm and Schneider (2017) argue that the agents themselves have little authority over individual cases and most of their work is conducted through symbolic power. The relevance of being local government agencies, both federal and Länder, have a perceived *discretion* to operate relatively independently in the processing of asylum cases, but are governed by something beyond Bourdieu's notion of the *bureaucratic field* (Bourdieu 1994). Schittenhelm and Schneider interpret this to mean that 'the bureaucratic field objectifies the authority of the state in acts of authorisation that shape officials' positions as well as their actions, beliefs, and discourses' (Bourdieu 1994, 12 as cited in Schittenhelm and Schneider 2017, 1699). However, I move beyond the frame of the single government agent in order to consider a social reality of the public imaginary, which is largely national but operates locally. Agents are not influenced so much by the broader policy, but interpret policies based on locally constructed realities that are produced inside offices, not necessarily regions; on the other hand, the limited authority of their position as agents also calls into question the state as an absolute authority, as Bourdieu suggested:

> It is the state, acting in the manner of a bank of symbolic capital, that guarantees all acts of authority – acts at once arbitrary and misrecognized as such ... The nomination or the certificate belong to the category of *official* acts or discourses, symbolically effective only because they are accomplished in a situation of authority by authorized characters, 'officials' who are acting *ex officio*, as holders of an *officium* (*publicum*), that is, of a function or position assigned by the state. (Bourdieu 1994, 12)

For local administrators working at BAMF, this notion of authority is contested in cases of disputed asylum claims and local figures' accountability for errors. Scandals and rejections of the authority of BAMF at the regional level since 2015 put the institution at odds with its local branches and the federal level of authority as well as THE regional courts (Kastner 2018; *Zeit Online* 2020). The milieu of immigration authority found throughout European asylum law (Jubany 2011; Eule 2018) can be seen in a broader context of the social imaginary of agents at BAMF that is constructed through media, personal job security, and a governmentality approach to refugee law that consists of what was discussed earlier as 'working conditions' as well as social perception (Ellermann 2006).

The government's capability to process asylum claims regionally influences refugee's choice of settlement region, as outlined in Chapter 1. However,

Syrian collaborators for my research also used their social capital to learn about the capacity of regions to organize emergency shelters and to provide access to housing, and offer language courses. Certainly, there was a regional approach that dictated how administrations began legal integration measures, but fluctuating Syrian networks allowed refugees to manoeuvre around and in between these measures to assert their agency.

While social capital and refugees are often framed in the access migrants or refugees have to labour markets (Cheung and Phillimore 2014; Eggenhofer-Rehart et al 2018), I am interested here in the discourse on social networks and their link to social capital (Sökefeld 2006; Ryan et al 2008; Erel 2010; Etzold 2017). Although there are ways to access labour markets early on in the asylum process both legally and illegally, quality work in Germany that would be more than the amount offered through welfare benefits is limited without a minimum of German language skills. Furthermore, applying social networks to access early arrival necessities, such as residency cards, housing, language courses, or to overcome a litany of other bureaucratic hurdles, may expedite, slow or directly influence later access to quality work. In other words, although the remainder of this chapter will discuss early arrival issues, this does not mean that the social capital used to access those pathways is mutually exclusive to such networks that would later be used or play a role in access to labour markets. I approach the conditional inclusion of refugees with caution so as not to reduce the experience of Syrian refugees to those valued by way of such neoliberal contributions to society. Instead, my hope is to engage with how they navigate the conditionality of being a refugee in Germany – or to relate to a broader discourse of 'performing refugeeness'.

Bureaucracies and time

While Michael Lipsky may have captured the framework for researchers of social work to establish discourse on bureaucracy, it was Michael Herzfeld's work that began to frame bureaucracies as a class-critical aspect of anthropology of the state (Herzfeld 1982; 2019). Herzfeld argues that bureaucracies are both indifferent to individual needs and at the same time function only when rules appear rigid, but in practice are flexible or, to put it another way, they have 'shared rules and strategic practice' (Herzfeld 2004, 167; 2007, 321). However, two other frames of analysis elaborate more deeply on the work of Herzfeld. Building on Herzfeld's notion that the 'government business' allows bureaucrats to control clients' time (Herzfeld 1992, 163), Hoag's analysis of time as a theme 'central to the experience and operation of bureaucracy' (Hoag 2014, 411) shows how time can be both 'linear' and 'circular'. In this circular understanding of time, there is hope for an end point, but complications can return individuals back to square one. Finally, prominent work by Gupta – informed by fieldwork in Indian bureaucracies characterized by rampant corruption – explores the contradiction between government anti-poverty initiatives and the failure of the state to effectively manage or reduce the millions of poverty-related deaths per year in India (Gupta 2012). Gupta later built on his seminal work *Blurred Boundaries* (Gupta 1995) by highlighting the reification of the state in the public imaginary, which is a concept that emerges through public understandings of the imaginary in his book *Red Tape* (Gupta 2012). In *Red Tape*, Gupta made a deeper argument about the administrative state, which asserted that low-level bureaucratic 'arbitrariness' – here praising but replacing Herzfeld's 'indifference' – produces and/or reproduces forms of structural violence.[1] Both can be helpful to understand how the Syrian research collaborators presented here experienced asylum claims and processing.

To this end, all research collaborators discussed the period of arrival with a fuzzy sense of time, yet they distinctly remember their impatience upon arrival. Reflecting on time, space and place, Jackson illuminates how memory shades events when 'the meanings we give to events eclipse and compromise our memory of them, so that while we go beyond the past in our new imaginings, rationalizations and narrations, engrained habits of thought and action persist, effectively binding us to the past' (Jackson 2005, 2).

The sheer volume of asylum seekers in 2015 made the process inherently chaotic. Mohammad's journey from Turkey to Germany took a matter of days, but was punctuated by memorable events. He casually brushes over the travel over sea to Greece, being caught once and sent back, only to set back out the next day. But when he recalled being in a train container with 50 other men standing up for six hours straight, he told me that "we had to stand there and not smoke and couldn't move, that was the worst part of that trip" (Mohammad, Saarbrücken 2017). They passed through a country he could not remember the name of, but remembered arriving in Germany and the police searching them for weapons, yelling at them to stay put while they waited. This first confrontation with a German authority, where he imagined a more nuanced democratic order, was significant. And of course, the bad food, the crowded halls, here and there for periods of time, health inspections, inoculations, waiting for a court appearance for his asylum claim – but when it was over, the first question in his mind was: *how long would he have to wait to be able to work?* Time compresses and expands in memory and experience, especially in times of limited ability to imagine a future, like an existential notion of stuckedness (Hage 2009). The layer of immobility to act and the immobility to influence the lives of relatives, no longer being over *there*, creates a duality of trauma while waiting for something to happen – in other words, a form of orientation stasis. A orientation stasis occurs when refugees were unable to clearly imagine a navigable future, which is not a loss of hopefulness, but instead a momentary lapse in control.

In Mohammad's experience he was offered a similar choice to Anas, with the freedom to move upon arrival to Germany and apply for asylum elsewhere. Instead, he used his social capital to navigate the fastest path to asylum. There is a distinct difference here in the traditional construction of the refugee experience. Mohammad was not part of the imaginary of those living in the squalor of refugee camps in Greece or Italy waiting for a relocation claim to come through in order to move on to one of the settlement countries (Rozakou 2017; Della Puppa 2018). He was part of a group with a certain level of means and movement that arrived before the Residency Obligation came into effect in early 2016, which restricted refugee and asylum seeker freedom of movement. He would go on to wait six months, travelling through several cities and living conditions, before receiving asylum.

Gaining asylum during this time was defined by the country of origin. The question of who would be admitted as a refugee was not of great concern for Syrians arriving, since it is was almost certain that they would be granted protection and residency rights (Pro Asyl 2018). However, as important as access to early social acceptance was, more practically, access to language courses was a priority upon early arrival because of the demands from the German state for language learning. Unlike Hassan, who arrived in 2014 and benefited from several people in the neighbouring village coming to teach him German in the months he waited for his asylum application to be processed, Mohammad only had contact with bureaucrats and then later on, a retired man came to check on him and others in the camp where he stayed. This was his only contact with a non-official during his first settlement. On the contrary, he remembered walking down the street in a small town and people in a passing car yelling racial slurs at him and his friends. It was an experience that would stay with him and others to whom he related the incident, informing other forms of racism against refugees, which drove home feelings of uncertainty. These punctuated events are part of the narrative that Syrians constructed during this time. Events reveal 'biographies as well as histories' (Jackson 2005, 13) from the singular perspective of experience, but help to formulate collective imaginaries.

Nazir was the only one in his family who went on the journey because his family could only afford to give him money to travel. One of the first times we met, he explained that "my mother and father were very afraid for my brother because he had his wife and two children with him. I said, 'I am young, I can come, no problem. It was too much money for all the family to come'". Speaking of life in Syria occupied at the time by ISIL, he explained, "there, young men can't live there because of Daesh". He was planning to study economy at a university, but because ISIL brutally took control of the area, it was no longer possible to study or work. He would have either been killed or forced to fight alongside ISIL. He searched on the internet with a friend for the best way to travel from Turkey to Germany. In 2015, he left Dier ez-Zor to travel first to Turkey, and then paid for a boat ride to Greece, through all the chaos of the massive migrant movements at blocked borders, and finally crossed into Germany. Then came the long period of waiting for an asylum decision and his identification cards. He would spend seven months sharing a small room with 12 other asylum seekers. Early on, his first priority was also to work once he finished his asylum process.

Rasha had to deal with long-distance German bureaucracy in order to gather all the proper documents for her and her girls to join a family member already in Germany. When Rasha joined Hakim after two and a half years living in Turkey, she told me: "And when I came here, I imagined I would be coming to paradise. And I thought everything would be good. But then I saw the container and I said 'Oh my god! At least in Turkey, I had a house.'" When she saw the situation after she arrived, she wanted to get everything done fast, but Hakim had to explain to her that things worked more slowly in Germany, that it was all a long process and that she must be patient.

Applying for asylum is in effect the ultimate submission to bureaucracy. As similar research in the field of migration argues, asylum seekers submit to authority indicating a *negative power relationship*, in which individuals are dictated to in terms of what action is appropriate at what time (Dagg and Haugaard 2016).[2] However, I disagree with the notion of other research which argues that recognized refugees somehow achieve more agency once asylum is approved (Dagg and Haugaard 2016, 398). Gaining asylum is only the first point of security and even that is not without some precarity. Asylum in Germany, with the addition of the subsidiary protection, is not something permanent, as it does not guarantee a residency permit to live and work in Germany – the subsidiary protection had to be renewed every year and was decided by a separate area of government. As noted earlier, the country-specific approach to asylum favours some groups over others, while at the same time access to work with a salary greater than social support is unlikely in Germany without recognized skills.

As a point of departure, the asylum seekers needed to learn the host country's primary language and, lacking resources, asylum seekers also arrived at the lowest tier of a hegemonic hierarchy of the welfare state, which made them vulnerable to exploitation and receiving limited state support during the summer of 2015 (Gutiérrez Rodríguez 2018). In reality, it would be highly unlikely for an asylum seeker in the German welfare state to go hungry. However, research carried out in around 2015 in Germany highlighted the limitations of the state to carry out diligent oversight to review the housing quality at asylum centres (Safouane 2017) as well as concerns about the overall health of asylum seekers and their access to healthcare (Schneider, Joos and Bozorgmehr 2015). News coverage in 2015 (Bartsch et al 2015) followed many reports of violence between refugees themselves in shared housing and the sexual exploitation of asylum seekers by security workers. Violence against asylum seekers and the destruction of temporary housing by right-wing extremists is well documented (Benček and Strasheim 2016) and is supported by research connecting violent action to violent discourse in recent years (Abadi et al 2016). In other words, there have been several inquiries into connecting right-wing attitudes and an increase in anti-refugee violence. However, I do not believe that it is at all possible to draw a direct line from rhetoric to violence, but in the same way as cultural violence makes other forms of violence look and feel acceptable (Galtung 1990), violent, racist rhetoric allows violence against refugees to become normalized. This is not to propound stereotypical notions of victimhood amoung asylum seekers; however I do seek to examine this structure, one that Bakewell (2010) warns places refugees in a precarious position of ascribing too much agency to refugees, lest their status be called into question.

Upon arrival, my collaborators attempted to negotiate their position and assert a level of control within the asylum regime. However, on many occasions they made decisions that would not put them in a better position in terms of a quicker asylum processing time or give them better access to language courses, work or housing. Hassan only benefited from early access to German language courses because he arrived by chance earlier than others and received language support through informal means. In other cases, institutional discrimination, limited access to housing and poor living conditions altered the ability to imagine the same future they had planned before leaving to apply for asylum. This early negotiation can be characterized by a form of social capital that is insecure in value because of the volatile conditions. It is also a failure of the imagined state to assert its power of authority over refugees as an accountable institution. Early reliance on networks of other Syrians instead of official forms of information is a cyclical pattern of interaction between the integration regime and refugees that would continue throughout this process. Although the means of accessing the benefits of the regime are unequivocally available, the 'knowhow' or 'feel for the game' in a sense of habitus is elusive when refugees invest their social capital in sources that are not necessarily reliable in times of volatility (Bourdieu 1993). In other words, the capital that is accumulated has a temporal and special conditionality that benefits some, while others apply the knowledge that may be outdated, inaccurate or incorrect for a particular region.

The performativity of asylum-seeker identities

Many of my collaborators imagined that once they arrived in Germany, things would get easier, but the impatience of beginning their new lives in the face of an orientation stasis was challenging for many of them at the point of initial arrival after applying for asylum. To complicate matters further, upon arrival the present and continued evolution of the imaginary of *refugeeness* was to be renegotiated without the refugees themselves being involved. The social construction was reproduced while its definition was in flux based on public events. This imaginary was influenced by political and social movements in Germany, which in the autumn of 2015 were largely in favour of and sympathetic to refugees in Germany. The work of Borneman and Ghassem-Fachandi (2017) analyses the volatile mood shifts (*Stimmungswechsel*) in Germany, using the German word *Stimmung* to frame a discourse of public events, which can mean both or either an internal mood or something more external like atmosphere. Beginning on 15 July 2015 with German Chancellor Angela Merkel's attempt to console a crying young girl during a 'Citizens Dialogue' (*Bürgerdialog*) event. The girl and her family were seeking asylum, but Merkel gave a relatively cold reply, causing public criticism. Months later, the outcry following publication on 2 September of images of Alan Kurdi, the young Syrian boy drowned at sea attempting to cross the Mediterranean and whose body washed up on a Turkish beach, drove greater sympathy for refugees. Finally – and what I have not discussed up until now – a drastic public mood shift towards xenophobia occurred on New Year's Eve 2015 in the city of Cologne, when reports of mobs of Arab men sexually assaulting German women emerged, which resulted in complaints against 183 men (Borneman and Ghassem-Fachandi 2017). Media coverage and aalysis of events across Europe not mentioned in the work of Borneman and Ghassem-Fachandi (2017), such as one of the worst terrorist attacks in European history in November 2015 in Paris, had also been used in public discourse to arbitrarily connect Islamic terrorists to refugees from the Arab-speaking world. However, instead of considering this as a form of *Stimmung* or *Stimmungswechsel* (change of mood), I suggest that the use of these events by media and politicians to reframe the discourse also motivated sections of the public and refugees, particularly when politicians made public statements that influenced where refugees wanted to apply for asylum, but more importantly shifted the public imaginary about refugees. In other words, my collaborators had planned to apply for asylum in Germany well before September 2015, at which time it was perceived that Germany would allow more asylum applications – from a historical perspective, media and public discourse return to this notion that public statements motivated more migration. Additionally, xenophobia had already materialized by way of the political party Patriotic Europeans Against the Islamisation of the Occident (PEGIDA), which emerged in 2014, and by way of the AfD 2013, although the latter gained more (albeit marginal) popularity in the following years (Marx and Naumann 2018). Finally, in the time that passed from the summer of 2015, and following what happened during the new year's eve celebration at the end of that year in Cologne, these events became discursively part of a spectrum of motivations for increased violence against asylum seekers, but the violence cannot be assumed to represent the mood of an entire population; rather, it indicates an increase in the boldness or motivation for such action (Benček and Strasheim 2016; Jäckle and König 2018; Vollmer and Karakayali 2018; Köttig and Sigl 2020). Vollmer and Karakayali (2018) note that when Germans provided support for refugees through volunteerism after 2015, they often expected something in return – a kind of quid pro quo volunteerism. As revealed though fieldwork carried out during this period, volunteers expressed indignation in interviews when their expectations that refugees should be grateful, made visible through conformity to volunteers' perception of 'German' norms, were not met (Vollmer and Karakayali 2018, 129). In other words, they performed refugeeness in a way that followed the social construction of the refugee as victim, but when the imaginary of refugee as perpetrator emerged as a possibility, the expectation of this performance changed or alternatively vanished altogether. The public frame of the *deserving* refugee emerged, and with it a reinforcement of conditional inclusion through integration. In a similar manner to the experience of my collaborators with regional volunteers, there was no marked drop-off in volunteer engagement nationally. However, the shift in public debate marked a symbolic turn in the public narratives about refugees in Europe. Shortly after many of these events that affected the mood in 2016, I spoke with Anas on the phone while he was waiting to join the integration course. I asked him how he was doing and he told me "you know, it is very hard to be a refugee in Germany right now, and *I am refugee*". It was clear that his situation had not altered much, but he was commenting on the change in discourse about his group identity.

Since the work of Malkki's influential discourse on refugee performativity and how refugees are defined, other research has expanded beyond analysis of state actors and has also turned the focus towards the function of NGO support in asylum claims (Szczepanikova 2010; Cabot 2013). Yet researchers often qualify asylum in terms such as an equivocation of speed and efficiency (Thränhardt 2016), so-called burden sharing (Soysal 2012; Hilpold 2017) or what this section concerns itself with: the construction and legitimization of the refugee (Zetter 2007; Zimmermann 2011; Gibney 2018), which includes the implication of xenophobic tropes in Germany (Ilgit and Klotz 2018) and analysis of how asylum-seeker narratives are portrayed and who speaks for refugees (Sigona 2014; Innes 2016; Schittenhelm and Schneider 2017).

Very detailed accounts of the asylum procedure in Germany already exist in the literature from ethnographic perspectives (Scheffer 2001; Gill and Good 2019) to locality-centred research (Hinger, Schäfer and Pott 2016; Schittenhelm and Schneider 2017). However, Safouane's analysis of asylum reception centres in Hamburg in 2016 specifically establishes the manner in which refugees reconstitute their narratives to adapt to the legal refugee frameworks in Germany and internalize 'the "foreign" language of the credibility assessment procedure', in which case 'applicants become themselves agents of the rules that alienate their subjective journey narrative' (Safouane 2017, 1930). This case speaks to a broader discourse in refugee regimes, in particular the paradox that Zetter notes:

> The refugee label has become politicized, on the one hand, by the process of bureaucratic fractioning which reproduces itself in populist and largely pejorative labels whilst, on the other, by legitimizing and presenting a wider political discourse of resistance to refugees and migrants as merely an apolitical set of bureaucratic categories. (Zetter 2007, 174)

There have been a multitude of asylum designations applied to asylum seekers resulting in asylum decisions by BAMF in recent years, leaving 'peripheral' country nationals in relative limbo, particularly those with a *Duldung* (tolerated person) status (Scott 2018). Noting the taxonomy of bureaucracies, Herzfeld argues that 'creating and maintaining a system of classification has always, so far as we know, characterized the exercise of power in human societies. What distinguishes the state is its ability to infuse the common terms of sociality with absolute meaning' (1992, 110). This is the case with the notion of refugees in the German social imaginary with reference to 'deserving refugees', but within the bureaucracy of the integration regime, there is another layer of coded classification that also carries meaning.

The majority of Syrian asylum applicants since 2015 fell into one of two categories in the few years following the so-called crisis: fully recognized refugee or subsidiary protection (BAMF 2018). It is also worth noting that 99.7 per cent of Syrian asylum applicants in 2015, 99.6 per cent in 2016 and 99.2 per cent in 2017[3] resulted in a decision that fell into one of these two categories (Pro Asyl 2016). But the increase of subsidiary protection after 2015, from a very marginal per cent of all asylum decisions among Syrians in 2015 to 42 per cent and 61 per cent in 2016 and 2017 respectively, brings to light two interesting points (Pro Asyl 2018), which accounts for a larger shift in the total cases from only 1,707 subsidiary protection decisions in 2015 to 153,700 in 2016 and 98,074 in 2017 (BAMF 2019a). The shift was based on a broader policy change by BAMF because of a successful false asylum claim in 2015 by right-wing extremist Franco A. Although Syrians in 2015 were considered a privileged group, this notion soured when a deeper collective image of 'the refugee' rather than the 'Syrian refugee' emerged in the public imaginary.

Refugees were put through the rigor of BAMF's procedural legitimation of asylum recognition, but still needed to perform refugeeness and present a 'good' personal narrative (Schittenhelm and Schneider 2017). Butler's understanding of performativity and precarity provides a helpful framing to understand how perceptions limited Syrians' subjectivity:

> Performativity has everything to do with 'who' can become produced as a recognizable subject, a subject who is living, whose life is worth sheltering and whose life, when lost, would be worthy of mourning. Precarious life characterizes such lives who do not qualify as recognizable, readable, or grievable. And in this way, precarity is rubric that brings together women, queers, transgender people, the poor, and the stateless. (Butler 2009, xiii)

The first wave of Syrian asylum applicants in Germany – the majority of my collaborators featured here – during the so-called crisis were also affected by an overwhelmed bureaucratic process, which included hundreds of thousands of backlogs of cases over a significant period of time (Thränhardt 2014; Schittenhelm and Schneider 2017).[4] In this way, Foucault's notions of governmentality and veridiction (Foucault 2011, 9–10) inform Butler's statement given earlier. The asylum decisions based on the conditionality of *who* was able to perform the role of *refugee* was governed by a constructed collective knowledge 'established in the individual procedure itself' (Schittenhelm and Schneider 2017, 1708). What is even more surprising is that before 2015 the interviewer was 'in considerable cases' not the person actually making the decision on the asylum claim (Schneider 2019, 290).

In relation to Butler's description, the situation for asylum seekers became more precarious as news stories, politicians and the public began to focus on imaginaries of 'integration', welfare use and border security (Marx and Naumann 2018; Rexhepi 2018), and largely ignored the crisis of violence against refugees in Germany (Benček and Strasheim 2016). Syrians were still recognized under subsidiary protection status; however, the state made concerted legal efforts to limit the legitimacy of such claims that only a year earlier would have been granted full asylum status, thus leaving the door open to potentially removing individuals at a later date, to possibly block family reunification and to reinforce an inherent precarity in settlement status. Finally, violence against asylum seekers and refugees had been adequately reported, but there was an institutional negligence to curb such violence. The law after the events on New Year's Eve in Cologne made it 'easier to deport [an] asylum seeker involved in criminal activity' and there was a 'ten-fold increase in arson attacks' against refugees, which shows a futher lack of protection for refugees under increasingly violent circumstances (Komaromi 2016, 82). Komaromi (2016) also notes the infiltration of neo-Nazis into the German security sector as a concerning level of precarity for refugees. The so-called refugee crisis and events following it not only informed how refugees as a subject shifted over time, but also how the foreigners as a subject expanded and returned to old notions of blood German versus foreigner (Sadeghi 2018). There was both a material shift in this period through the change in status and lack of security presence in asylum housing that is rooted in what was detailed previously in Chapter 1 in both bureaucratic constructions of the regime and the regional discord that lacks concrete basic standards for refugee housing. Finally, there was an existential shift that changed the narrative about refugees in the social imaginary and that directly influenced how refugees perceived their worth to be judged by the German public.

Although this section details the narrative and the bureaucratic aspects of the integration regime, it positions the social shift and the bureaucratic shift as indicators of how the coercive nature of integration is established. This perspective shifts focus once again from an institutitional one of integration to the experience of Syrians, which in the case of status would imply that refugee experience is often based on luck. Timing influenced refugees – those arriving before 2016 had no knowledge of the ramifications of new laws and their social capital was based on their ability to reach out to networks in order to position themselves to capitalize on the opportunities offered before legal changes took place. And in the case of social imaginaries of refugees, it shows that while the public narratives may not have had the implicit impact that historical reflections of 2015 would suggest, they did motivate an increased boldness – in other words, a legitimization of right-wing extremism and a drive for politicians to make arbitrary legal changes.

Before and after 2015

The implications of arriving before and after 2016 are far-reaching and currently ongoing. The Königsteiner Schlüssel and EASY systems mentioned in Chapter 1 were the starting mechanisms that the government used to maintain relative control over where and how asylum seekers should be processed. However, in practice collaborators had varying experiences during the peak of the events of 2015 and it was only after 2016 with the Residency Obligation that there was a strong control over who settled where, mostly due to the need to receive benefits through SGB II (Sozialgesetzbuch, Zweites Buch) – known colloquially as Hartz IV – which meant that refugees fell under the support mechanisms of the long-term unemployment scheme.

Asylum seekers were first registered with the EASY system and during the asylum procedure, applicants were required to reside in the assigned region (*Residenzpflicht*) in connection with the BAMF office while they waited for their asylum claim to be evaluated. Instead, many of my collaborators explained that they were told to choose where they would like to go to apply for asylum. After crossing the border into Germany, Mohammad explained they slept in a small city near Hannover:

'It was a big place that gave us a bed and people could sleep. The boss said, "who wants to stay in Germany? Who wants to go to Sweden?" I had a lot of friends here in Germany before I came and I asked one of them, where should I go? One friend said, "you can go to Horst, and stay in a Camp or *Heim*. There you can get an identification card or present your asylum case faster than in other cities". So we went to Horst.' (Mohammad, Saarbrücken 2017)

There is a subtle distinction that refugees apply when discussing housing; they often use 'camp' when referring to a large housing area, such as the abandoned army barracks on the outskirts of Munich, but use *Heim* for a smaller shared housing area that is more like a flat than mass housing. They then waited one month for their BAMF case to be presented and then they went to a hotel in Rostock and waited six months for the BAMF decision and their residency cards (Aufenthaltstitel). Anas, Nizar and others had similar experiences based on their networks and their ability to navigate bureaucracy. Outcomes from these inconsistencies were not particularly relevant; however, the Residency Obligation, which followed in 2016, stemming in part from political discourse over so-called parallel societies (*Parallelgesellschaft*) (Xenia and Kluge 2016), made the consequential interpretation of asylum and residency law based on decisions by administrations at the Länder level and not the federal level Chemin et al 2018, 49–57). Not only would variables like *bureaucratic discrepancy* effect integration protocols, but what was also relevant was the way in which the Länder chose to limit movement within the entire state or to force refugees to live in the city of their original asylum application, which would have a contradictory influence on the official integration aims. The integration regime is framed here beginning with the first residency permit refugees receive, which under normal circumstances would be valid for three years. As a result, if someone arrived after 2016, they would have had to stay in the same city unless they were given permission to move by the Ausländerbehörde or the Job Centre (Jobcenter).

But in the case of my collaborators whom I met early on, the rule did not apply and they had the ability to move freely and use capital to locate themselves closer to established networks, which influenced how they would later move around Germany in search of better language courses, academic and vocational training, and actual work.

Locating roots

One afternoon in 2017, Anas and I sat in his cramped room in Saarbrücken and he pulled out the paper contract we had discussed while walking through the city earlier that day. It was from a language school where in 2015 he had mistakenly signed a one-year contract to live and learn German. He told me how he hated that school for not making it clear what he would be doing there and for how long.

When Anas first arrived in Saarland, he was in a room with around 100 people for three weeks. But afterwards he would end up sharing a room with ten other refugees at the language school. He remained contemptuous of the school when we spoke about it later, but he admitted that he formed some of his best friendships during this time.

In Rasha's case, the miserable conditions of the container housing were amplified by both country of origin-specific reasons – in the more extreme examples overcrowded emergency halls with 1,500 migrants from around 20 different countries led to mass brawls and serious violence (*Zeit Online* 2015) – and by the behaviour of the residents. Residents would stay up late, drink alcohol and even use drugs, while Rasha was attempting to rebuild a life, learn a new language and shield her children from such behaviour.

Regardless of the forms of social capital upon early arrival and the way in which my collaborators began to feel the burden of precarious subjectification, they eventually found a location to stay after asylum decisions were made and began to form regional networks while living in transnational realties with family members still in Syria or Turkey. This is a period of transition, waiting and establishing new connections. Instead of a smooth transition from asylum seekers to recognized refugees, access to the integration regime remained elusive for many months, sometimes even years.

After asylum

Motivated by impatience, many of the collaborators I discussed in the previous section accepted the slow processes of bureaucracy after months of simply waiting. Hakim explained to Rasha that they must be patient here in Germany. Unlike other new arrivals, who after a successful asylum decision had to wait anxiously for their residency cards, Hakim had already undergone that period of waiting for a long time so that Rasha and the children could join him through the family reunification (*Familiennachzug*)[5] visas and only wait for residency cards upon their arrival in Germany. Nonetheless, they had already been separated for a significant amount of time and were ready to begin a new life. But the transition period entailed two levels of change. On the bureaucratic side, they had to change from the Asylum Applicant Support Law (Asylbewerberleistungsgesetz) to SGB II, which required the coordination at the Kommune level between the Sozialamt (Social Welfare Office) and the local Job Centre (Bogumil et al 2018; Bommes 2018); the federal government only gets involved when refugees are waiting for the review (confirmation) of an asylum claim after a period of three years. However, in a more existential reality, the notion that their security is relatively safe and they could now begin focusing on the life they imagined when they fled to Germany allowed my collaborators to believe that things would become easier.

Instead of falling under the supervision of the local Social Welfare Office or BAMF, once they receive recognition as a refugee or subsidiary protection, asylum seekers are directly under the authority of the Ausländerbehörde with regard to all matters of residency allowances and the local Job Centre for almost all financial matters. The emphasis on local authorities is prominent. Although politically speaking Munich is in the centre of the predominantly conservative Länder Bavaria, the city itself is rather liberal and the influence of this liberal attitude can be found in the administrative branch of the Ausländerbehörde.

The offices are notoriously unfriendly, but the head of the refugee department made a clear distinction during an interview when I met her in 2019 as to how their office handled rejected asylum claims as mandated by the city of Munich:

'Also, if they are rejected totally, we have to try to make them leave Germany or we have to look if there is any other reason for them to stay here. For the city and government of Munich, this is a very important point. First of all, we look if there is any reason [for the applicant] to stay here. Not say, *okay, asylum procedure is finished, you have to leave.* We have to say, *asylum procedure [is] finished, [if there is] any reason to stay, in case no, then we have to start the deportation procedure.* In case there is any chance, we have to investigate this chance. So that's the main thing that the Foreigner's Office of Munich has to do, because the city of Munich says this is important for us, not the deportation.' (Anja, Munich 2019)

In the ideal situation, once this early stage has been completed, instead of the Kommune maintaining responsibility for shelter (*Unterkunft*), usually collective or shared accommodation (*Sammelunterkunft* or *Gemeinschaftsunterkunft*), refugees can seek housing alone and the responsible Job Centre covers the cost of the accommodation as well as supplying cost of living funds depending on the household. Additionally, there is an immediate requirement to attend a 'language course' once this transition is made if a refugee does not meet the wage earnings threshold.

The ability to move freely based on social networks, housing opportunities, vocational and formal education, and job opportunities has, since the implementation of the Residency Obligation for the first three years of all protected refugees in 2016 (El-Kayed and Hamann 2018), raised a number of concerns that conflict with the aims of the integration regime (Büchsel and Schneider 2016; Xenia and Kluge 2016; Renner 2018).

The transition from asylum applicants to recognized refugees and bureaucratic reproductions within the integration regime highlights one of the fundamental indicators for the Syrian experience in Germany. In the case of Rasha and her family, as a larger family network, they are particularly limited in terms of their ability to use continued mobility and apply social capital in order to settle in areas closer to their friends and relatives. There are also practical limitations with regard to accommodation.

Housing limitations in Germany and soaring rental costs across large cities have limited where refugees can find accommodation using the funds provided by social support (Krajewski 2015; von Einem 2017). Furthermore, the municipal-level discretion makes funds available for housing in most German cities unattainable when hedged by the minimum square metre per person required by the Job Centre for approval of a rental contract.

Through empirical findings, two levels of distinguishable categories emerge between the majority of asylum applicants, young men and heads of households with more family members to consider. When retracing Mohamad's journey – negotiating new locations, and seeking friends and associated networks in order to find the best place to settle – he had the freedom to be mobile and, after receiving an asylum decision, to move again to the region of Saarland where he knew people. These decisions were not made out of necessity, but rather out of choice, whereby he sought the most favourable outcomes for seeking employment later. Conversely, Hakim's priority was to quickly establish himself as a refugee in Germany so that Rasha and the children could join him. But once he arrived, they were limited in terms of space and mobility.

These distinct experiential categories are not definitive, but rather fluid. Young men may use the ability to engage in networks to maintain mobility, but then, when they have family joining at a later point, they shift from mobility-based choice to one based on necessity. In practical terms, they may find a place while alone, but then face difficulties once their family arrives, or living in shared temporary housing may become a temporary reality without a foreseeable solution. This last point highlights the division of refugees arriving between 2016 and 2019 – in 2019 the temporary law mandating the so-called Residency Obligation was made permanent.[6]

The distinction between those with a Residency Obligation that limits movement and those without is a matter of timing and location, depending on where they arrived in Germany and if they arrived after 2016. The city of Munich can be distinguished by the highest rental costs in Germany reinforced by the Bavarian implementation of the Residency Obligation. The mobility of refugees was in this case truncated and group housing remained the only viable option. The quality of the housing remains not only loosely legally bound by quality standards (Wendel 2014; Hinger, Schäfer and Pott 2016), but what also emerged in interviews with Munich Job Centre employees was that if an inspector were to check whether the quality of this shared housing, it would meet the basic legal housing standards. However, the building I volunteered at in Munich, which was supported by Caritas, was very clean and well organized, but the larger housing areas, like those at the Bayern-Kaserne also in Munich, were rumoured to be of poor condition.

However, caseworkers have very little ability to check on the living conditions of the people whose cases they process. Researchers like El-Kayed and Hamann (2018) have shown through city comparisons that the effects of the Residency Obligation on asylum applicants are compounded by factors such as discrimination, high housing costs and bureaucracy. Furthermore, the Residency Obligation itself has been shown to hinder the idealistic notions of *integration* mandated by the state (Stukenberg 2017). In a sense of 'Catch-22' kind of irony, the state bureaucratic structures have both set the restrictions on *how* they must integrate and the *way* in which refugees go about navigating the bureaucratic processes.

Since the legal approach to refugee rights across Europe has shifted ideologically from multiculturalism to integration (or assimilation), terms like 'Leitkultur', 'parallel societies' and 'immigrant ghettos' (Williams 2014; Dettling and Rauch 2016) have entered the vernacular. The conditions in Germany have constrained Syrian refugees within a time and space where they are measured by and allocated to various arms of bureaucratic ideologies that each reproduce precarity through entanglements with the administrative state.

From the academic side of the integration regime, German researchers have attempted to refocus housing as a 'key indicator' for 'good integration' (Adam et al 2019); however, the implication is correct that many of the underlying social issues that have emerged after years of reductions in social benefits and affordable housing have only been made more acute for refugees.

Conclusion

Both Chapter 1 and this chapter have outlined the events relating to the record number of asylum applications in 2015 by Syrian nationals in Germany, and have done so through the lens of narrative interviews that reflect this time through the discourse that evolved around the so-called crisis. The phases of arrival, settlement and 'integration' have since been constructed and reconstructed, dictated not by the experience and precarity of the refugees themselves, but politically and ideologically. This assertion is not intended to inflate contrary political notions drawn from collaborators and activists against bureaucratic convolution, but rather is used to express the individual experience in relation to the broader research context. This aligns with BAMF's increasing designation of subsidiary protection status for Syrians and reduction of fully recognized refugees, as well as the development of the Residency Obligation concerning recognized refugees and those with subsidiary protection. Both show the tension in practical legal terms, which on the one hand may be in conflict with EU laws and on the other hand may be more immediate and impactful, is the leeway (*Spielraum*) and discretion given to German Länder in implementing such policy.

Work by Lisa Riedel and Gerald Schneider describes this system of federal variation as 'the Federal Asylum Lottery' (Die föderale Asyllotterie) (Riedel and Schneider 2017a; 2017b) in which the country's national asylum rates are shown to vary incredibly depending on German Länder and national origin, which made asylum regionally variable. Nonetheless, empirical interviews and policy changes outlined here have shown that asylum decisions are based largely on country of origin, but the regional approach to asylum decisions may have an impact on the coordination of federal and local offices. Thränhardt and Weiss (2017) outline the pressure put on Länder by the federal government following continual policy changes and highlighting the limited power of Länder to influence federal law and policy, although it is the local governments that assume the burden of implementing the majority of refugee and asylum policy. In other words, the legislation comes from above, but the method and tactic is produced at the Kommune level and, depending on the legal language, some laws can be discarded altogether. For example, only some Länder apply the Residency Obligation, and even fewer have outlined the basic standards for the housing of asylum seekers, yet from the federal to the village level, everyone has a *plan* for integration. The common theme is not the legal aspect of the integration regime, but the regional ideology that is negotiated between local authorities. The implication for refugees is that the integration regime produces arbitrary preconditions on inclusion that may be navigated by refugees, but do not necessarily produce favourable conditions depending on capital or habitus.

When my collaborators arrived in Germany, prepared to work and participate in life in this country, an early and lasting disillusion developed, in which it appeared that the state, despite vast support mechanisms through the refugee regime, did not have their best interests in mind. What begins to emerge is a double-edged, fluctuating transition of expectation and ambivalence in both the social imaginary *of* Germans and in the refugee imaginary *about* Germans (from Syrians). As Rasha exclaimed one afternoon, "They want to make everything difficult!" – the *they* in her statement being the imagined state.

For my collaborators, early on in this process, it was not a question in the legal system or the social imaginary of whether or not Syrians would be granted or deserved asylum; this was in large part decided by consensus. Nor was it a question of capital – should they not receive the official refugee status they applied for and wanted to take the case to court – but rather a question of taking part in the narrative or ability to perform what is conceived of as a 'good refugee', which would in turn have implications on their ability to access the benefits of navigating the integration regime.

PART II

Integration

Integrating integration: a prelude
A majority of young men in Germany

In the period from 2013 to 2016 there were a variety of media discourses highlighting the number of young male refugees who arrived in Europe. These discourses helped shape the imaginaries of refugees who became racialized and seen as criminal threats to order. The discussion was always framed by who had *integrated well* and who had not. This tension tended to be conceived of as social divisions emerging from the 'refugee crisis' and of perceived cultural differences (Richter 2016; Bangel and Thurm 2016; Bershidsky 2018; Abdelilah et al 2019). However, the fact remains that the majority of asylum applicants and refugees arriving from 2015 onwards were indeed young men living alone – a group I consider to be from aged 18 to 35 (BAMF 2019a). Nonetheless, much of the discourse was uncritically observed from a statistical perspective of male arrivals, and ignored the broader context of refugee arrivals. In the following chapters a more nuanced and less static narrative will be presented. In other words, Chapters 4 and 5 draw a rather decisive line between the group of young male arrivals and the family group arrivals.[1]

The distribution of Syrians who arrived in Germany can be analysed across transnational class divisions, temporal arrivals and the habitus of refugees themselves. There were incredibly nuanced cases in which refugees arrived in Europe and applied for asylum, but later had family members join them, or in some cases arrived after legal changes and received a status that prohibited a family reunification visa (*Familiennachzug*). There were refugees from well-educated, wealthy land-owning classes who were eventually able to have their entire large family of eight settled, and others who were the only family members sent to apply for asylum because the family could only afford to send one person to Europe. In some cases, young men overcame legal challenges of status by taking informal action that led to other legal mechanisms, which in turn were more favourable to their livelihoods. Unlike attempts that have been made by researchers, politicians and journalists – and often in the public imaginary in Germany – to essentialize both society and refugees as distinct groups, it is the aim here to present a spectrum of both experience and circumstances, where many paths and routes were taken in order to navigate the German integration regime. Nonetheless, the majority of the people who are included in this group of *young, male Syrian refugees* did end up living alone through the duration of my fieldwork. They are discussed here as young men, although they may have diverse and expansive family networks, which are both national and transnational. The fact that they reside alone is noteworthy for reasons I will argue in the forthcoming pages.

Constructing families

The way in which families emerge as a distinct network is through social connections that differ slightly from those of young men and, more importantly, the way in which they enter and navigate through the German integration regime. Families as a field are much more fluid in their composition; structures fluctuate over time, networks expand and contrast, new members join small families and others depart. They are also interesting because they are not as exclusive as may be imagined. Young men are not necessarily alone because they *live* alone. Their family may indeed live in close proximity, but they choose to live alone, as is the case of one of my informants, because they do not want to feel the pressure of performing hierarchies and norms that would be expected of them if they still lived in Syria. Indeed, this fuzziness or blurred boundary of stratified social imaginaries or imagined societies (Schinkel 2013) exists not only in the imagination of refugees and their social construction, but also in the struggle for symbolic power over 'naming' who belongs to codified groups (Bourdieu 1985).

My interest here perhaps is more precisely rooted in place and space – similar to that of young men – the collaborators I group as families reside together and as a result face daily lived experiences. In contrast, there are places explored in this book in which families are separated for extended periods of time, and dynamics of needs and motivations change. Hage's (2009) writing on *stuckedness* informs the times when the family members were spread across vast distances and the symbolic sense of movement was broken as a whole; perhaps one or a few of the family members were moving, but others were often 'waiting it out'. Yet, once reunited, there was a need for a clear vision for the future, one that was formed as a unit and was interdependent on the ability for all family members to *move forward* together. However, the periodic unreliability of the state as a legitimate authority, one that can be relied on in the refugee imaginary as accountable and democratic, produces continued moments of what I referred to in Part I as *orientation stasis*. In other words, these are the moments where the inability to find direction based on their previous knowledge and embodied realities, which in turn often requires informal, alternative modes to navigate bureaucracy or in some cases to give up altogether – in the case of turning to crime, violence or substance abuse. However, the primary point I highlight in the following discussion is the reliance families have on what I call *engaged volunteers*, usually working with a *Verein* or NGO, who act as a symbolic bridge from the network of families and are the main point of orientation.

It is through this distinction that I will outline families as a group that experiences the integration regime very differently from young men, albeit only while they remain in a family orientation. This group, as noted previously, is not static, but evolves and transforms over time and spaces.

Spaces

In one of the earlier calls for an anthropology of bureaucracy, Heyman asserts that bureaucracies should interest anthropologists 'because they orchestrate numerous local contexts at once' (Heyman 1995, 262). More recently, Gupta writes that ' "modern" bureaucracies are technologies of governmentality, in that they operate on populations and not on individuals' (Gupta 2013, 436) – of course, he is making this remark about how bureaucracies claim to function. He has worked specifically against the reification of the state elsewhere (Gupta 1995; Ferguson and Gupta 2002; Gupta 2012). Although the anthropology of bureaucracy has evolved since the work of Heyman and that of a more seminal work by Herzfeld (1992), the notion that bureaucracies are structured by unified idealism that categorizes and oversees – from a position that looks down on managers or street-level bureaucrats from above – fails to comprehend regional administrative power, in this particular case that of the German Länder and Kommunen. The notion that German law is evenly distributed across localities is not applicable because of its federal structure. And yet this section will challenge the notion that bureaucracies are in themselves somehow ubiquitous across localities and uniform in their governmental distribution. Indeed, they operate in localities, but their presence and visibility are almost completely arbitrary and are only orchestrated with uniformity across populations in the imaginary social conscience, not in everyday practised reality.

I do not wish here to compare localities in terms of the way in which the administrative state interacts with refugees across space, although that does perhaps have some relevance. Instead, I will illustrate why regional spaces in combination with family status shape the way in which refugees interact with the integration regime.

Syrian refugees are faced with both the consequences of mobility and immobility within the borders of Germany, and that experience is indeed shaped by the particular locality and the newly constructed 'internal border regime', which through legislation limits the mobility of refugees (El-Kayed and Hamann 2018). However, the driving factor is not how local regimes change the experience of refugees *because of the locality*, but the structural benefits of regionally based access to resources that make navigating the regime easier and the freedom for local governments to interpret and operationalize policy as they see fit. This work is interested in bureaucracies precisely because they do *not* represent numerous local contexts at once; they operate on individuals based on locality and not on populations. I am interested here in how local administrations implement and interpret 'integration' policy, residency permits and the temporary housing of refugees, how federal funding is distributed and prioritized, and who are the primary beneficiaries of these decisions. Bavaria's 'Work First' initiative and Saarbrücken's lack of a specialized department of the Job Centre to service refugees are indicative of both local political aims and the way in which bureaucratic structures function regionally.

Here I follow several groups of Syrian refugees, which are multisited and dynamic in form, but the localities are not definitive in the refugee experience. In other words, social fields *and* research fields are structured across localities and are often transnational – as a result, they have a significant impact on refugee *navigation*. However, the framework of local resources, administrative functions and social networks can be seen as more generalized. The following frames the experience in *localities* and *fields* while avoiding the pitfalls of essentializing all Syrian refugee experience within the described localities.

3

Young Refugee Men: Saarbrücken

Young men present an interesting framework for integration policy. They should be the refugees with the most hope in front of them. They have adaptability, mobility and intelligence. Yet, this chapter will outline how the narrow framework of the integration regime structurally limits the effectiveness of these 'benefits'. Through ethnographic fieldwork with primarily young men who arrived first in Germany alone, I will reflect their experiences through the various challenges presented by the integration regime.

The regional integration concept

Like many German cities, Kommunen and Länder, the medium-sized, western German city of Saarbrücken prioritized integration around 2003 following national legislation that adopted integration as the primary concept for the future of migration law, which was part of a broader shift in political thought, academic debate and the social imaginary (Schinkel 2017). Although there were extensive legal changes that developed after the enactment of the Integration Law in 2015 (Integrationsgesetz**)** (Ersanilli and Koopmans 2010; Bundesregierung 2016), it was merely the final touch of a legal framework that evolved from the early calls for immigration and citizenship reform in 2000 until the implementation of the 2005 Immigrant Law (Zuwanderungsgesetz) (Schneider 2007). From this point onwards, discussion of migration in Germany occurred primarily in the context of *integration*. From the national focus on integration, many regional governments took it upon themselves to organize and define a regional integration concept. This chapter begins with that idealist perspective and applies the ethnographic empirical research to analyse how everything played out when the regions were confronted with large numbers of asylum applications.

The framework outlined by Saarbrücken's Immigration and Integration Office (ZIB) in its reports between 2008 and 2014 largely highlights the collaborative efforts between interested parties: the city working with local arms of aid organizations like the German Red Cross (Deutsches Rotes Kreuz) and Caritas, and a broader network of organizations to assist with the integration of migrants into the community (Zuwanderungs- und Integrationsbüro (ZIB) 2014). To put the impact of a European aid agency like the Catholic Church associated with Caritas into perspective, they alone have over 25,000 branches across Germany. However, the report also envisions a concept of integration that requires broader community engagement by the citizenry with foreigners to achieve its aims. The ZIB distinguished itself by attempting to position what the city or Kommune can conceptually do to support migrants beyond the more practical measures, although primarily in a philosophical sense.

In ZIB's first report, focusing on the city's experience with its 'Integration Concept' up to 2014, it struggles to depoliticize the word integration – that is, grappling with the concept of *social integration* and *official integration*, the lack of space for the individual in the official indicators (work, citizenship or permanent residence) that signify 'good integration'. Additionally, the city struggled to collaborate with the local Ausländerbehörde, which is also associated with local government (ZIB 2014).

When I interviewed one of the office employees, they speculated that the focus on cultural exchange might be credited to the city's location on the German border with France, which has formed a long history of migration between the two countries. The interview partner also pointed out that the ZIB works closely with regional administrative authorities, but works less on the individual level and more on the community level; connecting agencies, leading committees and helping to organize cultural exchange events like the annual Orientalischer Markt (Oriental Market). However, the *need* for a city to develop, or have an integration office at the city level, was initiated and driven at the top of the policy structure that can be traced back to the integration shift in immigration law. Regardless of its more nuanced approach to integration – conceived as something that a receiving society can help migrants 'acquire' – the ZIB approach is still based on a neocolonial construction of others that need help to become more German or European, even if it is grounded in notions of enrichment of intercultural exchange. Furthermore, the well-documented experiences of racism and discrimination at all levels of life outlined in the final chapters of this book are not discussed in depth or accounted for in this integration concept. The basic ingredients of integration philosophy, which include language and employment, are most likely necessary for accessing a substance; however, the framing of support (*fördern*) and demand (*fordern*) makes the relationship one of unequal distributions of power.

Although the National Integration Plan (NIP) publicly included a range of stakeholders and was followed by a conference that included the participation of Muslim leaders, the government quickly moved to promote measures to evaluate integration indicators and produce more immigration controls (Aybek 2012; Boersma and Schinkel 2015). My position is that government policy on migration and integration was conceived at the top level by political leaders, who then used other 'people with migrant background' in a merely symbolic manner of inclusion to legitimize their policy aims, which reveals the symbolic power that false inclusiveness may produce. This approach is reproduced at the local level to frame what Schinkel calls 'moral monitoring' as a celebration of diversity and inclusion (Schinkel 2017). This kind of steering of migrant populations was also done in the scramble of 2015, when refugees arrived in Saarbrücken in large numbers for the first time.

The administrative centre of Saarland, Lebach, where under normal conditions asylum seekers would live while their asylum claim was processed, was quickly overwhelmed in 2015 and forced to decentralize. The asylum applicants arriving in Lebach were sent across the region after initial registration. The region then decided to apply its own version of the Königsteiner Schlüssel in order to distribute asylum applicants throughout the region. According to ZIB, the city worked closely with aid organizations and communities to establish emergency housing and evenly distribute asylum applicants, which would prevent the growth of *migrant enclaves*. This allowed asylum seekers to reside in neighbourhoods otherwise inaccessible to migrant or economically distressed populations. The jubilant *Willkommenskultur* materialized in Saarbrücken alongside many other regions through volunteer engagement with refugee arrivals, who, according to ZIB, supported the incorporation of refugee residents in the more affluent neighbourhoods of the city. The ZIB recalled:

'Every time in a neighbourhood where a refugee home was opened, we would invite the neighbours to an information meeting. This was also really important. We didn't have so many residents in opposition, quite the opposite. At these meetings we always had many people that came to us and said that they would want to engage as a volunteer.' (Interview with ZIB representative, Munich 2019)

Although ZIB uses a distinct approach to integration ideology, the organized distribution of asylum applicants was indeed in line with federal discourse that had warned against the rise of 'parallel societies'. Regardless of their regional efforts, once asylum applicants transitioned into recognized refugees, they quickly relocated to neighbourhoods with deeper migrant networks, the neighborhoods traditionally inhabited by migrants in Saarbrücken, where social ties were stronger than in other areas. In my interview with the representative from ZIB, she also referenced the work of Canadian journalist Doug Saunders (specifically his book *Arrival City*) to qualify migrant pathways into new cities very practically – they would settle were they knew people, where it was affordable or where it was easier to make connections there, indicating they had developed some deeper general conceptualization of who migrants are typically and how they function in a new country. However, these conclusions are framed in generalist imaginaries of unified migrant populations and host societies, producing homogeneous groupings of foreigners and locals.

The perceived and experiential perspective from the network of young Syrian refugees is pervaded by their interaction with institutions and other residents. In the early periods of travel, arrival and waiting, collaborators gathered knowledge and experiences that would dictate how they came to navigate bureaucracy. Since 2015, and made clear through interviews with the ZIB, the aid agency Caritas and extensive fieldwork in Saarbrücken, support mechanisms for refugees that were established to aid them orientate and navigate bureaucracy have been abundant. Indeed, there has not been a lack of information available, assistance or community outreach available for refugees; rather, this information had often either not reached my collaborators adequately or they focused on other more informal sources of information. Additionally, this chapter will address several questions surrounding the problem of bureaucratic inconsistencies that emerged from interaction with collaborators. How to find the *truth* from unreliable agents? How do refugees seek out information and further engage with institutions? What interagency tensions and conflicting motivations within various state administrations emerged at the expense of refugees, especially considering the inexperience refugees had with German government and bureaucratic processes?

Eule's work addresses the last of these questions in part by indicating that 'the "migration regime" might thus comprise more and more agencies with more and more sophisticated methods, but also see increasing frictions and structural deficiencies that hinder their successful implementation' (Eule 2018, 2783). In other words, although access and availability may structurally exist on paper, the capacity for key administrators to reach targeted groups fails to do so because they are impeded by the bureaucratic processes themselves.

Eule (2014; Eule, Loher and Wyss 2018; Eule et al 2019) was one of the few researchers able to access and thoroughly study a local migration office for long-period ethnographic fieldwork. One of his observations highlights the 'nonchalance' of bureaucrats and the way in which they approach cases of irregular migrants with an 'informed pragmatism'; caseworkers were lenient not out of empathy, but rather because of high caseloads and their unwillingness to have to carry out more administrative tasks (Eule 2018). However, the interpretation and implementation of the Residency Obligation, which is used only in some cases in Saarbrücken, and other

Länder policies that are applied at the administrative level, do not necessarily impact the collaborators featured here.[1]

Throughout my periodic visits to Saarbrücken from 2017 to 2020, I was never granted permission to do fieldwork at any of the offices that had a significant impact on integration policy and implementation. Instead, I have relied here on institutions like Caritas and ZIB to contextualize the broader social imaginary. However, the following sections outline the experience of a range of collaborators as they struggled to rebuild a life in Germany through the lens of the state apparatus. It focuses on three levels of interaction with the regime: first, that which is the most fundamental – seeking secure shelter, the ability to move freely, and the power of friendship and family; second, those that are demanded from collaborators – joining a language course, and getting degrees and experience recognized officially to gain access to work; and, third, gaining financial independence or attending postsecondary education. Finally, it deals with the most basic elements of daily life and future building: the ways in which the plans refugees had before arrival have worked out so far, changes to their social environments over time, and the way that they envision and plan for the future.

This chapter is the middle point in their story. It is where they face challenges, where they meet mentors and antagonists, and where they prepare for their final tests as new residents potentially seeking to build permanence after years of temporariness and at the same time dreaming of a homeland.

A place called home

When I first arrived at Anas' flat in 2017, we had not seen each other since we were in Turkey over two years earlier. I was somehow surprised by the small size and poor quality of the flat. The feeling was that of another country, another time, something that did not fit here in Germany. There was a sense of poverty tucked away in the social welfare state of Germany.

Anas offered to sleep upstairs in his friend's place and let me sleep on his couch, which could be converted into a bed that I could sleep on – with my feet dangling off the end. The room was a maximum of 16 square metres and had a small hot plate for cooking and a sink for washing. He gave me a tour without moving his feet: 'here is the instant coffee and hot water cooker'. He showed me the stocked refrigerator with instant meats and cheeses for bread and even cookies with a brand name 'American Cookies' (I thought to myself: *he thoughtfully picked out American cookies for his American visitor*). He moved on to the bathroom in order to make sure I knew how to turn on the hot water heater. 'You have to start it 20 minutes before you want to shower, then turn it off when you are done', he said. This somehow reminded me when we last met in Turkey, as if part of the atmosphere had been transferred here along with him, a kind of movable life with decreasing social status.

In front of the window hung a floor-to-ceiling flag from the Free Syrian Army that Anas used as part of the window curtain. At either end of the room stood two desks, one next to the window, where Anas said he studied German, and one to the right of the entryway, where an Apple iMac that was gifted to Anas sat alone, strangely out of place.

Other than a few books, German language handouts and maybe three changes of clothes, the room was relatively spartan. This would make much more sense to me a year later when his life back in Syria came up when we were talking about the human tenancy to accumulate more material possession as one ages.

The next year, when Anas was still living in that flat, he explained that back in Syria before the war his mother would say things like 'When you are married, I will give you these for your family', and would gesture to a piece of jewellery, a family heirloom. She would talk about what would be given to his brothers and what he would inherit: properties, furniture and other things of value. His father owned several pieces of land in both Deir ez-Zor and Damascus that would one day also be his. These and countless other things were now left behind in Syria or Turkey, destroyed or sold. Now, years had passed since the beginning of the civil war and since ISIL murdered his father and brother, and it sounded as if he took pity on the value given to such things. 'Since we left Syria and I saw how quickly all of these things can just disappear', he told me, 'I don't care at all to have so many things.' For him, all of these things that one may spend a lifetime collecting and worrying about could be gone in an instant, so it's better not to worry about material things.

Over the next three days, we would go on to visit three of Anas' friends in their flats and travel to a neighbouring village where his mother lived and eat dinner there. Anas explained that he had found his flat with the help of his friend Nizar, who already lived in the building. He only had to speak to the building's owner and the owner let him rent the room. I do not believe I once saw a neighbour living on Anas' floor; most of the other rooms seemed like small offices or *ateliers*. His friends, he explained, used (black market) housing brokers (*Maklern* [*Schwarzmaklern*]) to find their flats – always other Arabic-speaking foreigners, often Lebanese – who would charge a large fee for negotiating a rental contract for the refugees. The rental contract in turn was always the maximum allotment supplied by the Job Centre regardless of the size, location or quality of the flat, which depending on the region of the city of Saarbrücken cost from €364.62 to €390.80 per month for a single person with a minimum of 45 square metres and rising in increments of less than €100 per person or dependant with 15 square-metre increments and value per additional person (Aktionskreis Kindergeld und

Sozialhilfe Saar 2019). The 'dubious' practices by rental agents who charge 'immense commission rates' to refugees have been well established (Bogumil, Hafner and Kastilan 2017, 50), but continue because the conditions in the overburdened German housing market openly discriminate against recipients of welfare benefits and those of Middle East or North African descent. The discrimination in Saarbrücken was only exacerbated during the so-called refugee crisis and existed across Germany.

Nizar also lived in the building; as noted earlier, he had originally helped Anas get the flat. Nizar's flat was on the third floor, but faced a different wing of the building. There were more immigrants in this section of the building and his flat was larger than Anas'. Nonetheless, the feeling was also foreign, not necessarily poor, just transient and temporary. The smell of strong teas, Arabic coffee and secondhand furniture all made for a distinct environment. He also found his apartment through a black-market broker, for which he was happy to pay over €600 in order to leave the shared refugee housing where he shared a room with 12 other men.

Their other friend Mohammad also lived only a few minutes away by foot. The three of them live in the neighbourhood Sankt Johann, which encompasses most of the centre of the city and is within walking distance to supermarkets, restaurants or drug stores. Mohammad had been in Germany the longest and spoke the best German, so his younger friends often sought him out for advice. He was also older than the others, around 30 at the time, and unmarried, a not very common combination for Syrian men. Because of this, he was someone older, but without the typical conditions of hierarchy, family responsibility or authority, to whom the younger men could come for advice. Mohammad made light of this later that day when I asked how he felt when he met German women. They were cold to him and when I asked if he met any Syrian girls who he would like to date, he responded by laughing and saying "Syrians cannot just date a girl, we can only marry them". Anas also laughed and said "not me, I would not marry right away, I would need to date a bit first".

The exchange not only indicated their ability to distinguish themselves as young men, who did not live in a structured family that tradition would require, but also how it allowed them to keep their strong connections to other young men living in Sankt Johann, who rented these small single-room flats in the area. The fine balance between the size of the apartment and the rent allowance from the Job Centre, which was dictated and varied by region, city and district, cut families or those wanting to share a flat off from this region of the city.

As an example, take the case of Osama and his brother, who lived in another district of the city, a brisk 30-minute walk or infrequent 15-minute tram ride to the city centre. Their flat was much larger than the others in the centre of the city. It was immaculately clean, with a comfy black leather couch and big-screen TV. The area was one that had traditionally been a region of the city with a majority of migrants from other European countries. Now there was one more layer: Syrian foreigners. Osama told me every time I visited how he loved this neighbourhood because it reminded him of Syria. After spending months and sometimes over a year in shared housing, the young male Syrians were thankful for their independence and the ability to be close to friends. In many other German cities, it was much more complicated finding housing and refugees were better off looking in rural areas, but here they had quick access to their networks of other young men and did not need a car for transportation.

Recognized refugees, physically unable to work or able to work but attending language or continuing education (*Maßnahmen* organized by the Federal Employment Agency or Job Centre), receive the same welfare benefits as German citizens and residents – contrary to the conspiracy theory constructed by other unemployed Germans that refugees receive more than Germans (Schmidt 2017). This means that in addition to the limited cost of housing and heating, they may request extra funds to move into a new apartment and funds for furniture. The funds for buying furniture are given in the form of a voucher and they have to take the voucher to a store that accepts them in exchange for furniture.

Since 2013, there has been limited research on the housing conditions for refugees – how do refugees access quality private housing after asylum, for example (Baier and Siegert 2018)? Yet, there are few relevant works that will help contextualize the broader conditions for refugees in Germany. Living in a temporary emergency housing after a change of status from asylum seeker to recognized refugee or subsidiary protected (refugee) is colloquially called *Fehlbeleger* or 'wrong occupier'.[2] So-called *Fehlbeleger* are one of the byproducts of both the lack of available housing and the implementation of the Residency Obligation. In addition, there have been studies showing how discrimination plays a very large role in refugee access to private housing (Hummel et al 2017; Antidiskriminierungsstelle des Bundes 2020).

What survey data does not also indicate is the subtle differences between massive national aid organizations operating in Germany, such as Caritas or the German Rot Kreuz (Red Cross), and locally 'self-organized' groups; other research by Karakayali and Kleist (2016, 22) clearly shows a relationship between the exponential growth in 'self-organized' aid organizations or volunteer groups since 2015 and the percentage of these groups in smaller cities and towns. In other words, as the number of asylum applications grew, mostly women-led organizations registered as help organizations and worked independently from the larger established groups to aid refugees. This macro-data supports what my collaborators with larger families experienced when seeking housing. They often relied on people who were introduced as friends to me and who I would later learn were volunteer workers who were critical in securing independent housing for the families. Conversely, collaborators in the city of Saarbrücken were situated in the macro-data from these studies that related not only to access to housing convenience, but also to the way in which they accessed the housing market, mostly through friends, because they were seeking single housing, and only sought out aid organizations to help with rental contracts or other bureaucratic matters, if at all.

As von Einem (2017) comprehensively outlines in his assessment of refugee housing in the broader German context, the rise of cost in affordable housing, lack of financial discretion by Job Centre bureaucrats and the large quantity of houses that are vacant and are either rural or centred in Eastern Germany all figure into the complexities of housing by region. Finally, El-Kayed and Hamann (2018) highlight the role of racism and discrimination by landlords against refugees seeking housing, something that has been well documented elsewhere by researchers and activists in other German-speaking European contexts (Ehret 2002; Wendel 2014; Droste et al 2017; Hummel et al 2017; Horr, Hunkler and Kroneberg 2018) as well as reported extensively in the media (Böhne 2017). Collaborators in Saarbrücken and the Saarland region have discussed not direct discrimination from landlords, but rather rejection because they receive social welfare benefits – particularly, they explained, that the Job Centre always transfers the rent amount late, usually on the 20th day of the month, and therefore landlords argue the payment is too inconsistent and they refuse to rent to refugees.

The families in the area around Saarbrücken in the small towns also found housing relatively easily, but the defining difference between the families and young men was the fact that the families had to live further outside the city centre and often in more remote neighbouring villages. The three families that I have visited regularly since 2017 live in cities where most residents have a car, and to which access by bus is infrequent, resulting in long commutes to a city centre. The issue of the travel distance is coupled with family obligations, making it difficult arrive at the primary location of the Job Centre's focus at this early stage: the integration course.

Young men on the one hand benefited early on from their networks and access to affordable housing in city centres that eased the demands of the Job Centre to attend language courses or be present at required appointments. However, because of discrimination and landlords taking advantage of those supported by the welfare state, young men were also limited to specific neighbourhoods and quality of housing that lacked government oversight.

Fördern und fordern in times of trauma

After finding a home, access to integration courses was one of the key things that dictated how much bureaucratic pressure would eventually be put on refugees by the Job Centre. As language is seen as a cornerstone to 'good integration', the mandated attendance to integration courses enabled lawmakers to also add a so-called 'orientation course', which was aimed at increasing social integration and basic knowledge of German laws. Non-attendance of integration courses results in a reduction or even a loss of welfare state support – hence the coining of the term *carrot and stick (fördern und fordern)*. There are a number of complicated mechanisms involved in the distribution of and enrolment in the integration course, but what is relevant to this work is the basic access to the initial language courses, who conducts the courses and the quality of the courses.

Back in 2015, the growth in federal support for refugee support organizations together with a drastic increase in private donations fuelled an increase in refugee support programmes by merging public and private aid as well as social engagement (Karakayali et al 2018). Because the integration course, while designed by BAMF, was in effect outsourced to private language schools and public adult tertiary education centres (*Volkshochschulen*), recognized and subsidiary protected refugees were not *assigned* an integration course, but were instead given a list and told to enrol in a course within a specific time period – usually a few weeks. A catalogue of language schools is also available online where, depending on the city, there are hundreds of listings offered by a variety of schools and organizations; my collaborators in Saarbrücken often attended courses offered by Diakonisches Werk an der Saar, a 150-year-old organization supported by the Protestant Church. In order to develop such an expansive language course mandate, BAMF needed the support of private actors to facilitate the courses, but what emerged in 2015 was the social support mechanism through the civil engagement of *Willkommenskultur*, which engaged with the imaginary civic integration by supporting language learning through activities and, at the same time, provided a form of local *moral monitoring* of migrants.

However, during my first few visits to Saarbrücken in 2017, I was convinced that the language course offerings in this city were strangely limited. Interviews with both the local branch of Caritas and with ZIB revealed that a lack of integration course offers was not a known issue facing refugees. Conversely, all of the collaborators I spoke with said that there had been long waiting times to get a place on language courses, regardless of whether these were integration courses or higher-level language courses. Why did this discrepancy occur?

One rainy autumn afternoon, I sat with Anas and Mohammad as they rolled and smoked one cigarette after another and I sipped the extra-strong tea Mohammad prepared. It was a familiar configuration: one small room serving as living room, bedroom and kitchen, the kitchen being a sink and a hotplate with a refrigerator under the counter, and a very small bathroom. Mohammad told me about how he had travelled from Turkey, like the others across land and sea, to Germany. He described friends and adversaries who he met along the way and how he now found living in Saarbrücken 'okay'. He had a laidback demeanour and described many difficult situations with a surprising casualness. He had already finished his B1 language course and was enrolled on the B2 course. The Syrians I spoke with always talked about the integration course in terms of course level,[3] even when the integration course was over. A few years later, my informant Nazir told me with pride: 'I've already done my C1 course, that's good enough to get into the university'.

There is an imaginary ladder of language course levels that have a symbolic meaning, from A1 at the lowest level to C2 at the highest level. There are those that are based in law, B1 (as part of the integration course) to fulfil the requirements of BAMF and the Job Centre for an extension of residency and later permanent residency, and C1 as one of the requirements for a potentially earlier access to permanent residency and citizenship. Then there are the fuzzier courses, which are a mix of the socially symbolic and the legal: B2 for access to more complicated vocational training (*Ausbildung*) and C1 for access to university. Language course levels have become a kind of shorthand not only for intelligence and education but also for how engaged refugees are with 'becoming part of German society' and on their path to better supporting their families.

But when I met Mohammad, he was annoyed. He was waiting for another B2 course. I asked why he was waiting so long and he told me he had a problem with one of the teachers at his old language school, refusing to elaborate further. Later, when I looked back at one of my early conversations with Nazir, he was also always annoyed, but with the *instructors* at the integration course. He told me he would just go to one course and get annoyed and then just as quickly change courses:

'There aren't so many places in the language course and the teachers aren't very good. There are old teachers here, when these old teachers go into retirement they work for the private schools. They are foreigners. So, I searched a lot of schools, a lot of schools, then when I see the teacher isn't so good, I say, "no" and look for another. There is a big difference between the times when you register and when the new course starts and I have to wait one or two months.' (Nazir, Saarbrücken 2017)

There is always a period of waiting between courses, sometimes months, sometimes weeks, but when refugees drop a course, the wheels of bureaucracy begin turning: the school sends a letter to the Job Centre, the Job Centre sends a letter summoning the client, and then they are given a date by which they must find a new course or face a penalty of reduced funds for living costs (rental costs are excluded in this case).[4] In the event that there is no course available for a few months, they have to attend other language-associated activities called *Maßnahmen*.

Of course, identifying the actual wait times in order to access courses would be of merit in other contexts, but what is more relevant here is the conditions of the mandated course requirements and how the Syrians I have interacted with have reacted to the *conditionality* of the refugee integration programmes. Since it was implemented in 2005, the integration course has become the key feature that the overarching government agencies see as the foundation for migrants to integrate into German society. The integration sentiment is most directly stated in the BAMF report on the federal-wide integration course in 2016, where it explains that 'learning the German language is the foundation for successful integration' (BAMF 2016, 52). The official mandate of the BAs or local Job Centres is to get people working. Refugees are treated in exactly the same way as a long-term unemployed German through these agencies, and if they are not working, they must be engaged with *something*, be it an internship, a language course or continued education; in the end, all must be coordinated and approved by bureaucrats.

The logic that if one receives government assistance, one should in return be actively seeking ways in which to increase one's income is the foundation of the 'carrot and stick' principle of *fördern und fordern*. Unfortunately, the concept has long been criticized for making the *demand* stronger than the *support* (Wiesner 2018). In other words, for the normally unemployed residents of Germany, the relationship with the BA or Job Centre is precarious and uneven, but for refugees it is more desperate because they lack the external support networks and have a diverse range of issues that may not be addressed through the Job Centre. However, from the perspective of the Job Centre employees, they are not social workers but civil servants and therefore are not required to be sympathetic to particular cases; their mandate is to get the unemployed back to work. Both self-study and *Maßnahme* were organized and offered by the language schools. Unlike the integration courses, these short *Maßnahme* courses were intended to supplement the primary language courses and were therefore not regulated to the same standards. When I asked Anas about the *Maßnahmen*, he explained that in some cases "you just sit there and do nothing!". There is certainly more nuance to the situation, but many of the course options within the *Maßnahmen* offerings were completely unengaged with language learning, so from Anas' perspective, this was a quite literal critique of what he experienced.

The sanctions for not attending courses or missing appointments at the Job Centre multiply by offence, starting at 30 per cent and upon three repeated offences or inaction can result in a complete loss of financial support. Only in 2019 did Germany's highest court rule that these sanctions were against the German Basic Law and were finally limited in term of their scope (Groll 2019). However, for the most important period of this research (from 2015 to 2019), my collaborators faced the constant pressure of loss of support even at its most fundamental level: a sanction of a 10 per cent reduction in monthly funds can be given for failing to appear for an appointment.

The basic integration course consists of a language course (B1) and an orientation course, which amounts to 600 hours of German language lessons and 100 hours of information about German history and culture, respectively. Failure in either the A2 or B1 exam results in a repetition of a 300-hour language course. There were of course several variations of this course, which differed in terms of intensity and needs; in some cases, the course increased or reduced the number of course hours based on the intensity of course material. The standard to learn German within a period of three years was a tool intended to motivate language learning using the uninforceable threat of not being granted an extended residency permit. However, the *reward* – written into the legislation of the 2016 Integration Law (§ 26 Abs. 3 Satz 3 AufenthG)[5] – was fulfilling the requirement for permanent residency (*Niederlassungserlaubnis*).

Ingrained into the sentiment of *fördern und fordern* was that a person reaching level C1 in three years (along with meeting several other conditions) *may* be granted permanent residency. However, the basic expectation was to reach at least B1 within the period of the first residency permit, after three years, and then after five years apply for permanent residency. Failure to reach level B1 German could not alter the protection status of refugees, but could reduce the length of the residency permit, which added a layer of precarity.

Like other 'motivators', this approach is used to apply continuous pressure to learn the German language via shorter validation of residency permits and more bureaucratic hurdles to overcome, which neither works as a threat to residency status nor has any other strong negative implication. However, there was no legal consequence for failing to gain languages skills written into law; the cases were left at the discretion of the Ausländerbehörde employees, who could mostly exercise this to provide benefits for high language skills, but the tendency was for high levels of scrutiny, even when reward conditions were met.

When the bureaucratic hurdles of the Job Centre created complications for refugees, they often found informal ways around the control mechanisms for attending a course. Back in 2017, Mohammad was attending a language course and asked the instructor for more detail on a specific German grammar question; the instructor replied 'Here is the book, you can look it up', handing him the textbook for reference. He became disenfranchised by the way in which he was spoken to by the instructor and told the instructor that he wanted help beyond what the book explained, but the instructor refused to recognize his request. When he wanted to leave the course, an employee at the Job Centre informed him that the course had already been paid for and that he must see it through until it ended or receive a penalty.

The employee told him: "Either you go to the course or provide a doctor's note to explain why you cannot attend." He thought: *no problem*. As he explained in one interview: "So, I went to an Arabic doctor and said, 'I need a note so I don't have to attend this course where I have a problem with the instructor', and so they gave me a check-up and they gave me the certificate." Interestingly, collaborators usually began by speaking of the Job Centre as a whole, not the worker at the Job Centre, unless they differentiated how the individual treated them. The individual represents the broader bureaucracy of the nanny state in a way that similar agents and official records group 'refugees', 'foreigners', 'residents' and 'persons with migration background' together. In this case, Mohammad explained how the Job Centre both represented strict conditions and offered an informal way to circumvent the bureaucratic process by avoiding taking responsibility for the poor quality of the course. However, the ability to circumvent poor quality in the language course does little to solve the question of how to find a quality language course, which collaborators described as a matter of luck, or trial and error.

In 2019, Anas was working at the language school he had previously attended as a student. He told me what he thought about the conception and organization of the language courses, only now he was doing so from a privileged insider perspective. When he first attended the integration course, he was in classes with different age groups, different education levels and aloof instructors. Thinking back, he considered how things are now for his mother when attending a course and dealing with indifferent instructors: "Especially when you are an old person like my mother or the parents of my friends. Because they are old, they don't understand anything, they used to sit in the class and do actually nothing. They would just sit there talking or eating. It was chaos."

Finally, although the Job Centre enforces language training, it does not offer specific advice on where to find good courses. Complete listings of course offerings are available on the BAMF website, assuming one has working knowledge of how to access such systems online. BAMF has regulated the standards, outline and procedure of the integration course, but 'outsources' the implementation to local private and public institutions. Naturally, this outsourcing has implications on regional variation and ability to access integration courses. In my observations at different Job Centres, refugees were handed a sheet listing a few dozen local courses as an 'example' of the potential courses on offer, but would not recommend one over another, in part because in theory there should be no difference as the courses were alleged to be uniform in terms of their content and quality. There is also no way of finding the most immediate course; the refugees had to simply contact the language school individually and uncover the procedure for enrolment, which would potentially leave some courses unfilled and others overbooked. In the event of there being no course available, refugees would have to attend a *Maßnahme*.

To give an example, in early 2019 Anas wrote to me that he had passed the exam that would allow him to apply for a university place (C1), and he would begin looking for a job to fill the time between now and when he could start at a university. The next time we spoke, he had found a job – at a language school, teaching German. He found it very amusing, explaining that he had learned a lot about work culture at the language school, the inner structure of the bureaucratic systems, and his rather awkward position of authority over other refugees. But when I came to visit him later in April that year, he was already exhausted from teaching foreign students. He was responsible for students who had often failed the integration course and were required to attend a *Maßnahme* course. He explained his particular situation:

> 'The problem is when they visit the integration courses that are supported by BAMF and they fail the exams after they visit 800 hours of courses. They wouldn't even be able to write a sentence in German or to read anything. After 800 hours of German courses. So, we had to teach many of them the basics. There was the alphabet group, we had A1 group, A2 group, and B1 group. For me, I was teaching the A2 group.' (Anas, Saarbrücken 2019)

The alphabet course is offered by BAMF under the umbrella of the supported integration courses and is directed at refugees who need to learn the German alphabet as a prior step to learning the language. However, there were extremely diverse people randomly enrolled in language courses under pressure from the Job Centre, many of whom attended a range of courses and, according to Anas, had almost no understanding of the language after hours of instruction.

Anas' experience is not only verified quantitatively but also made more scandalous considering the amount of resources applied in these areas. Among those required to attend integration courses, which after 2016 became a majority, the withdrawal percentage was 79 per cent and 67 per cent in 2017 and 2018 respectively (BAMF 2019b), while the 'parental and women's integration course' had a withdrawal rate of less than 5 per cent and the 'intensive integration course' had a withdrawal rate of less than 1 per cent. In other words, specialized courses had drastically different levels of engagement and potential success.

Transnational trauma

To understand the complexity of the choice refugees made when deciding where to seek help, it is useful to consider the transnational social networks that shape and dictate the experience of the Syrian refugees that I spent time with during my field research. I consider previous traumas key to understanding the everyday experience and decision making among refugees who fled Syria beginning in 2014. I suggest that trauma can also be transnational, undiagnosed because of shame or unawareness, and thus untreated and made visible in unusual places.

Transnational trauma is the term I use to refer to the condition of experiencing trauma as a result of hearing news of members of one's social network in danger, which may trigger the experience of previous trauma to be relived through another or may simply create a traumatic situation upon hearing negative news. Refugees fleeing an ongoing war are indeed unique, in that they have often left family members or friends behind who are still in the conflict zone. The transnational networks of these individuals are characterized by those with families still in danger. The framework of transnational trauma is drawn from what Fassin and Rechtman described as 'psychotraumatology in exile', or the domain between activists and professionals who deal with the connections between asylum and torture (Fassin and Rechtman 2009, 223). Their original work traced the historical connections between trauma and particularly torture as validation for being granted asylum in France. The authors are quick to point out that psychotraumatology in exile is not a recognized condition, but rather a conceptual framework applied to the particular case of asylum seekers who continue to experience trauma after flight. This is unique because it frames trauma not in a single experience, but instead in the subjectification of refugeeness. In order to become subjectified as 'the refugee', torture became the key variable indicator to validate refugeeness, in which case, trauma had to become transnational in order to legitimize the construct of the refugee. Fassin and Rechtman's work carefully details how trauma developed in relation to asylum, particularly in France, since the 1950s from a condition that must be proven to a condition that was legitimized through a *governmentality* of asylum decisions. In other words, the connection between trauma and legitimizing asylum claims became governed by a normative praxis by professionals and in the courts, but was not explicit in French refugee law. Instead of considering how trauma is legitimized through torture as a means to validate asylum claims, I consider here the existence and reproduction of trauma through transnational ties, something that materializes in the daily life of refugees. This form of trauma could be legitimized through official channels of the state, but is often more nuanced and beyond the scope of the governmentality within the Job Centres.

When I spoke with Anas after he had completed his B2 language course in 2018, he told me that they had a break in early December that lasted until January. During this time, he said he locked himself inside and did not visit his friends or family, and closed himself off almost completely socially. I remember him telling me a few months before this, as he pointed to his computer that he used to report on the war in Syria: "Sure, I am here, but my computer is in Syria." He explained that it was like that for all of his friends: "Their bodies are here, but their minds are in Syria." I asked him why he had closed himself off to everyone during this time and he explained that he was like this in Syria after ISIL killed his father – he just stayed alone: "At this time I thought of so many stupid things." I did not press to ask what he meant by this, but it was clear from his expression and mood that he meant he considered harming himself, perhaps seriously.

This is not as extreme as Hage's notion of social death, where the individual has lost so much of their *illusio* that they cannot imagine a worthy life (Hage 2003, 79), but instead, like the *orientation stasis* outlined in Chapter 2, refugees could no longer perform everyday tasks in the refugee imaginary without being guided. The constant movement and coercion that they experienced in the prior few years suddenly halted and they could no longer autonomously function with so much time to reflect independently.

A few months later, we visited our other friend Osama and his brother across town. Osama was always gracious and smiling when we visited. When I asked about his family, the laughing stopped and he grew silent for a time. Finally responding, he only said one word, "yeah". I changed the subject to his brother's job. For some, the memory brings back the trauma of the past, while for others, the thought of family still in Syria produces such a complex range of emotions that they cannot speak. My collaborators explained that regardless of their reaction at the moment, under the surface there is a constant torment of the past, the present and weak hope for the future of family members in Syria. In most cases, they cover up the deeper emotional part of the trauma until an event triggers the reaction. These traumas are not fully explored here, but are set in the context of the performative expectations within the conditional inclusion of integration. I wish here to emphasize two points: first, the traumas and experiences outlined in this section are not found in the statistical reports or measured in the repertoire of quantitative analysis – the experiences cannot be measured and are therefore discrete in nature; and, second, because they remained discrete, they were not considered by the state as imperative to differentiate the measures for 'integrating' refugees and the measure for 'integrating' 'normal' migrants. From the perspective of the state, these two categories should have fallen under similar conditions of welfare state carrot-and-stick approaches. Yet the refugees at risk of subjectification should have welfare benefits that take greater care to ensure that mental health is prioritized over integration measures.

The trauma of war from a transnational perspective is not something that Anas would have felt comfortable talking to a professional about, nor was it something for which he could have sought out assistance from other people, but he nonetheless managed to push through it and drive himself forward. However, these peripheral factors, ones that cannot be accounted for by the bureaucratic structures or measured in statistical categories, change the trajectory of my collaborators and influence in some cases how they navigate bureaucratic hurdles and their personal realities. It would only be several years later, when Anas was close to finishing his bachelor's degree, that he would suffer a crippling psychological breakdown.

'Little Syria' in Saarbrücken: the foundations of a diaspora

During my interview with ZIB, we discussed how asylum seekers arriving in 2015 were spread strategically throughout Saarbrücken in emergency shelters that included shared flats in wealthier neighbourhoods. However, once they gained asylum status, the refugees would inevitably relocate to more affordable areas or those with stronger migrant connections. Anas, Nazir and Mohammad all live only a few blocks from the city centre where one finds a typical foot traffic-only promenade, which runs from the central train station to the Saar River. Osama and his brother live on the eastern side of the city.

Osama surprised me when he showed me how much of an affinity he had for Saarbrücken. When I asked him how long he would stay in Saarbrücken, he told me: "This city reminds me of my city in Syria. It's like a copy of Deir ez-Zor. I would stay maybe ten years here." He grinned widely and he told me and Anas over strong coffee and cakes that he could do anything he wanted here. The narrow streets of his neighbourhood are lined with brick apartment buildings. Like many cities, the area saw waves of different immigrants; before the Syrians and Lebanese, the neighbourhood was dominated by a population of Eastern European origin. We walked the streets and saw few 'native' Germans.

Certainly, the impact of Syrians and Arabic-speaking migrants is felt in this area, which was already a majority migrant neighbourhood in Saarbrücken. But for those like Osama, who intend on making Saarbrücken their home, this area is developing more features of the cities that may only exist as they were before the war in their memories. Although the aims of integration reform were idealistically constructed – those developed by the city of Saarbrücken at ZIB and the legal reforms of integration law all aimed to avoid so-called parallel societies – the neighbourhood in Saarbrücken has come to life and it remains questionable how officials will reconcile the idealistic with the legal. Refugees like Osama have more than met the quality standards for legal 'good integration', but they would seem to remain living and supporting a 'parallel society'.

We walked down the small hill from Osama's house one evening and Anas explained that this neighbourhood was very different when he first moved to Saarbrücken: "You see Syrian bakeries here and another shop, all of this was not here a few years ago." He spoke in the same way when we were in Turkey and saw an electrician working in his shop around midnight when the streets were empty in Reyhanli: "You see how he works through the whole night? He must be Syrian." There was a mix of pride and hope in his voice when he told me about how things were in Syria before and now when he saw something that bridged his two worlds.

After visiting Osama, we always walked a few blocks to the local Syrian restaurant that was always full of customers. The street outside was also filled with Syrian sweet shops, bakeries, convenience shops and clothing stores. As we entered the restaurant, Anas shouted a joke to the young man behind the counter in Arabic. "He is my friend, we have German course together", he explained. The waiter came over and it turned out he also knew Anas. He ordered extra food because another one of his friends was coming from Mannheim to visit us for dinner. He was another Syrian and already studied at a university. As the dishes of *Kibbeh*, roasted chicken, *shawarma* and hummus were served, Abdullah arrived and greeted us amiably. He was tall, had a full beard and wore his long hair tied up in a bun. The three of us ate and Anas told us how the restaurant owner is always trying to get him to work as a waiter because he speaks such good German. When I tried to pay the bill for everyone, Anas told me that his friend's father owns the restaurant and they would not charge us for our meal, so I left a tip for our waiter anyway. There was an ongoing fight between us as to who was allowed to invite the other and pay for a meal or groceries. For Anas as a Syrian, it is ingrained in him that I am a guest and he has to host me in some way.

Here and there

We left the restaurant because we also had to prepare to visit Anas' family in the neighbouring village. I asked Anas if we should bring some sweets along. Anas told me that it is not good to bring sweets for dinner. "You only bring sweets if something bad happened", he explained. Over time, since arriving in Germany, Anas has held on to certain traditions strongly and has let others go. With no one around to tell him otherwise, he does not want to live with his family outside of Saarbrücken. He told me: "If I go there, I will have to order my brother to do things, I don't want to do that so it's better for him and for me if I live close by but not together with them." The youngest siblings in a Syrian family are usually at the bottom of a deferential hierarchy. I remembered when we were in Turkey and Anas' other brother, the one who would later be killed fighting ISIL, served all the guests and the other brothers tea, coffee and sweets. For the rest of the Syrian households, I experienced a similar hierarchy. But not in Germany, under the freedom and anonymity of a new place – Anas did not want to continue this hierarchy (at least not in everyday life), which he may be pressured to perpetuate if he lived with his mother and brothers. Yet, over time, he took on more responsibilities for his family. His oldest brother was still living in Istanbul and the next oldest brother had a family and spoke poor German, so many of the responsibilities in terms of dealing with bureaucracy in relation to his family fell upon him.

The last few times I visited Anas, when he still lived in Saarbrücken, he always had to help a sibling with some issue. He would accompany his brother to the Job Centre appointment or would be constantly writing messages on his phone to his older sister, who was separated from her husband.

We visited Anas' mother later that evening. She still spoke almost no German, so Anas sometimes had to translate for her because the siblings and Anas all spoke German with me. Because she had difficulty with German, she relied mostly on her two daughters and one son who lived in the house for anything written in German. But she also finally had a chance to join a German course at the school where Anas was teaching later in 2018. Nonetheless, she was a widow, who was over 50 years old with little formal education; even if she would learn better German, she would still rely on her children and the state to support her financially. Unlike the other family that I spent time with, where the children were younger, the father was working to get his medical specialization as a paediatrician in Syria recognized in Germany and both parents planned to work eventually. In the coming years, they would again be able to support their children. However, Anas was aware of his commitment to his mother (he was the middle child in a family of seven siblings), but in this new context he would most likely become the 'patriarch' of his family, despite existing tensions.

The evolution from *foreigner* to German *citizen*, in the most participative sense in relation to recent discourse (Balibar 2009; Gibney 2015; Scherschel 2018), shows how Anas had not only shifted networks of Syrian friends and responsibilities to his family, but had also come to terms with the duality of being *here* and *there*. Indeed, much of his everyday reality was in the context of the utter boredom within migrant groups who were coerced into attending language courses, but he had a singular aim of gaining a university degree and working in Germany. How reaching the first goal would transform things for him is explored in Part III, but what I would like to emphasize here is the one-sidedness of this dynamic change.

Although Anas defined what it meant to him to be *integrated* in Germany, he remained beholden to many of the social constructs of 'the refugee' and 'the Syrian'. When he met a German girl he seemed to like, he quickly became annoyed by her questions on religious beliefs – he is not a practising Muslim – and how he treats women. He said "when I met her, she started asking me how I thought women should be treated, do I believe this or that because I am a Muslim". At this time, he came to terms with the notion that more so than other minorities, there was a range of assumptions that his background carried with it. No matter how much he followed social norms, he would always be a foreigner and an Arabic man. But he had also developed his own construction of a 'good refugee'.

We sat by the river in Saarbrücken one summer evening and he saw a group of Syrians he knew talking and joking loudly. He looked at them with pity: "They don't even know any German." "You know them?", I asked. "Yes, I have seen them around", he said, "they just stay at home and do nothing and take the Job Centre's money. Did I go out on the street and protest against the Assad regime just so they can come here and act like this?"

Mohammad also constructed his version of 'a good refugee' when we spoke over the phone one day. It was 2019 and he was working now. I told him how many Germans would see him as a good refugee because he could speak German and had a job. He agreed that refugees should be working and paying taxes instead of just taking taxpayers' money. He said: "I ask myself: *did you flee Syria just so you can sit at home and not work? Or do you support your family during this time of war?*". The two of them have consciously or unconsciously co-opted some of the ideological foundations that would be used in many of the contested integration debates. They are reframing this conceptualization to create a hierarchy of refugees within their own national background. They formulated an understanding of refugee duties that includes notions of what researchers would refer to as *welfare chauvinism*, but is contextualized by the transnationality of refugee families, living in places where there is no chance of work. There were times when life reached a standstill, consisting of basic survival and pressures from the way Syrian refugees were being socially constructed in collective imaginary. If they wanted to be considered social citizens and also belong to German society, not only did they need to 'integrate', but they also had to prove they fit into a *Leitkultur*-based welfare state system of values. The conditional inclusion of Syrians by *Syrians* requires that they assert themselves by showing that they have acquired the means to be a part of society through the aims of the regime – language and work – but as second-generation migrants in Germany, the pressures of their social construction from outside dictate that they must strive to be 'perfect' migrants and refugees, even when those taxonomic categories no longer apply to them.

From policy to reality

In terms of effectiveness, the *fördern und fordern* policy approach to the integration regime produces arbitrary outcomes for young male refugees and is based in reality on personal motivations and external familial pressures.

Refugees who are highly motivated by a complex network of evolving circumstances will take advantage of learning the German language and access to employment, regardless of whether it is forced upon them or not. This section has shown that despite the efforts of the state to reify itself by producing policy that can somehow produce 'proof' that integration courses cause refugees to be more engaged with work and civic activities, Syrians manoeuvre around bureaucratic roadblocks, using informal means when necessary. Syrians who are unable to navigate through bureaucracy are adrift in it. They attend the integration course, but learn little from it; the information revealed by other refugees delegitimizes the state's authority in the imaginary of refugees. In other words, the European subject, what Chakrabarty describes as the entangled narratives that make European history the centre of 'modernity' (Chakrabarty 2007), is tarnished over time in the experiences of Syrians, but at the same time is reproduced through their own narratives. This indicates a fluctuation in the way in which *illusio* is produced within refugee groups.

The experience of my Syrian collaborators in Saarbrücken has been one of subtle locality-based adjustments, which provides insights into life in Saarbrücken and Saarland, but is not indicative of the whole of Germany. Collaborators free from Syrian social constraints, or avoidance of familial hierarchies, are more present in this newfound home. What would be perhaps socially taboo in Syria – and still was when I first met collaborators in Turkey – can be done in Germany discreetly, which was representative of change in times when we shared the occasional beer and talked about the possibility of them dating a German girl. Anas sought to distance himself from familial hierarchies and yet make himself available directly should they be in need. Mohammad revealed to me how he tried pork occasionally (although he did not like the taste of it). A very individual formulation of their new identity is created for some, while others are beholden to more collective Syrian traditions, but adapt to the material aspects of German life and increase their reliance on networks of other Syrians living in the new country of residence.

Some of the collaborators in Saarbrücken, like Osama and Nazir, will undoubtedly stay in Saarbrücken, but others, like Mohammad and Anas, have already left. Yet the families I know have logically not moved on. Work from Boese, Moran and Mallman (2018) highlights the 'multilocal' experience of migrants, highlighting the 'unsettledness' of migrant experience. In my fieldwork, this multilocality emerges through a balance between necessity and cognisant decision making. Young male Syrians have moved much more often than families, but more importantly their lifestyles and networks have changed drastically following these moves. The families have been much more pragmatic and slow-moving, drawing out their connection to the integration regime. However, this is all occurring in the narrow reality of local environments, especially concerning bureaucracies. Once certain bureaucratic mechanisms are overcome, the manner in which my collaborators construct their future in Germany is dictated by these factors and the local construction of refugees rather than by national sentiments. Chapter 4 will outline and underscore some of the lived differences between these two groups, focusing on the different forms of social capital used and the separate set of challenges that families face, plus the strategies they use to overcome them.

4

Families: Osnabrück and Hameln

In Chapter 3, I applied ethnographic fieldwork conducted from 2016 to 2019 to frame the experience within the integration regime through the perspective of young men who arrived in Germany mostly alone. In this chapter, I will highlight the experience of several families that I collaborated with during the same fieldwork period. Their experience with integration mechanisms was markedly different from that of young men – for both obvious and not-so-obvious reasons. What emerges from this are structural issues that further question the unitary concept of goal-oriented integration.

Villages and small towns

The following sections are primarily concerned with collaborators who live in small villages next to Osnabrück and Hameln. Rasha and her family settled in a village called Westerkappeln, located 14 kilometres west of Osnabrück, and Abdul and Adel are now living 9 kilometres south of Hameln in an area called Gross-Berkel, which is an unincorporated part of Aerzen. Unlike the cities in which I conducted the rest of the fieldwork in this book, these small villages are characterized by much fewer resources. There is no office for integration that drives the local integration ideology or any specialized office for refugees inside the local bureaucracies of the BA or Job Centres, and no Ausländerbehörde. These are Kommunen (or Gemeinde) which are part of a district (Kreis), which means it is at the district level that the aforementioned bureaucratic functions operate. However, aside from the structural differences, several distinctions emerge from their experience as a family as opposed to the experience of young men in Chapter 3.

"They don't want to give refugees houses"

The issue of secure housing is a topic that has emerged several times in this book, yet under different circumstances, because it is the most basic condition of settling in a new country. However, I emphasize the time refugees spent in what should be temporary emergency housing even after being granted asylum, which is largely based on regional policy, local housing costs and support networks. This goes beyond the basic categories of city, small town and rural, and considers the entire social environment (*soziales milieu*). The type of housing available for refugees is distinguished between families from young men, as well as the means by which that housing is accessed, yet the search and security of housing in both cases often strengthens previously formed relationships. In terms of basic access to housing, other research shows that refugee access to housing is limited on several levels.

Most relevant to this work is a study from the Federal Institute for Research on Building, Urban Affairs and Spatial Development (BBSR), which contextualizes many of the experiences present here and which details landlord discrimination, late payments by the Job Centre and repercussions from the Residency Obligation, but also – and most relevant to what follows – the variables of region difference as factors contributing to securing good housing (BBSR 2017). The study points to the 'appropriateness criteria' (*Angemessenheitskriterien*), which determines the funds available to welfare recipients for housing costs and varies by city or region, as a point of regional difference and flexibility by Job Centre employees who agree in interviews that the allowance is not sufficient for larger families. Survey-based studies can indeed provide insight into the wider context, but fail to access target groups living outside of larger cities and limited numbers in private housing (Worbs, Bund and Böhm 2016), and only address the abundance of black-market real estate agents by way of news media investigations (BBSR 2017) or fail to address the issue altogether (Baier and Siegert 2018). Thus, the actual number of real estate agents working in the black market (*Schwarzmakler*), who charge up to €600 per person to arrange private housing, and their impact on distribution of funds by the Job Centre remains under-researched (Werner and Khello 2016). My collaborators only secured initial private housing through three pathways: by getting help from close friends, by using a *Schwarzmakler* or through the assistance of a local aid organization. While collaborators would later find ways to access housing, upon arrival and at the most vulnerable point, none of the Syrians found their first house by contacting a landlord alone. Furthermore, the housing that families did find tended to be in very rural areas.

When I first met with Abdul and Adel, like Rasha, they continually referenced their friend Kim. When I asked how they found their current apartment, Abdul said: "Kim helped us find the flat and talked to the landlord, and then helped us move here." Adel added: "Kim would be visiting them in a few days. They were looking forward to it very much." Again, I thought it was great that they were able to find such a close friendship with a German after only being in Germany a short time. However, I soon worked out that Kim was an *engaged volunteer* who they met early on in Germany. Should this exclude her as a labelled friend? Certainly not. However, there is a much deeper relationship in this situation than that of an agent of the Caritas aid organization. When I talked about Kim with him later, Abdul said "yes, she works for an organization but she has always done so many things for us that are not part of the organization, she is a good friend".

During another visit with Rasha, she was clearer about her relationship with Julia: "our friend Julia always helps us. She is really nice. She works for an organization called Wabi. And they take care of refugees. We make activities for children, for women, they make kitchen for men sometimes and cook and eat together".

Julia had helped the family since they lived in the container; she was working for a local organization that became more engaged with refugees in around 2015. She came to visit when I was there one afternoon long after the family had settled into their new house – it was clear that she and Rasha had a close relationship. The women snuck off together to smoke in the back garden after dinner so that they could talk with no men around. Julia did not help prepare the meal because she was a guest like me.

In a traditional (or perhaps a more conservative) Syrian household, the kitchen is indeed the women's domain – no men allowed! Back in Turkey I experienced a range of this behaviour, from an absolute restriction, where the kitchen was something so sacred to the domain of women that I was discouraged from attempting to peek inside with interest to learn how to cook Syrian food, to the more liberal, where I was allowed into the kitchen, but was not allowed to help cook. For families that I met again and for the first time later in Germany, the variation was even wider. Some families allowed me to stand in the kitchen and chat, but in Rasha's household I waited in the living room until the food was ready. Anas laughed one time when my family joined us for dinner at his mother's house. My wife made the mistake of standing up and getting her own water: "as a guest in a Syrian house, you should do nothing, just sit and enjoy!"

At the dinning table, other forms of transnational life emerged. The men smoked heavily at the table after dinner, but Rasha waited for Julia to join us before going outside to smoke a cigarette with her. When they returned, Julia often turned to Rasha with a knowing look as if they were sharing some silent joke together. Julia also understood and spoke quite a bit of Arabic, worked with many other families in the small town and organized a weekly women's meeting group. The organization she worked with also set up several day events for men, families and children. But it was clear, and perhaps not surprising, that his relationship had developed beyond what one may think of as 'volunteering'; the volunteer women acted as a support network and a bridge to insight into life in Germany.

In both families, volunteers also replaced the need to pay a *Schwarzmakler* to find housing and served as gatekeepers for parts of the social world.

Rasha nonetheless blamed the housing difficulties on discrimination – being a family, being Muslim and being a refugee. "They don't want to give refugees houses", she told me. "I would call the landlord and say, 'I have four children' and they would say, 'sorry I cannot rent the house to you'". The only way that someone finally rented a house to them was when Julia went to the landlord and said that she would be responsible for them paying the rent.

Abdul and Adel did not face the same circumstances as Rasha, who lived in a shipping container for several months; they arrived through the refugee relocation programme after they were in a Greek refugee camp for over a year. Yet they relied completely on an engaged volunteer to facilitate housing in lieu of other social networks or paying someone to assist them.

Finally, the limited housing available to families adds a layer of isolation to several levels aside from the practical access to language course and social circles. Unlike work that shows how sparsely populated villages were sometimes overburdened by the changing population of refugees (Bock 2018), the isolation has much to do with the 'special access' (Cass, Shove and Urry 2005) that characterizes full inclusion. Cass, Shove and Urry (2005) argue that limited '*spacial* access' to 'activities, values and goods' determine how (social) citizenship and participation are accessed. Access to social citizenship practices is distinct from activities organized by aid organizations or participation with the help of *engaged volunteers*, which require someone to facilitate the way in which refugees participate. The special form of inclusion and restrictions will further inform the way in which refugees consider their relationship with Europe as a subject in their imaginaries. These islands of social isolation, and at times exclusion, are also a unique layer of refugee interaction with the bureaucratic state. There are networks of families which are symbolically excluded by way of differing access to social capital than that of male youth and physically by being bound to locations that are isolated and usually require a car. In Groß Berkel, there is only one bus on the weekend that can take them into the city. Families distribute energy towards their children, time spent in public transportation, and demands from the Job Centre, while remaining in a relative black box of bureaucracy. Parents often expressed stress that they do not have enough time to support their children who are also struggling with German. The burden of the isolated location and integration regime does not leave sufficient space for the luxury that allows notions of social citizenship to develop. Take from another perspective, they are not engaged in the transition Balibar called 'transitional unities', which has to do with individuals transitioning in order to gain political agency and be politically engaged citizens (Balibar 2012). What I mean here is a process of becoming visible engaged communities, which eludes Syrian refugees.

Negotiating a 'good' language course

As noted previously, the guiding principle of *fördern und fordern* is one of action based on support. Receiving support from the Job Centre or BA is contingent upon regular attendance of an integration course or potentially a *Maßnahme*. Similar to the bureaucratic blindness outlined in relation to the transnational trauma described in Chapter 3, the limitations of families are not recognized by 'uniform' integration mechanisms. The wide range of integration courses offered, including those with potential childcare, do not account of the burden of travel distances in a family context. The threat of losing benefits does not convincingly serve as a tool for motivation within the field of refugee families, but rather increases their stress as they attempt to learn a language and adapt to a new environment. Nonetheless, put under scrutiny, the broader context of state accountability shows deeper flaws than merely difficulties based on assumed uniformity.

In the first longitudinal evaluation of the integration course, led by researchers with support from BAMF, the variety of courses developed for migrants is described as an overall success. The report not only argues that the mandated language course positively influenced course participants' motivation for language learning but also served as a tool for migrants to find work and access social spheres of German communities (Schuller, Lochner and Rother 2011). However, contrary findings show the flawed assumption of the 'heterogeneous' integration courses, accounting for nuances in mixed education backgrounds, demographic differences and previous language knowledge (Ehlich, Montanari and Hila 2007; Schroeder 2014). The implication is that the German government does not have a mechanism to evaluate and publicly discuss the integration course curriculum (Schroeder 2014). While a 2016 internal evaluation has also acknowledged importance of the heterogeneity of course participants and the drastic changes in the resident status of participants, it falls short of prescribing approaches to address the issue and furthermore constructs a language and social interaction narrative that largely ignores discrimination (Buhlmann et al 2016). The concept of a *federal-wide integration course* (BAMF 2015) leaves the nuances required for addressing the diversity of course participants in the hands of the instructors (Buhlmann et al 2016). However, the quality of language courses is by virtue variable; due to a lack of data using a locality-based analysis to assess the quality of integration courses, it is not possible identify a distribution of high-quality courses. From a broader statistical perspective, it makes little sense to judge the quality based solely on passing tests – this speaks more to the quality of the students or the difficulty within the testing procedure. Alternatively, I consider here the way in which collaborators react to adversity in the course, the resources they must collect overcome this adversity and later how they apply the language learned in these courses.

In contrast with my collaborators in Saarbrücken, who discussed how to find the best language courses among networks of young Syrian men gain, the way in which families have accessed the quality of courses relies on meeting other refugee women to coordinate finding the best courses.

Rasha attends a regular women's meeting organized by Julia. One of the subjects discussed at their meetings was access to high-quality integration courses. "We go to different courses and test the quality at different courses", Rasha told me. Over time, many of the women had attended courses in the area and had coordinated to find the best language school available.

Indeed, Rasha and her group have not taken on a passive approach to the so-called uniform integration course, but have developed a strategy to overcome a state mechanism that they deduced was unreliable. This informal approach is a way of not only overcoming the hegemonic relation to the administrative state but also producing a reliable pathway towards a hopeful future. Although the collaborators here are past the point of direct crisis, they nonetheless lack the position to act effectively against authority.

Proximity

Why didn't I see signs of transnational trauma in the homes of families? Certainly, they described traumatic experiences. Adel described being separated from her husband for over a year when he was in Turkey and she was trapped in Aleppo after intense fighting broke out and the roads became deadly. Adel and their son tried on one occasion to cross into Turkey, but were turned back and ended up having to go by boat and land over several days to reach Istanbul. When she told me this story, I was very emotional, but she only smiled faintly – a show of strength that they had survived that experience now in the past. But they carried on. Rasha did not talk about Syria or the war much, she only spoke of the time after the war while in Turkey, and the time that Hakim was in Lebanon and walked from there through Syria and all the way to Turkey. The other heads of households I met with also did not outwardly express trauma, which should not be particularly surprising. Parents rarely focused on themselves without considering the impact on their children first. However, from my experience in Turkey and in Germany, as well as other supporting studies (Sim et al 2018; El Arab and Sagbakken 2019), the tension of living through the war in Syria had resulted in an increase in domestic violence and led to a drastic increase in child marriage abroad. The families who came to Germany faced many of the difficulties presented here, but their way of coping with the issues was more destructive. The sister of one of my collaborators fled from her husband after she was a victim of continued physical violence at home and his problems with addiction became too much for her to handle. Substance abuse was also common, but the parents among my collaborators that I came to know were at least in their mid- to late thirties and came from at least middle-income households, which made the transition into German life more manageable. Generally speaking, the trends of substance abuse and violence were of course similar to those found in most societies, affecting the poor and hopeless in greater numbers.

The factor of a more immediate responsibility to children in a household narrowed down the ability to broaden networks between other Syrians and by virtue strengthened the reliance on family closer ties. This is not to suggest that younger Syrian collaborators did not have a greater sense of responsibility and relationship to family members in Germany – they certainly did. However, what occurred was a shrinking of available time which may have been spent involved in attempts to establish relationships and procure vertical social capital. For this reason, I argue that families were enriched by increased social bonds within the household and their relationships with *engaged volunteers*. Their daily routine was rather structured and more predictable, and they did not have much time for spontaneous interaction that could open up new experiences in the way that was experienced by some of my younger collaborators.

Anas moved fluidly through his wide range of relations. One minute he would be on the phone with his brother trying to help him register at the Job Centre, then he would be arranging a meeting with his friend later that afternoon and later on impersonating an ISIL sympathizer on the messaging application Telegram to gain information for a report he was making on his brother's online media organization. He was able to reach across several networks, between young men and families. Indeed, Syrian families have a normative structure, including deeper responsibilities to children and a spouse, but beyond the practical implications, there are expectations and investments in the future that have symbolic and tangible implications.

"You have to forget everything you did before"

Up until this point in this book, I have done little to address the pervading question that may have arisen in the mind of the reader: what actually occurs during the *integration course*? My descriptions seem to focus on the peripheral perspective of refugees' relationship to the bureaucratic foundations and implementations of this course. The reason for this is twofold: first, there is not much that occurs during the integration course that is of great relevance to this volume; second, engaging with the nauances of the language course and the dynamics there did not provide insights into how the integration regime produces arbitrary outcomes. I seek to understand how Syrian refugees act and react to the German integration regime. Having spent hundreds of hours on German language courses (around 880 from A1 to C1), I can attest that it is an exhaustive and monotonous process with little variance occurring from day to day. For refugees, the regular integration course is 20 hours a week, which is five hours a day, four days a week of learning German. This is around the same amount of time that a student seeking a bachelor's degree in Germany would spend in the classroom. In both cases, this does not include the extra time spent studying outside of classroom instruction. It is more important to consider these conditions in context rather than to consider the actual content. With reference to the previous comparison, it should be clear that those with university experience would excel in an environment with similar expectations to a university study. For my older collaborators, the desire to become an engaged student, as it were, was negligible in comparison to the desire to find work and provide for their families.

When Rasha and her daughters first joined her husband in 2016, she struggled to find a house, lived in temporary housing and felt discriminated against by local Germans, after which she expressed her great frustration to me about the administrative mechanisms that excluded them from access to work. They were particularly frustrated with the Job Centre, not only because they were beholden to the institution financially but also because of the indifference displayed by the Job Centre towards refugees.

One evening, as we all sat and talked after eating a large dinner prepared by Rasha and the girls, she told me about how her expectations had changed since she had arrived in Germany. It was the first time we had seen each other since I met her in Reyhanli in 2015. Much had changed since then, but after a year in Germany, many of the family rituals that are followed to greater or lesser extent by Syrian households had continued here. This contrasted with the experience I had with the much more scattered family members of Anas and those young men living alone.

But perhaps certain things had begun to change. We all sat at the table and used utensils to eat instead of using our hands. In Turkey we peeled a slice of flat bread to scoop up portions of meat, vegetable or rice, while sitting on the floor or a small pillow. During that time, I was invited by households which ranged from the extremely 'traditional', as my Syrian friends would explain, to the much more liberal. The workshop coordinators and I were invited to a very large dinner one night at a wealthy family's house. The men were quickly whisked through the dining room where the women would eat, and were sent to the terrace to join the other 15 men for the meal. Edgard, my colleague who joined us from Spain, and I did not see the three women from our workshop until the end of the evening. In other houses we ate casually, with men and women sharing the same communal plate. In all these situations, I tried to make sure I behaved appropriately and did not break any norms that might offend my hosts.

As a visitor is where I find myself often now in Germany with families *here* and no longer *there*. I was attempting to navigate norms that may be based on a family structure that could be national, local, nuclear or perhaps an adapted tendency from the old into a new place – norms that may be forgiven if they are not Syrian, or part of this family from Deir ez-Zor for that matter, but ones that nonetheless inadvertently strain relationships.

When I arrived that night in Westerkappeln in 2017, after not having seen Rasha for two years, I thought I had made some error because Rasha was rather put off by me and somewhat cautious when I first arrived. But a few days later, I called my close friend who first introduced me to Rasha to explain the situation. As it turned out, Rasha thought I would bring my wife there was well, so she had prepared extra food and was only disappointed because there would be too much food now. As I continued to visit more families, I realized how strange it was for them to see a man arrive as a visitor without his family. For me to visit young men was normal, but when I went to visit families, they would always ask after my wife and if I had any children. When my wife was pregnant, they began to ask "was the baby born?" every few months. I finally tried to plan my visits to families with my wife and son. But at times I was still often left at a loss as to how to be a guest with people who were living across cultures and time.

Expectations and norms were shifting and unpredictable. My collaborators were constantly trying to balance the multitude of their past and present identities, hinting at what Sökefeld's (1999) discussion of multiple identities expressed, developing an everyday transnational reality that has been more explored in the context of *cultural transnationalism* (Kirk, Bal and Janssen 2017; Myers and Nelson 2018). To that end, it cannot be taken for granted that refugees were not simply in transit from point A to point B.

Hakim was in Lebanon when the war broke out, and walked with a group of men to Turkey. He stayed there for several months before travelling via smugglers to Germany, leaving Rasha in Reyhanli for another six months before they were all finally reunited in Germany. Rasha and her family left everything behind with the assumption that should they finally make it to Europe, a better life for them and their children would be possible, but she soon found that perhaps only the latter would be possible. They then had to navigate and balance these identities towards outcomes that might determine their livelihood.

Rasha and her husband met with the Job Centre many times early on while searching for a house, an integration course and planning how to find work. First, her husband was told by one agent that he should just try to work at a factory or work in elderly care. Rasha told me about her husband's meeting with the Job Centre agent in disbelief: "they said he has to finish his language study and then maybe he can look for work. But this employee in [the] Job Centre told him, 'you just have to forget everything you did before'". As will be outlined in Chapter 5, the agents are not trained as social workers with a deep ability to individualize or have compassionate responses to particular cases. The general outline for agents is a bare minimum: attend an integration course and then seek work or additional work training, which can be in the form of specialized language courses for particular labour sectors.

I asked Rasha if there was any potential for her to have her previous work records and certificates recognized here. She then explained how things unfolded when she was at the Job Centre asking this very question and adding a bit of revealing dynamics of how the relationship with the Job Centre was felt early on:

> 'So, the Job Centre organized our language study, our money and we also talk a little when we visit them. Last week I had [an] appointment with them and I talked with them. I wanted to get my teaching certificate valid in Germany, it is called in German *Anerkennung*. So, it's like I would get my certificate in Germany to be equal as it was in Syria. I asked the agent if maybe I could work here with the certificate? And he said, "hmm, I don't think so". He talked to me like this. He is Arabic man. He is from Morocco. "We will see", he said. He can't even give us a hope.' (Rasha, Westerkappeln 2017)

Of course, there are three distinct things at play in this case. First, there is the power dynamic, one in which the Job Centre agents have an overarching impact on the lives of refugees. At this point, most refugees are only engaged with the language courses. So, money, language courses and advice for future prospects combine to form a relative hegemony of coercive power to motivate refugees to work, but the question is *what kind of quality will that work be?* Second, Rasha's recollection of events is one that reflects alienation on the part of the institution that is a gatekeeper for access to work. The dismissive nature of the agent's reaction to Rasha's desperate hope for a future in which work could be meaningful, and her wish to engage with the possibility, was quickly dismissed. And the final point to note is that the agent was from the Arab world, not a Syrian, but rather a Moroccan, which is a notable point in terms of character evaluation. In other interactions, collaborators have mentioned the national background of the casework to frame the context of the situation. Arab agents *should be* more sympathetic to other Arabic-speaking or Muslim migrants. This touches on the idea of betraying one's heritage that was discussed among my collaborators. Rasha was convinced that she and the agent had a shared identity and the failure of the agent to provide a more sympathetic level of support disappointed her. This raises a different perspective of Herzfeld's notion that 'indifference' is one byproduct of the 'refusal to respect difference' (Herzfeld 1992, 181). One perspective is that other ethnic minorities in positions of power may be seeking to distance themselves or assert their authority above those with a similar migrant background. However, it is worth noting Herzfeld's further remarks on the way in which the taxonomy of bureaucracy functions towards a client makes the position of insider and outsider more distinct:

> Successful clients are those who manage to persuade their bureaucratic interrogators to accept what makes their case 'different' as belonging to the bureaucrats' 'own' social world. They succeed in persuading the bureaucrats that they, the clients, are insiders: kinsfolk, fellow patriots, spiritual kin, coreligionists – in short, 'one blood'. Those who fail are other, outside, beyond the pale. (Herzfeld 1992, 181)

However, from the perspective of collaborators, there is a bitterness or even a betrayal when other 'non-Germans' do not show special support for refugees. The issue of perceived ethnic background revealed itself several times, whether it was Mohammad mentioning that his first German teacher was Turkish and that he was "a good teacher" or Anas commenting that "so many of the workers at the Job Centre are foreigners, but there is one guy there, he is an Arab, a Moroccan, and he has helped me several times". When other Arabs are also rude or indifferent to Syrians, there is an extra sense of frustration through betrayal. According to Herzfeld's position noted earlier, this means that there is a blurred line in relation to which side the bureaucrat may align themselves. The social world is one that is clearly constructed at the individual level; more particularly, Syrians must cope with agents who hold a shifting duality of being both German and part of another ethnic or national imaginary.

Much like my misconceptions in attempting to navigate the fluidity of temporal culture, my collaborators constructed their reality by a compiled experience involving their own experiences and those from others which informed future interactions. Rasha explained that even if her certificate would be recognized here, there were still cultural barriers in place. She related to me the experience of a friend in this respect.

Rasha recounted that the friend had wanted to do an internship at a nursery school, but "she said no, you wear this Muslim headscarf and we are Christian and we don't want the children to see something like this". Rasha later hedged the many complaints by saying that not all Germans are so bad. Julia, for instance, had helped them in so many ways. But nonetheless, the negative experience with institutions builds a strong perception that they are all like this and spills into the social sphere by creating a scepticism about discrimination.

Like other collaborators, Rasha questioned why people would not greet them in return on the street – perhaps they are discriminating against a woman wearing a headscarf or perhaps they are merely unfriendly. Regardless, the fact that Rasha and others ask themselves this question following regular interactions indicates much about the lasting effects of discrimination. Certainly not all Job Centre employees are callous in relation to refugees, but they are simply overworked or understaffed, and lack the capacity and knowledge to address refugees' specific concerns. Work by the Institute for Employment Research (IAB) shows the complex position that the Job Centre and BA employees occupy (Boockmann and Scheu 2018), which highlights the difficulty for agents in terms of identifying clients experiencing trauma, the scramble to restructure their local offices during the increase of clients in 2015, and diverging regional work culture attitudes and approaches to the changing migration landscape. However, the experience Rasha had with agents and through these formal bureaucratic gatekeepers of information shaped her distrust of institutional knowledge and social perceptions.

There is a rather complicated dissonance between a bureaucrat demanding that the refugee attend language courses to gain employment and, in turn, the client demanding the agent's assistance in finding a high-quality language course as well as career-specific advice. From the state's perspective, the integration courses are regulated by a unified approach to course material and quality assurance because these are conditions to conduct courses that are regulated from above, in which case there should not be any variation in the quality of integration courses. As for employment advice, the method may differ depending on the employment office, but administrators working here advise clients as to where to submit education and qualification documents; the two main bodies being the broader network through the Federal Ministry of Education and Research and the Integration durch Qualifizierung (IQ) (BMAS 2018).

However, researchers before the refugee influx in 2015 found that in North Rhine-Westphalia, a tension between clients and Job Centre or BA workers already existed, which drove many to seek career advice from other unemployment experts (*Erwerbslosenberatungsstelle*), in part out of fear of being sanctioned and having benefits reduced (Neureiter et al 2017). This is of course only part of the larger critique of the broad autonomy of agents, which causes case managers at the BA to have an unequal and rather unaccountable level of authority over the unemployed (Börner et al 2017), or structural issues between different arms of the Job Centre or the BA (Strotmann et al 2011) – much of which we see playing itself out in this book.

Much of the process of getting work quickly depends on the ability to apply 'informal qualifications' to work in Germany, as would be required for both Rasha and Hakim. As outlined by Etzold (2017), the recognition of informal qualifications is extremely limited in scope, but that is not to say that there are not in theory a wide range of specified labour market integration programmes.[1] However, these specialized programmes are funded on a rolling basis, meaning that a person may find a perfect programme to have their skills as an artisan recognized, only to discover that funding was only from 2015 to 2018 and they are now too late to enrol. Moreover, a study by the Friedrich Ebert Foundation (FEB) into the qualification programmes organized by the state together with trade unions and industry backers explained flatly that:

> The design of the mandatory training programs and projects reflects less the needs of refugees and is more a way to demonstrate the ability of actors to work together and cooperate. The actual function of such combined projects works together poorly, not because of the inability to work together or unwillingness to compromise, but rather because of conflicting institutional rationale. (Knuth 2016, 3)

In other words, there are the branches of varied integration courses that are designated for certain groups (language courses for parents of young children are one example of this) and the wide range of courses that are included in *Maßnahmen* in which one must take part as a condition for continued welfare support. *Maßnahmen* are often taken in lieu of German language courses when there is a gap in availability for a course or when a refugee wants to change courses and must wait for the next available course, but *Maßnahmen* are also used as a supplement for additional career-specific language training. There is a loophole in the language course administration of certified instructors created by a lack of qualified and regulated instructors in *Maßnahmen* courses. Unlike the highly regulated integration course, *Maßnahmen* are short-period courses, the costs of which are subsidized by the state, and are conducted by instructors who do not require a formal qualification, most of which is administered and regulated by the language schools themselves. It should be noted here that independent organizations, often associated with religious organizations such as the Catholic Diakonisches Werk an der Saar in Saarbrücken, are engaged in career-based language vocational education and offer a wide range of support programmes and social activities at the regional level.

The network of refugee families is characterized by waves of insecurity, much like what Michael Jackson describes when he applies Bourdieu's notion of habitus, for instance the idea of *illusio*, by thinking of the 'forthcoming, that which is brought forth, or brought into being, or built in the course of one's present, as oriented to a possible future' (Jackson 2005, xxiii; Bourdieu 2000). In other words, the investment in hope became a disappointing aspect of this social field because of the limited ability to apply their cultural capital. Conversely, Jackson also relates to the Bourdieuian concept of *conatus* (Bourdieu 1992), or 'a condition of wellbeing' (Jackson 2005, xxii), that can be used to consider a loss of habitus, in terms of a destruction of lifeworlds.

The security of what is known to be built by one's habitus is broken down by inconsistencies in normative structures like the state or intense trauma. Back in Turkey, collaborators spoke of Europe and America as standard-bearers for democracy and justice; the opposite of Syria's Assad regime. I observed people mad with frustration at German bureaucracy yelling at no one in particular through the halls of Ausländerbehörde and other agencies. On the other hand, there were others who more calmly contemplated their flight only to be buried in bureaucracy or have doors closed in their face without reason, which reflected a sense of illiberal form of governance for refugees. As a representative of the state, and by virtue part of the cognative imaginary of the ideal European as a pinnacle of democracy, this betrayal of ideals, or overplayed *illusio*, caused a breakdown of Rasha's perception of her cultural capital. Jackson again notes:

> Though the migrant may have an illusio founded on the hope for a better life in the country to which he or she has migrated, this illusio may prove to be based on unreasonable expectations and false hopes may prove to be based on. 'La misère du monde' defines, for Bourdieu, the condition of hopelessness that follows from this widening gap between expectations and chances – this failure of hope. (Jackson 2005, xxiii)

The social fields here do not necessarily end or have the high life-or-death stakes that Jackson relates to the concept, but I rather question the habitus related to a positive form of *illusio* that instils faith in institutions. As he points out, they seek *illusio* elsewhere, like 'joining clubs and churches' (Jackson 2005, xxv) – some relatives of collaborators have spiralled into lives of crime in Germany, and have begun using and selling drugs, becoming abusive to their wives and children, leading to the break-up of the family. However, in the case of Rasha and Hakim, the social field of the integration regime in the institutional state has been replaced by an *illusio* that favours social welfare organizations and family ties over faith in the state as a reliable source of wellbeing and value. Like the concept of orientation stasis described earlier, the uncertainty in an imagined future does in some cases cause hopelessness, but the case of the families described here more accurately describes a momentary questioning of the situational boundaries that become unclear – or, as Treiber describes the learned practice of informal action in the face of failing systems, 'searching for predictability and reliability, migrants blunder into certain forms of actions, which they actually try to flee' (Treiber 2014, 117). The way forward is a deepening scepticism that although the social welfare state does supply financial support, it may not have its clients' best interests at heart.

Is there hope here?

Since I began speaking with Syrian families in Germany, I was often interested in whether they think they wanted stay in Germany or one day return to Syria. This was perhaps an unfair question when there was continued violence by various governments and militant groups throughout the country, but the question arises when we talked about a time of peace. But what would such a 'peace' look like? Unlike the young men I had talked with, whose answers were more definitive, families responded with greater difficulty. In the first few years in Germany, they immediately said they wanted to return to Syria. There was always a hint of romanticism to the homeland. At some point, all of my collaborators gave me deeper, more nuanced accounts of Syria that included simple, functioning lives. So, the first answer was always "of course, when it is safe or if Assad was gone, we would go back". But this was almost immediately followed by the consideration for their children. There was acceptance that the children had spent years in Germany, learning the language and developing friendships, and that memories of Syria for the younger children were now distant and vague, as they had spent relatively equal amounts of time in both places. In the end they were torn. The reality was also that the war in Syria was still ongoing at the time of writing, and at least with regard to personal security, many collaborators had sympathies that lay with the rebels and had histories that may have documented such active views and engagement. For those who stood up to the dictatorship, there could certainly be reprisals if they returned to Syria. Neutral families who fled the war out of fear of conscription into the Syrian army would most certainly face consequences should they return, in addition to loss of land and destroyed property. They asked themselves whether they were willing to rebuild a life in Syria under the same regime. It was indeed the case that the longer the families stayed in Germany, the more they came to terms with not returning to Syria in the foreseeable future.

In the end, the families often realized that it was more important to build a better future for their children in Germany. Rasha had relatives in Sweden and Hakim had a brother in the neighbouring region of North Rhine-Westphalia and more relatives in other areas of Germany. They either had plans to visit the families living further away or were making trips to nearby relatives fairly often. There was a broader connection between family ties that were being reconstructed in Germany and becoming more normalized. Although families had been left behind in Syria and Turkey, the transnational networks were at times reachable and in direct contact.

One afternoon, as I sat with Rasha in the living room talking with the children, the news in Arabic was playing on the television, and Hakim was on a video call with one of our mutual friends in Turkey. The friend was attending a university and was planning to apply for Turkish citizenship. There was a shrinking of distance between friends and relatives that eased the construction of a new life away from what was the old life. The more time I spent with my collaborators, the clearer it became that it was common for family networks to spread across Germany, other European countries and even to the USA.

The oldest son in one family outside Saarbrücken would ask me questions about life in the USA every time we spoke. He wanted to study there, either for a semester or for his whole course. His father looked on anxiously when these conversations come up and I proceeded cautiously. Nonetheless, some of these families became even more internationalized over time and shed many of their Syrian ties. The same holds true for Anas and his siblings. When asked when they would go to see their brother and sister remaining in Syria, they often shrugged with uncertainty.

Neoliberal integration

The foundation of the neoliberal approach to the integration regime discriminates against heads of households that support children enrolled in school or on their way to university. There are a range of legal procedures emerging as part of the reforms since 2015 that have indeed served as discreet ways to discriminate against the viability of long-term settlement of refugees in favour of 'highly skilled migrants', the clearest obstacle being the ambiguity of one of the principal requirements for permanent residency – the declaration that 'livelihood is largely financially secure' (Bundesregierung 2016). The interpretation of this law remains at the Länder level and calculated regionally in terms of rent and cost of living per household. In order to receive early permanent residency (three years in the case of recognized refugees), the law requires 'highly outweighing' (*weit überwiegende*) livelihood, which would calculate to a large excess beyond the stated minimums per household. Finally, those with subsidiary protection are further excluded by adding a requirement of 60 payments into German state retirement insurance (Rentenversicherung) (Bundesregierung 2016), which would require those who gained subsidiary protection to begin paying into the national retirement scheme from the moment they applied for asylum in order to gain the benefit of waiting a minimum of only three years for permanent residency instead of the standard five years. The class hierarchy underscores the national hierarchies that are only partly incorporated into the immigration law. As one agent at the Ausländerbehörde reminded me with a broad smile when I was worried about extending my residency, "at the end of the day, don't worry, you are American after all". His statement confirmed that not only were certain nationalities privileged in gaining *entry* to Germany, but also, more importantly, certain country nationals were privileged when it came to *staying* in Germany.

Syrians were prioritized by BAMF early on, but after the vast majority fell into the subsidiary protection category in 2016, many would not enjoy the security of permanent residence within five years and would have to wait until they had also made 60 payments towards a retirement scheme. Unfortunately, the law did not calculate periods of unemployment due to childcare, and the framework was in general relatively ambiguous. Officially speaking, priority was given to those who contributed to the social welfare system over those who might be giving informal contributions to social welfare through unpaid work, such as childcare and taking care of a household. Gender discrimination – working under the basis that women overwhelmingly conduct the majority of the aforementioned tasks – is in this way written into the official law. However, from many cases presented here, we can see that the arbitrariness of the application of law raises the need to consider both the symbolic power of how law is conceived by politicians from a heteronormative perspective and the institutional power of the application of law.

The orientation towards future building and imagining is met with legal restrictions that often prove arbitrary. This goes beyond what would be considered a basis for belonging (Simonsen 2018) and addresses a more fundamental issue of security. The symbolic security to build and imagine a future requires a strong ability to perceive state institutions as fair and just. There is a certain ebb and flow surrounding a family's ability to apply some of its social and cultural capital to institutional security, and outcomes are too often arbitrary and inconsistent. The rewards for heads of households in the German integration regime are often exclusionary based on gender norms, this institutional blindness being similar to the nuances of transnational trauma experienced by young men. How can such a regime calculate the social contribution of a widowed mother of eight children? The question offers only elusive answers that themselves produce insecurities that ripple down to other family members, some of the outcomes of which are explored further in the following chapters.

Conclusion

Although both chapters in this part of the book have a concluding section, this space serves to compel the reader to consider how the two chapters can be tied together beyond the practicality of their placement. This concluding section explores the overarching implications of the German integration regime. Within this regime, there are bureaucrats, social ideologies and governmentalities, and the refugees themselves. The chapters explore two diverging networks of refugees that express both the temporality of their lives in Germany, which fluctuate through space and time, and the benefits (capital) and shortcomings belonging to their described social networks. They also explore the bureaucratic tensions that emerged on the side of the imagined state.

If there is a through line to this section, it combines some of what Vigh (2010) conveys in his concept of social navigation and the application of social capital within networks. My collaborators often navigate the existential reality by imagining a future based on their ability to recapture an *illusio* in which they may reassert their place in the quality of life in Germany with strong transnational ties and existential reality with memories and contacts abroad. They gain support through various actors in their networks – young men through their peer networks and mentors, and families mostly through other relatives and *engaged volunteers* – and they cope with the different stages of their lives in order to prioritize responsibilities and find a way to move forward.

As Chapter 3 demonstrated, the bureaucratic state is not merely the *imagined state* but a network of policies produced at the federal level (by the state), interpreted at the regional level, and then filtered down to various administrative bodies at street level, where officials operate as dictated by local governmentalities, influences from the media and their own social networks. This leads to a state only partially reified through policy application.

In turn, and to address the unreliability and inconstancies of the state, my collaborators sometimes use informal means to bypass temporary unpredictability to gain a beneficial outcome for themselves, which is to say that they often only follow the official policy under coercion. They construct their parallel social imaginaries and hierarchies, much like the German public imaginary, in which there are 'good refugees' and 'bad refugees'. Although they do not name it themselves, they have indeed constructed integration in their own terms and have abided by much of the same ideology. Yet, for young men, this is embodied in support for families abroad and for families, it is not concretely established at this early stage, but will be explored in more depth in the following chapters. This has more to do with not settling for being average and being able to apply previous skills, but at its heart is centred on the responsibility of refugees to support their families. The chapters in the final part of this book will show how my colloborators' identities have been reimagined over time and the limits of the practical concepts of social incorporation. The focus moves beyond the narrow implications of the refugee regime and shapes a reality for what an 'independent' life in Germany might look like.

Stagnation, Independence, Dependence

5

Institutionalized Integration: Munich and Kassel

Inside the regime

In Parts I and II of this book I narrated the arrival, asylum application and early experiences with the integration regime from the perspective of refugees. In Part III, I shift focus to two areas: first, how intuitions were operating during this period, the challenges they faced and the way in which they incorporated themes of the integration regime; and, second, how this institutionalization of the integration regime impacted Syrians attempting to permanently settle in Germany. This chapter takes many of the themes featured in previous chapters and applies them to ethnographic work conducted within several federal and local government intuitions. Chapter 6 will outline many of the structural challenges 'well-integrated' refugees face, as well as challenges for refugees who are outside the scope of mechanisms created by the integration regime.

When I began undertaking my fieldwork, meeting up with the contacts I first met in Turkey in 2015 and then in 2017 travelling around Germany in order to reconnect with them, the bureaucratic theme almost immediately emerged. I was just beginning my inquiries, so it was unclear at the time why BA played such a vital role the experience of Syrians in Germany. Once this finding was made, I sought to join research collaborators on their visits to in the Job Centre in order to gain insights into the bureaucratic processes and observe the tensions that my contacts recounted to me. Early on, I was faced with difficulties contacting the Job Centre in Saarbrücken and near Westerkappeln (administered by the district of Steinfurt), and was later denied access to BAMF's central office in Nuremberg. However, a colleague referred me to someone close to him at a Job Centre in the city of Kassel and they agreed to let me observe and conduct interviews. I was also, after much effort, able to access the Job Centre, BA and the local Foreigner's Office in Munich. The offices of various bureaucracies in Munich were particularly supportive in providing transparency to researchers like myself.

What follows is a complement to other references to these agencies given throughout this book. It attempts to frame localized variation in the legal interpretation and structure of agencies in the context of their regional resources, as well as some of the ways in which agents work with clients to achieve differing Job Centre agendas. I will additionally explore my short experience in the Munich Ausländerbehörde in the final section of this chapter, which provides a unique perspective to research presented in previous chapters and adds a new layer that highlights the tensions that emerged between powerful bureaucratic agencies.

As has been highlighted throughout this book, there is a great deal of regional autonomy, but local offices are also able to structure their offices, based on available resources, in different ways. The discretion of offices at the Ausländerbehörde at the Kommune level is thoroughly outlined by Eule (2014) in one of the most comprehensive studies of German bureaucracy available. Contrary to Eule's findings and perhaps due to the changes since the so-called refugee crisis, employees within bureaucracies are increasingly political, especially in Munich. In other words, there are regional differences within these bureaucracies that are nothing new, but the establishment and dissolution of specialized branches to address refugees specifically reveal some of the symbolic ideological shifts.

In Kassel, like many German cities, there is a dedicated branch of the Job Centre that works with refugees. While in Munich the Job Centre is more deeply structured, based in part on the historic influx of Afghan refugees in the early 2000s to Munich, in Saarbrücken there was formerly a dedicated office for migrants, but, according to ZIB, this was discontinued because it was found to be superfluous.

However, in Munich there is not only a specialized department for refugees but also a specialized branch for recognized refugees living in shared emergency housing, or what the refugees often call a *Heim*. Regular unemployed refugees are also supported through the Munich-specific initiative between Munich's Sozialreferat (Social Services Department) and the Job Centre, called the Sozialbürgerhaus, where the federal and Kommune come together as part of the broader framework of social help for refugees (Bogumil, Hafner and Kastilan 2017). In addition, like Saarbrücken, Munich has a 'Masterplan for the Integration of Refugees' (Sozialreferat München 2017), which reads much more like an academic or legal document than the ideologically founded, lighter tone of Saarbrücken's masterplan. Furthermore, Munich has two particular aspects that are relevant to the discussion that follows.

First, during the *long summer of migration* in 2015, as thousands of Syrians passed from Hungary through Austria and on to Germany, many also passed through Munich, where, as outlined in previous chapters, officials encouraged them to continue through to other Länder and Kommunen. As a result, there are relatively low numbers of Syrian refugees in Munich – the figures hovers around a few hundred Syrian recognized refugees (Sozialreferat München 2017). Second, Munich is one of the largest cities to implement the Residency Obligation and has the most expensive rental housing in all of Germany – both these points were outlined in the previous chapter, but will be contextualized here.

This chapter will also shift the focus significantly towards the processes within the inner workings of the integration regime. Although I have attempted to structure this book as a path that loosely follows those who arrived in Germany from 2015 onwards, the reader should consider this chapter a slight detour and a preview into what refugees will experience in the following chapters. The empirical work is assigned a separate section here because I will attempt to show how the structural problems that emerge here will have a significant implication on the way in which research collaborators attempt to settle in Germany.

Camps and restricted free movement

When I spoke to Rasha in Westerklappen, she referred to the refitted shipping container housing using the German word *Heim*, which was used in other areas as well, but refugees called the larger housing areas a 'camp'. More specifically in Munich, *camps* were the larger areas used for emergency housing near Munich, most notable of which was the Bayernkaserne (Bavarian Military Barracks), the old empty army barracks that have been converted in order to house thousands of refugees and asylum seekers.

The area, a distant bus ride outside the city, was gated with 24-hour security guards on watch and had the feel of an abandoned city. The tree-lined streets were devoid of cars; instead, children roam the streets, and in the windows of the flat stone buildings the occasional curious head of an inhabitant pokes out to see what's happening on the quiet street. The numbers varied over time, but partial numbers from the city of Munich in 2018 indicated over 5,000 refugees living in shared housing, although the report does not provide the number of recognized refugees (Böhle 2018). Alternatively, an article in *Süddeutsche Zeitung* noted that 400 refugees were living in shared housing at the time who also were so-called *Fehlbeleger*.[1] *Fehlbeleger* were recognized as refugees without private housing who were still living in shared housing; in 2016 the number was estimated to rise later that year to 4,000 (*Süddeutsche Zeitung* 2016). However, at the time of my research at the Job Centre in 2017, most of the employees agreed that the clients under their care never exceeded 300. As noted in Chapter 3, the number of *Fehlbeleger* is directly related to the lack of affordable housing.

Other research has previously drawn out the complexities of this case (BBSR 2017), with several regions containing much higher rates of *Fehlbeleger*, which cannot all be attributed to high rental costs; instead, they were associated with periods of high-status change rates, from asylum seeker to protected status. Nonetheless, as observed in Munich, it was very much the case that most refugees cannot afford to pay for housing with the money supplied from the Job Centre, in conjunction with the Residency Obligation that restricts movement to a cheaper neighbouring city.

The Job Centres

Throughout this book I have repeatedly attempted to emphasize three continuous elements at play with the Syrian experience in Germany: first, pressure from above that pushes refugees to conform to standardized norms that are written into law, contrasted with practices which do not always adhere to the idealistic foundations of the policy; second, the desire of recognized refugees to have security and wellbeing, while at the same time fulfilling the administrative requirements in order to receive welfare benefits and residency-related rewards; and, finally, the temporary pressure to achieve the preceding aims within a specified timeframe. These elements were never more present than in the period I spent at the Job Centres in Munich and Kassel.

What follows is an account of some of the things that I observed during my time at both locations. Unlike other research on bureaucracy in Europe, which focuses on gatekeepers and bureaucratic discretion, access and law (Cyrus and Vogel 2003; Eule 2014; Tuckett 2015; Dahlvik 2018), what emerges here is more a muddling through. I found familiar themes of arbitrary paperwork, overburdened staff and an often-bewildered clientele, but there was less legal wrangling, and more advising and coerced motivation. The bureaucrats I observed only had the power over refugees' financial security, but little influence over their legal rights, which were usually administered through the Ausländerbehörde. However, they were at the centre of the integration regime because they actualized the principles of *fördern und fordern*. In other words, even though refugees may not have been aware of the principles of the so-called 'support' but 'demand' that was fundamental in welfare state reform, they were subconsciously aware that agents who facilitate support should also support the means by which that support was materialized before they began to demand how it was being used. Recent studies on the limited access to private housing highlights this point – housing support was financially given through the Job Centre, but because of discrimination and high rental costs, refugees usually had to apply informal tactics or social capital to actually find housing[2] (Adam et al 2019). For this reason, tensions emerged out of misunderstandings and the demand on agents to provide support for tasks they were not necessarily prepared or willing to handle.

I was invited to spend a few weeks with the section of the Job Centre Munich entitled Zentraleinheit Flüchtlinge (ZEF), which in the years before my fieldwork had grown to 30 specialists who are part of the Job Centre's refugee-focused branch. In 2017, the social welfare office of Munich reported that the Job Centre's refugee centre (Zentrum Flucht) supported over 4,000 refugees with SGB II,[3] but during my fieldwork, caseworkers at the ZEF noted the number under their care to be only a few hundred (Sozialreferat München 2017). This meant that the number of people registered with the regional BA could fall under a range of categories for those who received support, but it also indicated that many of the recognized refugees who had arrived since early 2014 were still living in shelters administered by the government.

Although there were limited numbers of Syrians in the care of the ZEF, I tried to primarily sit in on meetings with clients of Syrian nationality. The ZEF only focuses on young people aged 18–25 without children, which meant that most of the clients were so-called *Fehlbeleger* and male. I sat in on appointments during December 2017 and conducted interviews with both bureaucrats and refugees, as well as returning to conduct follow-up interviews with the caseworkers the following year.

Each caseworker had a different approach to their clients, but Max, the one I spent the longest periods with, spoke freely with me, and was the most sympathetic and emotionally engaged with the clients he had under his authority. As he reflected to me one morning, "I have the feeling that the most of the time I spent here is doing social work". This is an interesting point because bureaucrats at the Job Centre are not social workers; they have diverse educational backgrounds, but the majority have an education in administration. In our follow-up meeting, I reminded him of what he said and he nodded in agreement, but his colleague said he didn't agree – "it depended on the client's needs", who in his case were mostly Somali and who in his opinion required more practical support; they needed a more pragmatic approach rather than a more nuanced and emotionally sensitive approach.

Because of the housing situation in Munich and many recognized refugees living in 'camp', a huge amount of Max and other caseworkers' time was devoted to bureaucratic idiosyncrasies. In one appointment, half an hour was wasted because the letter from the Job Centre had been lost in the mail. In the camp there is so much movement of people that letters from the Job Centre are frequently lost in the post. Letters from the Job Centre are almost always a request for the client to come to the Job Centre and present a document of some kind: documents for language course enrolment, documents for language course certificate of completion, documents for medical-related absence from courses, documents for rental contracts, documents for a notice that persons under 25 are not under the care of their parents. Refugees would face a reduction in benefits from the social welfare office, and a range of other possible consequences, should they not respond to a summons from the Job Centre.

In the case of this particular appointment, it was only a request to present a document showing that the refugee had enrolled in an orientation course. However, because the document had been lost in the post, he was facing a penalty for failing to attend a required appointment, which would mean a reduction in benefits for a period of time – first offence being a 10 per cent reduction of benefits for three months. Max explained after the client left that he tried to avoid applying the sanctions against benefits: "I try to be humane about it." As an authority, the Job Centre had the right to reduce benefits by 30 per cent for three months of support for refugees over 25 years old – which could double and triple for repeated or unresolved issues – for failing to attend courses and 100 per cent of benefits for three months for those under 25.[4] When I asked my contact at the Job Centre in Kassel for her opinion about discretion on giving fines, she wrote back to me: 'There is no discretion. It just needs to be checked if an important reason is presented or not'. This raises a question of office or personal philosophy, but what is clear are the differences between local resources and work environments that I had observed.

When I arrived early on the first morning of my observation at the ZEF (it was in a temporary building because the regular offices were being remodelled), I was met by security guards who asked who I had come to visit before allowing me to go upstairs to the offices. It was less chaotic than other offices of the Job Centre I had visited, in part because the ZEF was part of other specialized groups that were in these offices at the time, but also because of the way in which the structure of Munich differed from other cities. I was there at 8:30 in the morning and waited in the empty hall for 15 minutes until the employees started shuffling through the corridors. Everyone was late because there was a blizzard and all the trains were delayed. Max had a relatively short client list and our meetings ran relatively long; at least 30 minutes for each person and no long lines of other clients waiting to be seen. In contrast to Kassel, Maria was responsible for over 300 clients at the time because her colleague was on holiday. There clients came and went with a greater briskness and Maria's tone was more 'tough love' than sympathetic.

The first client of the morning in Kassel asked if he could have a cup of tea and Maria looked a little unsure how to respond, but offered him water, with a thin tone in her response. The appointments came in 30-minute blocks, which meant we should have seen four appointments before lunch, but there was one 'no show'. In another interview, an older female refugee asked for an interpreter and Maria pushed back, explaining that she could understand, she had passed A2 and she should try. "When you study every day, I guarantee you will learn", Maria encouraged her later. After the interpreter arrived, the woman complained that she could not attend the German course because of back pain, to which Maria responded: "Yes, my back hurts too, but you have to still go to your German course." It is not from a cold, unsympathetic place that such responses arise, but rather a mix of overwhelming numbers of clients and confused expectations on both sides. Maria noted her frustration with the refugees before the morning of appointments started: "they come in and expect that I find them a job". This put a strain on the caseworkers because the refugees would fall into familiar patterns, get annoyed with the German course, stop attending, work for a while in seasonal or temporary jobs, and then have to start the process all over again after being laid off.

The path to work through language

One morning, Max calmly explained to his client that they had to be careful with the transit card that they had, it was only valid after 9 am, otherwise they could be fined up to €60 for riding 'in the black'. This is the kind of information Max has to convey to clients on a daily basis. As in interviews that I conducted with NGOs in Germany, workers at the Job Centre gave refugees everyday advice, such as cautioning about signing up for mobile phone contracts, using illegal housing brokers and how to avoid legal fines. In the particulars of individual cases and nuances, it goes without question that Syrian clients also commonly had health issues, which compounded all the other challenges involved in settling.

In one meeting, nearly two hours were spent simply clarifying that a client who had had four surgeries on his injured leg needed a letter from the doctor, which differed from the letter he had brought on this occasion, and had to take the letter to the social welfare office so they could verify the doctor's note to the Job Centre, and be excused from attending the required German course. In this case, like others, Max attempted to make offers to prioritize learning German – the client could have a German tutor come to his house since he was unable to travel to German courses. Instead of only offering the required German integration language course, agents at the Job Centre in Munich offered language 'cafes' or other programmes to help the support language learning.

In Kassel, the caseworker often had to focus on the next steps after the initial language courses were completed. What would they like to do next? The options were often *Maßnahme* or vocational training, or finding work. Often clients in both cities dropped their German courses and took part-time seasonal employment, only to be quickly let go shortly afterwards and return to the Job Centre for funds, where they were required to join another integration course. Of course, there are many external factors that may influence the motivation to drop an integration course and take part-time work – transnational financial obligations, disputes with instructors or dissatisfaction with the quality of the course.

Nonetheless, Max always encouraged clients to plan to attend some kind of vocational training or apply for official recognition of work experience and job certification, but there was resistance from clients who were determined to work directly. And when I asked if they would like to move to a different city, some surprisingly responded that they would like to stay in Munich – the most expensive city in Germany. Another female caseworker also confirmed this, adding that most of her clients want to stay in Munich. Others have family or friends in other regions and would like to move there once they have the freedom of movement: either after the three-year residency restriction, through a job or through vocational training. This is all with the understanding that if they want to participate in vocational training, it will take more time to go from B1 German to C1 German, then either in parallel to or afterwards spending two to five years in on-the-job training or apprenticeships through dual education.

Some Syrians planned this very strategically: one client in Munich wanted to work for two years and, after working, attend the integration course in order to apply for permanent residency, then go back and access more education. Another wanted to do an internship while improving his German in the hope of improving his chances of landing a position in competitive vocational training. But these strategies were conceived with little oversight by the bureaucrats at the Job Centre and mostly through the knowledge of other refugees with whom they either had direct contact or through a culture of rumours. Additionally, there is a virtual 'black box' of what refugees are dealing with outside of the perception of the Job Centre agents. The extensive descriptions of particular cases in the previous chapters provide a glimpse into the everyday lives of refugees that bureaucrats rarely personally address. Although these are social welfare offices, it becomes clear that the neoliberal, or rather biopolitical, shift of the social welfare state in Germany, which also placed the Job Centre as a key bridge between refugees and the integration regime, fails to adequately address the very specific needs of refugee groups. As Gupta notes, the indifference of bureaucrats is important, but the indifference to the production of 'arbitrary outcomes is central' (Gupta 2012, 6). Similarly, Eule points out that despite the severity of the implication of their decisions, bureaucrats 'went about their tasks with a certain casualness' (Eule 2018, 2790). Yet, the agents at the Job Centre were not unmoved by their client's needs, they were just blind to the symbolic implications of their work and to the particular outcomes in cases – there was no deeper understanding of 'success' beyond routine meetings. There was no way to find out if the job their client was recommended for ended up helping them to financial independence, if the language course attended enriched their client's social life, or if their client was able to move out of the emergency housing and find a private flat. Instead, most of their work served what Bourdieu called 'mental structures', which works as a way to distribute the mechanisms of bureaucracy, like integration courses, that reinforce state classification and 'national character' (Bourdieu 1994, 7–8).

It is clear that the caseworkers in Munich were familiar with a range of situations. Perhaps as a reminder of this, Max raised his eyebrows during one of my interviews after his time with the client. He was a Syrian from the city of Hama who described the trauma of spending three days lost at sea on the way across the Mediterranean. His older sister also joined him at an appointment – it was common practice for refugees to bring a relative along to an appointment at the Job Centre. She arrived in Germany only a year and a half ago and had found her own housing with her husband, who also worked; she spoke very good German, was studying part time at LMU Munich, and was in the process of finishing the university preparation course to become a full-time student in a year, while at the same time working to pay rent without any social support. Conversely, her brother had been in Germany for two-and-a-half years and was only at this stage enrolling on a B1 German course – still part of the integration course – and spoke very poor German. His sister explained that she and her family were in emergency housing in 2015 for six months and were able to have a great deal of contact with other Germans; they were able to quickly learn language and get work. They were from the same family, but had had very different experiences, something that should have alarmed Max, but he casually moved on to the next case when they left. It was not his job to find out *why* such huge differences existed between members of the same family. Perhaps this would be the job of someone working for a private institution, but the two sides are systematically divorced under the *fördern und fordern* framework – attempting to seek out what are the conditions in particular cases that allow for 'good integration'. However, caseworkers were also familiar with the informal ways that refugees circumvented state bureaucracies and had little interest in them or surprise when methods that may be illegal became known.

The young Syrian from Damascus with the issue of his leg operations explained to Max that because of his residency status, he could not have his wife join him in Germany through the legal means of family reunification, so instead they spent €6,000 to pay a smuggler to help her enter Germany and apply directly for asylum. Max nodded along, unsurprised. As noted elsewhere (Fassin 2011, 218), when bureaucracies create more complicated access to immigration, it increases the reliance on illegality, in this case supporting smugglers. Finally, I will now discuss some of the tensions that emerged within the Job Centre between caseworkers and clients.

I arrived one morning for the first meeting to find such a situation, despite Max cautioning the day before that it would not be of interest to my work.

As I walked in, tensions were boiling over. The client was raising his voice in frustration with Max: "This is Germany here, not Assad in Syria!" Max calmly responded that the man needed to provide certain paperwork, as though he had been repeating something similar for the last half an hour before I arrived to observe the situation. In the end, he told the client that they were both upset and it would be better if they met again on Monday after cooling off. When he left, Max said he had tried to do all he could with this man and yet it always ended in a similar conflict with him. Additionally, there are cases that make the staff at the ZEF unable to respond because of the nature of the situation. This was the case when one client presented such a wide range of questions in a matter of minutes to the most experienced caseworker in the department, Noah. First, he explained that he would like to begin receiving benefits again because his seasonal work at Amazon was ending. A minute later, he began asking if he could learn English instead because he didn't like German. He proceeded to inquire first if he should perhaps take a job working in Canada, before finally asking if he could possibly return to Syria for a one-week holiday. Noah carefully explained that as far as he was concerned, it didn't matter, but BAMF might call into question his refugee status if he returned to Syria as someone who had sought protection from the state there, and explained it would be hard to retain his asylum claim after returning to a county that he claimed was persecuting him. But despite the challenging work environment, the bureaucrats had all chosen to work in the specialized refugee departments.

Max explained how the employees had requested to work with refugees at the ZEF when the branch opened and were not simply assigned there. He was tired of working with people who "just have no interest in finding work", referring to the long-time unemployed in other departments of the Job Centre. He previously worked in the information technology (IT) sector and said he suffered from "burnout" after a few years, being overworked and overstressed. In Max's case, he feels like he has the flexibility at the Job Centre that protects him from being in such a stressful job. He said that if he feels overburdened, he can take a day or two off, or come in later in the day. If he feels that he has conflicts with certain cases, he can hand over his appointments to another worker and complete office-related tasks for a period. In other words, there are considerable factors that support caseworkers' affability to clients and their ability to handle diversity and complexity. As noted earlier, the role of the caseworker at the Job Centre within the integration regime is essentially to facilitate information and monitor that clients are keeping up with their commitments. To do this, they must not only be good at delivering information, but also filtering through the bureaucratic paperwork to find the right information for a particular client. Within the vast network of which programmes are available, caseworkers have to navigate and find the exact match for each client. At the same time, they hold the authority over what *truth* is. As Maria noted earlier, there is a black-and-white line between whether someone has presented a good enough case to avoid a sanction against their benefits.

During my time at both Job Centres, I found that there was always an exchange of documentation taking place: a letter summoning a client, a certificate of enrolment, a certificate of successfully passing a course, a doctor's note. As Hull notes without explaining it outright, documents are a way for administrative bureaucracies to reify the state: 'Writing establishes the stable relation between words and things necessary for bureaucracies effectively to implement regimes of control' (Hull 2012, 256). In the same fuction, Susan Sontag describes the development of photography as an art form that captured truth; unlike the painting, which is interpreted, the photograph *is* 'reality which is scrutinized, and evaluated' (Sontag 2005, 67), Contrary to the Weberian notion that documents signify order within a bureacracy, Foucault argues how documents hold a value of truth, which is made a reality through negotiation by those who hold power over truths – in the most Foucauldian sense, the German state fuctions through governing by 'the production of truth' (Foucault 1991, 79). In other words, the production of truths is a way to prop up the bureaucratic apparatus in order to create a symbol of power which reinforces norms. It is difficult for such systems to effectively support refugees' needs when the main function of the Job Centre is often simple regulations.

While there is an abundance of well-funded programmes, the question regarding the effectiveness of these programmes should be: how many of these Munich specific programmes are facilitated through caseworkers? When caseworkers had a client who wanted to participate in a programme to improve their German, employees often relied not on a searchable database, but rather on flyers that were found shuffled in stacks or displayed like local brochures in a hotel lobby. The caseworkers' responsibilities are so broad that it is difficult to not only be aware of these programmes, but then also remember when all is said and done to pass on the information to the refugee. This occurred with one client in which the main discussion was sidetracked by other bureaucratic details; Max then realized he had not passed on the language course information to the client by the time the latter had left the office.

Conversely, Maria in Kassel, despite a heavy caseload, was quick to remember a colleague looking for engineers when a qualified client entered. After a few phone calls, she was able to send the client's curriculum vitae on to her colleague who might have work for the man. He was middle-aged, but was one of the lucky people to have brought all of his work history documentation with him from Syria, from degrees to international certificates. He explained to her that everything else he owned was destroyed along with his flat in Aleppo. I recognized the change in Maria's demeanour during this case – she was visually excited that there was something positive she could do. She turned to me afterwards, smiling: "you see, this was one of the good ones". The caseworkers with a stricter approach still find validation in small successes. Yet, there was no mechanism for her to follow up with the man to see if the job had worked out.

Unfortunately, these victories are short-lived as the next appointment comes with more anonymized issues that conflate clients into a temporality that feeds into Gupta's (2012) accounting of 'arbitrary outcomes' in bureaucratic government programmes. Caseworkers at the ZEF do not know how many of their clients have left behind their *Fehlbeleger* status and found private housing. When I pressed them again on this point in a follow-up interview in 2018, two of the caseworkers shrugged and guessed that almost none of their clients would move on to find private housing while still receiving the benefits from Hartz IV. The implication was that if caseworkers had the goal, driven from aims to legitimize the integration regime, to help refugees secure their livelihood and 'integrate', there was nonetheless not a viable mechanism for them to evaluate how their work influenced 'good integration'. The Munich Job Centre does publish detailed reports, such as the Work and Integration Programme (Jobcenter München 2019); however, these broader statistical reports do not engage with individual refugees in the same way social workers do, so are unable to draw the same nuanced conclusions. Although Max had the feeling that the majority of his work was social work, the structural environments and measured outcomes were adversarial.

Finally, the characterization of bureaucracies, which was referred to earlier as 'arbitrary outcomes' (Gupta 2012), is clear in the priorities of the Job Centre. Bogumil, Hafner and Kastilan are critical of the fact that after asylum seekers are recognized, their status changes from support under AsylbLG to SGB II or SGB XII,[5] and the Job Centre is not required to support a housing search, but it would 'make sense to have a job inside the Kommune administration … that renters can contact cases of insecurity or concrete problems' (Bogumil, Hafner and Kastilan 2017, 81). Indeed, as noted in Chapter 2, landlords claim they are apprehensive about renting to people on SGB II because of late payments, a view that has been supported elsewhere (Adam et al 2019). The problem is rooted in the double standard between the expectation to attend language courses and the Job Centre's lack of accountability to support refugees in terms of securing housing – although it is the agency that must regulate this housing – with the clear knowledge that living in a camp or even in shared housing hinders integration.[6] As a point of pragmatics, agents must deal with the practical elements of lost paperwork through mail delivery going awry, or melodrama caused by a 'rumour culture' within the refugee camps, where refugees rely on what they hear 'via the grapevine' rather than on official information. Before one client left the appointment, he complained that the Somali refugees at the camp always received the preferred housing arrangements. Even within different groups of country nationals, there is tension and perceived favouritism. Problems are not resolved in the camp, so refugees bring their complaints to the nearest authority. The burden is on both the agent and the client, and time is wasted through unnecessary bureaucracy as well as extended discussions resulting from mixed expectations and misunderstandings.

This section details how time spent on such activities is a normalized reality in which tasks become so routinized and their outcomes so obscured that they no longer attempt to individualize their approach. Unlike other authorities, the power of the agents here rests on their ability to drag out the bureaucratic controls of time and monitoring. They are part of a larger network of integration ideology, but little thought goes into this narrative in their everyday tasks. While the Job Centre in Munich has a strategic vision and more resources than other cities, it is clear that an underlying frustration is present between refugees and caseworkers – something amplified in other cities, where I found workers less sympathetic to refugees. Nonetheless, how the Job Centre influences the other bureaucratic actors in the regime was of interest. During interviews with caseworkers at the Job Centre in Munich, I was also interested in how agencies communicated with one another. Agents did not have great objections to interagency work, but it was not central to their work. Conversely, when I engaged with the Ausländerbehörde, I quickly discovered this was not the case. There was considerable tension between these agencies because of a key impasse that does not exist between the BA and BAMF or the Ausländerbehörde because the other agents are the ones that give access to the resources that the BA and Job Centre distribute.

The Ausländerbehörde

I first gained access to conduct interviews at the Ausländerbehörde in Munich with the realization that the city of Munich had a different approach to transparency and the support of researchers, which had become a clear connecting policy with the city's vision to incorporate migrants. There are many thorough ethnographies on Ausländerbehörde (Cyrus and Vogel 2003; Eule 2014; Eule et al 2019), and I will not attempt here to capture the incredible complexity of these local administrations. Instead, I will highlight the internal tension that has increased between federal and local agencies since 2015, and will fill the gap missing in this work so far that focuses on the impact of refugees specifically rather than immigrants at large.

It took a long time to be granted access to speak with the department head in Munich. Anja explained at the beginning of our interview that although the office is responsible for all asylum cases after BAMF makes an asylum decision, she made a clear distinction that the decision by BAMF is not considered settled once a file arrives at their office: "If they [asylum seekers] are rejected totally, we have to try to make them leave Germany or look if there is any other reason for them to stay here. This is for the city and government of Munich a very important point."

This clarification was indicative of the top-down influence in Munich, in that the city and regional politics took precedence in the interpretation of law and furthermore how this approach was taken seriously in its application by the department head. As Eule (2014, 16) notes, Ausländerbehörden are funded by the local city councils; thus, the city has an influence on how immigration policy is administered, which reflects the position of the local government. Munich is dominated by the Social Democratic Party (SPD) party, although the rest of Bavaria is dominated by the conservative Cristian Social Union (CSU) party. Local policy makers are trying to remain more liberal than the surrounding right-wing-leaning politicians, and to distinguish themselves from the populist, radical right-wing AfD party, which grew briefly in popularity from 2015 to 2019.

The extra attempt to ensure that the correct asylum decisions were made makes the point regarding the reinforcement of the humanitarian principles of asylum. However, it should also be noted that the Ausländerbehörde assumes limited responsibility for simply reviewing the asylum decision. The asylum decision has already been made by BAMF, which means the Foreigner's Office is reviewing ways of changing the refugees' residency status (*Spurwechsel*), for example to a student or employment residency permit. Although the asylum procedure is completed by BAMF, as mentioned earlier, there is the possibility to challenge the decision in the courts, but the position of the Ausländerbehörde in Munich adds another layer of potential protection that does not rely on the refugees' social or economic capital, but rather pure luck based on regionality. The statement by Anja can also be taken as a point of tension between agencies, one that emerged after I raised the concern of BAMF's legal obligation to review revocation procedures (*Widerrufsverfahren*) for all refugees three years after individuals *applied* for asylum – a law that has since been extended to five years (Pro Asyl 2019).

The intersection of these two agencies and a relatively obscure legal change that continued to evolve following the original legislative changes on immigration reform in 2008 has caused a relative collapse in the accountability of local bureaucracies to execute the legal integration reforms. I have tried to argue in earlier chapters of this book that the German integration law is based on access to the welfare state and a reward-based conditional residency legislation contingent upon adherence to bureaucratic standards. However, this is only the case in theory. A border or migration regime application to integration highlights the following discrepancies: the tension between these two agencies, which has resulted in a deadlock since 2019, renders this conditional inclusion to a point of Kafkaesque arbitrariness.

Anja recalled her experience with the policy since 2008, which at the time reviewed the statuses of permanent residency, while also adding the condition that BAMF must review all asylum cases and permanent residency must not be issued until the Foreigner's Office receives a decision of 'yes' or 'no'. The BAMF later objected to the burden of evaluations and the law was changed to require only BAMF to notify the Foreigner's Office if the status of the individual needed to be upgraded or reviewed. Anja explained that more recently in August 2019, the law was changed yet again under the Datenaustauschverbesserungsgesetz (2. DAVG),[7] meaning it would influence all the asylum decisions from 2015 to 2017. The BAMF has to give the Foreigner's Office a formal 'yes' or 'no', returning to the previous policy, before it may grant permanent residency. Furthermore, she explained that caseworkers were told not to contact BAMF regarding these decisions. To complicate things yet further, the law allows for recognized refugees to apply for permanent residency after three years if they have met the assigned requirements, yet this timeline does not begin with the first residency card, but rather the moment one applies for asylum. Anja explained her frustration with the new rules – "It's a good idea; that the days of the asylum procedure should count" – but they created a mismatch in the timeline between the period that BAMF should have provided a letter confirming the asylum decision and the time that refugees may have applied for permanent residency. The implication is that it was to the refugees' benefit that the timeline would begin when the asylum seeker applied, but the lawmakers had failed to calculate that the review could in the end take place after only three years. This means that if the asylum procedure lasted eight months and they lived in Germany as a recognized refugee for a further 28 months, they could apply for permanent residency, but BAMF's deadline to review the case would be another eight months. Nor had they calculated that BAMF lacked the capacity to handle this volume of decisions. This was clear to Anja because she recognized that BAMF had let the added contracts of employees who were hired between 2015 and 2016 handle the increased caseload to expire, which made it clear that there were not enough staff to execute these decisions.

To put this into context, so-called Blue Card residents, highly skilled migrants (degree holders with a job offer with a salary above €55,200 per year), are able to pay into the social security retirement system for less than two years (21 months) with only level B1 German and gain permanent residency (§ 19a Absatz 6). However, should a refugee wish to use this principle, it would only apply if they *first* changed their residency status to that of a 'high-skilled' labourer, then the timeline for residency would begin for that particular classification of resident card. If there is a biopolitical element to immigration, in which neoliberal-style governance can be used to reify state sovereignty, then it certainly does not consider the arbitrary outcomes produced by such a policy (Ong 2012). The taxonomy of residency status, in practice, has little to do with its biopolitical foundations that serve old notions of welfare state prosperity, but have more to do with legislation that forms a relative *ouroboros* of eternally relived bureaucracy.

Finally, as in asylum decisions, the only way to address waiting for a response from BAMF in order to apply for permanent residency is to appeal to the courts. However, the responsible authority in this case is the Foreigner's Office, so in fact a refugee may only make a claim against the Foreigner's Office, which in turn would only be able to again request a decision from BAMF on the case under review. Even with various resources, the democratic function of law fails refugees in this case. The only possibility is to wait and hope.

However, once a refugee attains permanent residence, they *should* no longer be counted as a refugee. They can only lose their status if they were to leave Germany without notifying the Foreigner's Office and receiving permission to do so for a period over six months or in the case of a criminal-related removal, such as terrorism. In Anja's opinion, the situation for most refugees and subsidiary protected is that the vast majority seek to obtain permanent residency. They seek it not in order to apply for family reunification rights or other civil liberties, but for the simple fact of security: the security of not being removed, the security to build a future, and the security of not re-entering the bureaucratic machine of the nanny state.

In essence, within the German integration regime, the Ausländerbehörde attempted to solidify its legitimacy by following the local motivations driven by populist movements, followers of the welfare chauvinism doctrine, which were taken more seriously by political gains made by the AfD in elections since 2016. Unlike the bureaucrats at the Job Centre, who follow a federal model driven by monitoring refugees, the Ausländerbehörde is characterized by shifting political power that employees can use to adjust their interpretation of the law. Although the government of Munich makes a point to liberalize the residency permissions for refugees, it is both limited in its capacity to act independently due to the structure of the federal authority and by its limited influence on the broader regional approach to refugee policy in Bavaria. This policy was constructed on the principles of welfare state reforms that demand long-term unemployment benefits be coupled with broad sweeping ideals of labour market integration. It is not, however, one that has the capacity to establish consequences, beyond those attached to welfare benefits, for those who fail to follow the integration mandate. Nor does it aim to integrate refugees into civic forms of state mechanisms. In other words, the legal and theoretical rewards for 'good refugees' who are 'well integrated' are not connected to democratic inclusion by way of citizenship – in Germany only citizens may vote in federal elections, while EU Member State citizens who are residents are allowed to vote in local elections. Citizenship is only available to refugees and subsidiary protected after obtaining permanent residency and a standard period of eight years, which can be reduced to seven with an integration course and six with excellent German language comprehension in addition to other conditions. However, all foreigners must also pass the citizenship test.[8] According to the German government, as of 2019 only 8.8 per cent of refugees have permanent residency (Deutscher Bundestag 2019) and only 2,880 (out of over 100,000 foreigners) Syrians received German citizenship in 2018 (Destatis 2019). In general, the majority of foreigners receiving German citizenship have been resident for over eight years (Destatis 2019). The implication of these statistics and the consideration of the fieldwork presented here should make a case that the security of permanent residency for refugees is a hard-fought aim with arbitrary decision making involved, and the rewards for early permanent residency and citizenship are seldom realized by those who aspire towards them.

Conclusion

Doing research in institutions, attempting to capture some of the functions of the local state institutions, presents a number of theoretical and methodological challenges that are, from a governmentality perspective, most thoroughly outlined by Gupta (2012) and Andersson (2014). Many of the themes they outline are presented throughout this book, but Gupta's critique on 'the translocal nature of the state' as a point of difficulty for researchers is most relevant (Gupta 1995, 375; 2012). Most of the fieldwork was done with refugees and through their experience with the state. But in order to gain an understanding of the inner workings of how policy functions, it is important to spend time inside institutions. Like Gupta, I was engaged with the 'lowest levels of administrative hierarchy' because it was the level of greatest contact to my research group, and knowing that the 'higher one goes in the bureaucratic hierarchy, the less such interactions are likely to be found' (Gupta 2012, 64). As to the problem of 'pluricentredness', and similar to the contention that the ubiquity of state has no centre, time and space are issues that need to be addressed. How can one compare local levels of administration without observing actions at the same time in another area, and at what locale should one observe them? To that end, this section of the book is focused on the administrative aspects of the integration regime not at the location of my primary research collaborators, but at the area where I was able to gain access at a point of practicality. In part this highlights what Sökefeld and Strasser (2016) discuss in more serious cases of danger or precarity in ethnographic research 'under suspicious eyes', where state surveillance raises a number of ethical and methodological questions. It became clear in some cases, aside from outright rejection or unresponsiveness from administrative agencies, that there were political and social implications of talking with researchers. The impact of the BAMF investigations at the time (Deutsche Welle 2018), in which over 1,000 asylum claims were allegedly falsely approved, cannot be taken for granted. Accusations of bribery and pressure from above led to the dismissal of the BAMF head Jutta Cordt. When I arrived for my appointment in Saarbrücken, which I had arranged through the press office of the Job Centre, no one in the office was aware that I was coming and the head of the department refused to help me arrange an interview. One of the workers asked me for a *Dienstausweis* (employment badge), an identification card usually reserved for public sector employees or law enforcement, and shook her head, wondering who would want to be interviewed for this kind of work. She told me: "I wouldn't want to be interviewed!"

To address both these methodological questions, it is important to consider the fieldwork presented here in various bureaucracies as part of the social field of the German integration regime, where different forms of capital can be exchanged and accumulated. They are not representative of the reified state, but rather of the everyday practices of how administrative policy ideals interact with the vast network of factors that come into play when these ideals reach individuals, and how people in this social field may react to institutional tensions between agency mismatches and become victims of arbitrary legal reforms in a hegemonic structure.

As was mentioned at the beginning, this chapter moves away from the refugee experience with the perceived state and focuses on the bureaucracy itself. In doing so, it should be clear that this is a peripheral part of the broader context of the integration regime. My focus has not been to present an exhaustive outline of how bureaucracies function; instead, I present the shifting expectations and constructed imaginaries that both refugees and the state have produced since 2015. Additionally, my position as a researcher provides bureaucrats with the opportunity to steer part of the political narrative. Although the administrations in Munich provided a generous amount of transparency in comparison to other regions, this cannot be taken as a negative representation of the other regions as intransparent government administrations, nor can it be considered apolitical. In the following chapter I return to the framework focused on the lives of refugees and the implications of some of the themes explored in this chapter – more precisely, the ability of refugees to move beyond bureaucracy and the integration regime to reassert their livelihood in Germany.

6

Pathways Forward and
Pathways Uncertain

This chapter is primarily aimed at presenting the various outcomes of refugee interaction with the German administrative state. What impact did the integration regime have on the everyday lives of refugees? What did the refugees in the best possible position to 'integrate' achieve in terms of being accepted into German society, having met the official goals of integration? Among these questions, this chapter serves as the conclusion to the final part is what I consider the integration regime. After navigating arrival, language learning, private housing and relationship building, refugees should be in a position to find work and consider settling in. The integration regime promised, among other things, a livelihood through language learning. Here I will examine how refugees were rewarded for following the legal and symbolic frameworks of integration.

Ephemeral integration

In the previous chapters, the state and policy were discussed in terms of local administration, deploying Gupta's 'blurred boundaries' approach that pushes back against the reification of the state by arguing that the government often enacts policy to reaffirm the interests of 'powerful minorities' and that the actual state only exists in the 'social imaginary' (Gupta 2012, 56). However, Sökefeld adds another layer to the discourse, differentiating 'the state' and 'government', and noting that 'the state-idea is closely linked to the idea of the nation which on such occasions is celebrated through its symbols and heroes' (Sökefeld 2016, 10). In doing so, he presents an important distinction that questions the universal understanding of how the state may be interpreted. He frames 'the state-idea as a container' with particular importance to the analysis of Gilgit-Baltistan, while at the same time concluding that 'the walls and borders of the container are often negotiated and made penetrable by the state-system' and that 'the container system is very leaky' (Sökefeld 2016, 13). Similarly, both anthropologists (Ong 2006) and geographers (Darling 2017) have reinforced notions of the scale and space of citizenship; that is, they attempt to free citizenship research from attachment to the state. However, Tuckett argues that 'cultural citizenship' actually 'reinstates the legal-political aspects' of citizenship, which means it is from encounters with the state and institutions that refugees form their 'culturally specific modes of behavior' (Tuckett 2018, 74). These blurred distinctions serve as a point of emphasis in an attempt to use this section to synthesize many of the concepts and theories utilized in the previous parts of this book.

The concept of the *border regime* has recently been taken up by researchers in Germany as a tool to consider the negotiated space of EU borders and the limits of mobility within German borders (Tsianos and Karakayali 2010; El-Kayed and Hamann 2018). The regime approach, which has long been accepted by development studies researchers as the framework for considering migration research (Betts 2009; Horvath, Amelina and Peters 2017), has been used in this book to understand the German integration regime. Finally, the regime approach is also used as a tool to understand constellations of policy and policy-related actions along the lines of what Tsianos and Karakayali describe as 'the "reversion of sovereignty": the concept of regime makes it possible to understand regulations of migration as effects, as condensations of social actions instead of taking regulations functionalistically for granted' (Tsianos and Karakayali 2010, 376). This approach allows the German government's integration programmes not only to be conceived as a transnational negotiation of policy – the EU-Turkey negotiation by the Merkel-led German government comes to mind here – on refugees, but also as a way to incorporate the influence of the 'social imaginary' of both policy development and policy application. In other words, migration policy at the top level of governance has served to consolidate the power of ruling elites by attempting to placate the most radical social elements of the social imaginary since 2015 – most notably, the development of CDU's Interior Minister Horst Seehofer's so-called 'Master Plan on Migration' and Bavarian CSU leader Markus Söder's policies[1] that called for faster deportations, a special unit of Bavarian border police and the 'Ankerzentrum' concept for asylum arrivals, all of which reinforced a policy turn towards anti-immigration instead of welcome culture (Schuler and Götz 2018). In this way, the perceived social imaginaries that political leaders believe can help them maintain power influence the development of often symbolic legislation, but at the administrative level of government, I have shown that this policy is carried out based on the governmentality of local caseworkers – mainstream norms coupled by appropriate behaviour within the regional management. Here I am attempting to produce a view of governmentality that shows 'how the role-model of the enterprising self is connected with theory of human capital in an elementary way, and how this role-model is diffused and becomes hegemonic within present-day regimes of subjectification', which begins at the local level (Brockling, Krasmann and Lemke 2011, 12). Conversely, Syrian refugees themselves have been influenced by the narrative polity within their networks and by the narratives spread by members in their social groups, forming both the national and transnational social fields of Syrian refugees that flow along two distinct but interacting lines of young men and families.

This chapter is about the way in which potentiality in the Syrian imaginary has been disturbed along the way from time of flight, through the period of integration courses and thereafter. The subjectification of Syrian refugees has remained in a state of flux since 2015, as have the means by which they have been governed. The way in which governmentality has been shaped has been through an imaginary society, which share normative characteristics (Anderson 2013, 4). Like the old model of 'the migrant who is a utility-maximizing individual' (Collins 2018, 965), the formulation of a uniform integration process has been taken up by the younger Syrians to mean that they would be rewarded for adhering to norms and conditions. Older heads of households have taken a more pragmatic approach rooted in insider knowledge from *engaged volunteers* and positioning their previous class status. This is the potential period where refugees exit bureaucracies and the integration regime, asserting their independence. Again, two diverging paths emerge between those who have accomplished this and those who have further stagnated.

Higher education

According to the Federal Ministry of Education and Research (Bundes-ministerium für Bildung und Forschung [BMFB]), the arrival of Syrians from 2015 onwards is one of the reasons why the number of refugees enrolled in a university has increased from an estimated few thousand in 2014 to over 40,000 in 2020 (Fourier et al 2018). There is no exact number of refugees enrolled in German universities available because of data protection, but through estimates from the Hochschulrektorenkonferenz (HRK) survey, there was a jump from 205 refugees enrolled in the 2015–16 winter semester to 2,915 newly enrolled in the 2017–18 winter semester – a 98 per cent increase in the case of Syrians living in Germany (Fourier et al 2018). A review of the funded postsecondary education preparation for refugees shows that participants had slightly better test scores than those in normal integration courses, but at the same time notes that the primary reason for rejection into an area of study is lacking prerequisite qualifications, along with a limited number of student places (Fourier et al 2018; BAMF 2019a).

Anas was one of only two of my collaborators who by the end of my fieldwork was attending university. He arrived in 2015 and was able to excel in his German language studies in part because of his experience as a student, but also because he benefited from the help of an administrative person at his language school. He once reminded me that he had no idea what it was about at the time, only that the deadline was near, so the administrator just told him to sign the paper. After our failed attempts to enrol him in the *Integra* programme associated with Saarland University, the paper the mentor had had him sign granted him enrolment in a private language course for university preparation. The scholarship would allow him to reach C1 German (the level needed for study) and fund not only the course but also his living costs.

Anas began the advanced language course in 2018 and was enrolled on a university's bachelor's programme for the winter semester in 2019. He told me that one of the highlights of having the language grant was that he would no longer need to go to the Job Centre. When his course ended in the spring of 2019, he had his language certificate and needed to apply for the university, but he wanted to increase his chances of gaining the coveted security of the permanent residency card and remain free from the Job Centre, so he worked at the language school he had attended before as a teacher of *Maßnahmen* courses in the intervening period. However, being unaware of the complexity of the law, he was denied permanent residency because he did not have an unlimited work contract.[2] When I asked about this situation at the Ausländerbehörde in Munich, Anja confirmed that it can be difficult for refugees to receive a permanent residency after three years because in most cases, people have limited contracts, which means they would ask the employer to provide some kind of written statement that they would hire the person under another contract after the first one ended in order to receive the unrestricted residency permit. According to Anja, the caseworker can also estimate based on past work history: if applicants have had continual one-year contracts, caseworker can use their discretion to grant permanent residency. However, according to the Munich office, this should be considered a rare exception rather than the standard.

When I spoke to Nazir in 2019, he said he had also attended courses full time during the winter semester at the university. I asked him about having his education documents recognized in Germany and he proudly explained that his secondary school grades were so good that he could have studied medicine in Syria. It had been several months since I had last spoken with him, aside from a few SMS messages just to check in, so I was surprised by this news – the last time we spoke, he had failed his German B2 exam and was waiting for a new course. He didn't answer calls and texts from Anas when I came to Saarbrücken in early 2019. Anas said they were no longer as close and that he wasn't sure what Nazir had planned, only that he thought he wasn't taking things so seriously and needed to study more.

However, since then, he had passed the B2 exam on his second attempt and circumvented the Job Centre by finding a C1 course outside of Saarbrücken in a neighbouring town where he was able to find a course more quickly.

Nazir explained to me that he was lucky. He had a strong group of Syrian friends who he could rely on when he first started his course. I asked him how he found this group after he had begun his study and he struggled a bit to find a way to describe how these networks of young Syrian men operate. He told me "if you were Syrian, and I went to a new city and didn't know anyone you would only have to ask another Syrian friend and there was no question they would know someone in your new city. It's like that for Syrians". And that's how it was with his study group. It only took a matter of days before every Syrian who was studying informatics at the university had been brought together so they could make a collective effort towards completing their bachelor's degree.

When they were studying German and receiving money from the Job Centre, they lived in drab, claustrophobic, rather transient single-room flats in Saarbrücken. Even when Anas had his grant from the language programme and was later working, he stayed in his original flat. Since moving for his university study, he had moved into another flat with some students from his bachelor's programme, as did Nazir.

When we talked on the phone after Nazir began his studies, he told me that he couldn't send money back to his family in Syria at the moment because the money he received was less than he received from the Job Centre. However, he was hopeful that after his studies were complete, he would continue to send money to support them and that they understood the situation. The prospect of them leaving Syria in the meantime was not likely, since they had tried several times to travel to Turkey, but had experienced violence along the way and had been forced to return. He recounted several stories of how even in rural areas outside Deir ez-Zor, there was still fighting between ISIL, the Kurdish army and the Syrian regime forces. When this kind of thing came up in our conversations, I tried to be quiet and let them show me how to continue. I am indeed cognisant of the critical discourse on the 'business of anthropology' (Cabot 2019) and the radicalness of listening (Kumaran 2014) – that is, the humility to be open to contradiction and to recognize the privileged position of the researcher as an observer in situations and, at times, the imbalance of power exuded from the ability to remain quiet. To this end, I cannot point to specific trauma or claim to put a kind of *measure* of it in focus. I can only attempt to make sense of what my collaborators have described to me over time and in context.

The situation for Nazir and Anas had visibly improved in a number of ways, one of which was that at moments of stillness in their lives, they would not retreat from people close to them – Nazir had never reacted so strongly in this way – but more than this, when difficult subjects came up, they would describe them with a hopefulness towards the future. Something tangible was materializing.

However, Favell's critique of integration underscores how narrow measures of conditional inclusion are arbitrarily used to legitimize bureaucratic hurdles:

> Any kind of measurement of attainment vis-a-vis a 'national mainstream' will inevitably smuggle in with it 'cultural' markers of attainment that are no longer required of translucent global individuals, who by definition have an la carte relation to the national cultural requirements which need to be plebiscited ('democratically') every day … and which are imposed on newcomers in the society so that they must prove they belong (i.e., in conditional integration 'tests'). (Favell 2019, 6)

This means that the presence of state pressure and the 'public philosophies' (Favell 2001) was a constant form of pressure to conform to nationally imagined citizenship. With many of their accomplishments invisible in the public imaginary, Anas and Nazir wanted to continue to build their new networks but carried experiences of exclusion with them to new experiences with adversity. The lives they had begun to build were now shielded from previous elements through stronger networks of solidarity and inclusion, but their previous experience drove an existential exclusion that was embodied in tangible permanent security mechanisms, like residency or citizenship, which was rendered symbolic through hierarchies of status in Germany.

(Anticipations of) discrimination in the labour market

The motivation behind social science-based research on discrimination against migrants attempting to enter the labour market should serve as a welcome affirmation to what has recently emerged in the social imaginary and political spheres – an increasingly anti-immigrant sentiment, rising politically in the form of the popularity of the racist, anti-immigrant AfD party. The impact of racism on a refugee community using a social capital framework can be helpful in terms of seeing how racism can produce both stronger social bonds and distrust in the dominant societal group (Deuchar 2011). The foundations of integration ideology and law are framed by the notion that migrant groups choose not to integrate and thus form 'parallel societies'. However, when viewed through the lens of racism and social capital, it becomes clearer that it is as a result of discrimination that refugees have increased distrust in institutions, which prioritize White majority groups, and seek to shore up their recourses within their social and cultural groups as a means for both mental and physical survival. In the most extreme version of this, Wacquant (1998) explains that the structural limitations and isolation of government institutions in Black neighbourhoods in the USA actually produce a negative form of social capital. Thus, the orientation of the inquiry should not be to what degree racism *exists,* but rather what are the lasting and symbolic repercussions of experience with racist actions?

The experiences of discrimination are exponential considering class difference. My collaborators who decided upon their arrival in Germany to work in unskilled jobs, which was the case for Osama and his brother in Saarbrücken and Hakim in Osnabrück, experienced little exclusionary structures to enter their lower paid forms of labour. But the higher they moved up the labour class stratification, the more discrimination from gatekeepers they experienced.

One afternoon in 2020, I visited Hakim and Rasha outside of Osnabrück and they told me how Hakim had found his job. He took his remedial level of German and was able to save the money to obtain his driving license. He looked online at the 'help wanted' section of the used German Ebay-Kleinanzeigen (Ebay Classifieds) and was quickly able to find a job as a delivery driver. Since then, he had been relatively content with his job as a driver and was not seeking to have any of his former skills verified in Germany, which would give Rasha time to finish her training as a pharmacist.

When Rasha and I were discussing how she experienced tension from other Germans at their daughter's daycare – the other mothers had stopped greeting her – Hakim shrugged and said that all of his co-workers and clients were very friendly. Rasha returned to the notion that it was because she wears a headscarf.[3] Indeed, there is both normative class function for Hakim as a driver and a man with no visible symbolic indicators that can be immediately associated with being a Muslim. Rasha was not only training to work in a new profession, but was also feeling that she was excluded from the social groups of other parents, which in part was drawn from her experience and those of her friends that wearing a headscarf implies an immediate indication of the 'other', who is outside the social norms.

The next morning, when I went to visit another family in Hamelin, Abdul explained how the 'typical refugee' found work in Germany – it was almost the exact same story that Hakim had outlined the day before. Abdul explained: "They usually work as drivers." Abdul had no interest in working as a driver, but saw it as an option because he had recently felt the pressure to find work quickly.

Abdul and his wife Adel are relatively middle-class Syrians who worked as an accountant and a civil servant for the Syrian state (respectively) before war broke out. There was such sudden violence when they first fled Aleppo that they were unable to bring anything to provide support for their skills along with them. Now after a few years in Germany, both had excelled in the German language, but questions remained over how to provide for their families. Abdul expressed his frustration with the situation. He wished there were a way to just spend a short period learning specialized German for his career and then have an opportunity to take a test to confirm his skills. But he knew that in order to earn real money, he would have to invest years in the process. "But then I will be too old to get a job", he told me, fearing that after he finished his training, employers would view him as too old to start in that field again in Germany, so at the time I spoke to him. he faced a choice of double negatives; taking the typical route of working *now* or investing in education with the calculated gamble that he might not be hired afterwards. However, he reminded me several times: "Well, we just have to look forward now, not backward."

Although the large-scale quantitative studies on refugee 'integration' clearly show that the vast majority of refugees find their first work through social contacts (Woellert, Sievert and Neubecker 2016, 11), these are low-wage jobs in underpaid sectors, and the studies do not fully outline the influences driving the decision to take such low-income work. In other words, these are temporary fixes for some of the problems addressed previously.

Unlike similar ethnographic work in Denmark (Pedersen 2012), which argues that economic class in a new country is part of a 'downward class journey' for refugees, I argue here that it does not serve the issue of inequality of migrant capital to consider class equally across borders. Living standards for the Iraqi or Syrian middle class living in their country of origin are not the same for those in North America and Europe. The neoliberal consumer culture of the Global North overwhelmingly favours greater forms of symbolic material wealth over savings. By framing class transnationally, a consideration for global inequalities and exploitation of previously colonized regions is taken out of focus.

Many of my collaborators had family members spread across Syria, as well as ownership of properties that have now been wiped away by war: what they miss now are more practical things. Rasha spoke of buying a bigger car that could accommodate her husband and five daughters, and provide them with the ability to visit her sister in Sweden. Abdul and Adel were thinking more simply. They wanted to buy a car once they started working because they lived in a village that had no public transport services over the weekend. Abdul wanted to travel to Lebanon to shorten the time it would take the visit to his father, who was still living in Aleppo. The prospect of buying property in Germany was not even in the furthest fathoms of their imagination or future plans. To attain these more practical aspirations, there were deep postcolonial, international inequality legacies that impacted the way in which cultural capital might be considered in the transnational context.

The country-specific variation in cultural capital for university degrees, for example, has more to do with international relations than actual academic rigour. In this form of capital found in the 'institutionalized state', and although Bourdieu does not directly discuss the international symbolic power of degrees, I am thinking here about how well skills travel across borders. He explains that the 'bureaucratization goes hand in hand with the interest in culture as an instrument to access to the bureaucracy' (Bourdieu 2014, 156). He was of course considering the 'meta-capital' that the state possesses the right to legitimize power, but I want to draw attention to how transnational migration is stratified by the ability for states to enforce the institutional power of cultural capital. The degrees and documented vocational training of Syrians, especially in the German context, extend their need to acquire skills through the investment of time because they cannot be directly used to apply for work. Unlike younger men, families seek stability through symbolic capital that would allow them agency to return to doing meaningful labour that would fit their previous training. For young men, quickly entering the labour market often indicated a motivation to earn income to send home, limited education prospects, or a lack of knowledge of the dual vocational training system. However, in terms of class, Syrian refugees evaluate determining factors without state interventions of the integration regime. Those committed to learning German and earning income, or gaining training, in order to send money to their families indicate not only that they are 'good' immigrants but also that they have more aspirational abilities and imagination for the future. However, in many cases, the ability to imagine the future positively comes down to family circumstances and discrimination.

Rasha was well aware that if she could have conducted her pharmaceutical training at a college or university leading to a degree as opposed to vocational training, she would be able to earn twice as much income, but that this would have taken her four years instead of two. Being a mother and over the age of 30 made it unrealistic to spend an additional two years not earning a full salary. However, my younger collaborators who were in the middle of their bachelor's degrees were already considering enrolment on a master's degree course.

Nonetheless, the calculation that refugees can quickly contribute economically or that the notion of measuring unemployment of recognized refugees as an indicator for imagined integration does not contribute to or completely capture the situation of different groups of refugees and the nuances between individual families. What is relevant is how discrimination and self-ascribed status play into decisions about how and when to seek work in Germany. Discrimination leaves scars that influence how to cope with adversity and rationalize the inability to apply one's habitus successfully in new environments. Abdul and Adel never mention discrimination or being a Muslim minority in Germany – Adel wears a headscarf, but never mentioned it as a cause for conflict or unwanted attention – but they have also experienced so much trauma on their journey. In order to remove the symbolic return to the trauma of stuckedness in Turkey and in the camps in Greece, they avoid the existential immobility and focus on the next step even if there is not a tangible one available. While explicit recognition of experiences of racism was variable among my informants, the interplay between class, age, trauma and gender is an important intersectional aspect that is not explored in this text, but presents an opportunity for future research in integration regimes.

Continued training

Relevant work addressing the positionality of immigrant and refugee status upon early arrival in Germany (Söhn 2013; 2019) focuses on how symbolic status, such as EU membership, opens up pathways to employment, while state-designated stratification reinforces migrant stereotypes. This is a useful framework to expand upon in order to consider the differences between refugees with recognized status or subsidiary protection, those with longer processing times for asylum applications, and those with more complicated asylum decisions. However, the generally well-educated group of Syrians I collaborated with for this study had a recognized protected status and should be considered within the framework of a deeper social milieu in the migrant or refugee community and in terms of discrimination. On the other hand, inequality researchers in Germany have shown from a more quantitative perspective how migrants and their children face difficulties in terms of not only gaining access to equal education but also to vocational training (Pielage et al 2012). As is outlined throughout this book, the positionality of refugees shapes how they will adjust to the conditions presented to them – for instance, the optimism of young people to be flexible in terms of investing in a long period of continued education versus those with family obligations who are weighing up deeper family responsibilities.

Tuckett (2016) frames this notion in the limited mobilities of those migrants who have successfully moved on, but uses the concept of *transnational habitus* to present this problem as one of globalization. The ability to navigate some of the more complex environments with improvisation (Amit and Knowles 2017) using various forms of connectedness (Harney 2013) allows Syrians to distinguish themselves from other migrant groups. There is an ebb and flow of perceived agency that has shaped Syrians' experience. Like other migrant groups, the collaborators I worked with on this study experienced a great deal of 'deskilling'. Additionally, employment opportunities that reached them were often influenced by constraints of time and expectations; young men benefited from strong connections to other refugees. Anas and Nazir maintained a balance of family responsibility alongside deepening friendships with other students at the universities where they studied. Although parents had to learn German *and* enter into continued training, they lacked the social connections that gave them positive agency, building hope for alternative outcomes. They lacked the 'investment, directionality and intensity of reality' (Hage 2013) provided by *illusio*.

Unlike the immobilities in Italy expressed in the work of Tuckett presented previously in this chapter, parents had the means to move to better economic areas in Europe and had the skills to take on well-paid jobs, but the structural mechanisms made navigating access to these forms of capital more challenging than for young men. Once they entered training, they remained socially excluded from professional connections with other Germans as the dynamic was based much less on solidarity (as was the case for students) and more on competition. Indeed, since beginning her training, Rasha had not gained new friendships with those she trained with as a pharmacist. Julia remained her most valued advisor since support from the Job Centre, other refugees or even 'native' Germans did not offer advice on how to move forward.

Remittance and work

The Job Centres prioritize German language learning for all unemployed refugees. However, all of the bureaucrats, NGO workers and engaged volunteers I spoke with during my fieldwork agreed that the level of German that the integration regime demanded was not sufficient to participate in vocational training and certainly not for attending university or technical university. The consensus among aid workers who I spoke with while I volunteered and spoke with colleagues working in the IQ Network (Integration durch Qualifizierung) programme is that in most cases they should have had B2 level at a minimum in order to participate in an internship or a vocational training programme. This included the specialized German Dual Education (Duale Ausbildung) training, which is much more formalized. University faculties vary according to the study programme, but generally speaking they require a C1 level or the common certification of allowance to enter university study: Deutsche Sprachprüfung für den Hochschulzugang (German language test for admission to college) (DSH-2). The structural decision to base the integration course and the benefits associated with passing it on a B1 level is presented as a gateway to further language learning and deeper social interaction. However, the experiences presented here show that there are groups of highly motivated refugees and groups of marginalized refugees who do not fit into bureaucratic codification.

In addition to a language certificate shortfall based on the minimum requirement from the Job Centre, the structure of the German higher education and job markets is dictated by documentation-based evidence of work experience, which means that it is difficult to apply informal training[4] into the labour market. Furthermore, there are a number of interested parties who regulate the certification of skilled labour in coordination with

German labour unions and semi-public chambers of commerce (Industrie-und Handelskammern and Handwerkskammern) (Busemeyer and Schlicht-Schmälzle 2014). The strong influence of labour unions and local labour authorities created tension among refugees because there was no guaranteed path for their previously uncertified training to be recognized. As noted elsewhere, 'the majority of [r]efugees come from countries where their job training does not exist in Germany. In these countries one is either an academic or uneducated. Because refugees don't understand the value of the German Dual Vocational Education, it's difficult to convince them of its usefulness' (Knuth 2016, 9). The framing of this statement is relatively neocolonial, but the implication is nonetheless helpful in understanding the German labour perspective. Indeed, some refugees have regionally specific skills, but in the case of Syrians, it took *time* for them to understand the nuances of the complicated vocational training programmes available. Those who did indeed arrive with well-documented training were required to overcome another bureaucratic hurdle, and needed these documents translated into German and then in most cases officially recognized by regulatory institutions.

Recent research by Paulsen et al (2016) adopting a psychological perspective to a vocational skills recognition programme argues that language courses alone cannot achieve 'successful integration'; rather, entering into the labour market supports mental health by strengthening social contact outside of 'refugee homes' and provides the opportunity for independence from welfare allowances and stigma attached to the use of these benefits of the social state. In the same way as a purely economic perspective of success removes any ethical considerations, this magical thinking that labour market success equals 'good integration' does not remove the barriers presented by regulatory gatekeepers – particularly unions and politicians – whose interests lie with the status quo, or the barriers erected by sympathetic businesses that think that refugees should join the labour force, but are reluctant to take them on as employees. Furthermore, the 'colourblindness' and 'nonracialism' (Goldberg 2015) is found through labour market integration discourse. Nonetheless, refugees who enter the labour market do indeed benefit from deeper, nuanced language practice, broader potential social interaction, and financial independence. The road to employment hinges on a broad web of conditions, which range from the personal to the structural.

Access to labour markets and 'good work' plays out for refugees in a transnational way. The transnational experience, either trauma or a *multilocality* of existence *here* in Germany and *there* in Syria, means that refugees' motivation in relation to work and career planning is based in transnational relations. It took Anas almost eight years to arrive at a similar position to that he occupied when he left in Syria in 2011 at the beginning of his study programme – gaining a position to study at a university – although his experiences of fleeing first Syria and then Turkey drastically changed his study and career goals. Anas' family also moved to Germany, but he lived through *transnational trauma* from the loss of his father and brother, reporting on casualties of war in Syria, and punctuated periods of existential immobility. In many ways, he pushed these traumas out of his daily life by not fully reflecting on the painful experiences and yet he would still have to deal with the trauma of war and violence through his journalistic engagements.

Conversely, Nazir, Mohammad and Osama were the only ones in their immediate family to apply for asylum and settle in Germany. There were of course always relatives nearby; a cousin or an uncle seemed to visit regularly or they would go to visit relatives living in a town nearby, in contrast to Anas, who saw his mother once a week during this period. Nazir was often aloof about any responsibility to work quickly, but he, like all others, told me he sent money regularly to his family who were still in Syria, where he earned money working part time or from social support funds from the German government. Nonetheless, this was during the time when international governments were making a push to retake areas in Syria from ISIL and his family had been forced to relocate several times due to the violence. Several family members attempted to go north and cross a border into Turkey, but were either robbed by smugglers or arrested and sent back into Syria by the Turkish military. Every time I spoke to Osama, on the other hand, he made the point not to discuss his family in Syria, and it was only Anas and others who would tell me how most Syrians were all constantly worried about their families still in Syria and occupied with how they could support them. Those who did not support their families were labelled by my collaborators as 'undeserving' to live in Germany or 'not good Syrians'.

The third time I went to Osama's house to visit, he told me that the situation with his family had not improved. He and his brother had begun working almost immediately after he finished his integration course. Osama worked at a warehouse outside of Saarbrücken at one of Germany's largest supermarket chains. Anas joked: "Every time I talk to Osama, he has some new idea of what he will do." Indeed, he was incredibly active but also strategic in his plans – as time would tell.

Before finding a job in logistics, Osama needed a driver's licence, which would cost up to €2,000 on average and could take several months to complete. He also knew that by working nights, there would be no train to take to work and he would need to get a car. He saved for both a car and a licence, and after the first time we met. I later saw his post on social media that he had passed his driving test and bought a car. Working at the warehouse, he also knew that the salary for this position was not going to increase, so he began planning how to build on this experience. He attended a specific language training course focused on logistics work, and was thinking of doing a vocational training programme for logistics work as well – all of which he did while working full-time. But he loved football (soccer) and had the dream to be a football referee for the German Bundesliga, the professional league football in Germany. To become a referee, he would have to start by attending training, then working in the minor leagues and slowly accumulate enough hours until he could eventually be referee in the top league. But the immediate focus was to be able to send as much money as possible to his family who had to move from his home in Deir ez-Zor to Idlib because at that time ISIL occupied the area. For this reason, the brothers never considered enrolling in a full vocational training programme that would lead to a career earning a better wage; they did not have the time. Yet, Osama had been engaged in many levels of German life and he made a point of telling me every time we spoke how he felt completely at home in his neighbourhood in Saarbrücken.

Conversely, Nazir was not particularly motivated or driven by a specific goal. Each time we met or talked by phone, he slightly altered his future plans and had only reached level B2 in German and failed the examination back in 2018. Anas always complained about him, saying: "I tell him he needs to study more". He had little faith that Nazir would end up reaching level C1, which he did, and ended up enrolling in university at the same time at Anas in the autumn of 2019. But there was some kind of competition between the two of them and a bit of tension that arose later in 2018 over religious conservatism. They were not talking when I visited then. Anas said it was because he commented on something Nazir posted on Facebook. He had written that he thought the regional identities that Syrians associated some themselves with were 'stupid'. Nazir took offence, among many others on social media, and he was mad at Anas for a period. But even later when I told Anas I was surprised that Nazir had made it to the university and passed all the tests to enter, Anas said "well, he always acts confident, like he is okay but really he doesn't know what he wants to do and is not happy with his study programme". Some of the tensions that come from life in Syria transformed over time in Germany, while some were forgotten altogether. Nonetheless, there were hierarchies that Syrians constructed for themselves and other Syrian refugees, which followed some of the modes of thought that were reproduced within the integration regime.

We visited Mohammad once when he was working as a waiter while waiting a few months for the next German course. In Syria, he worked as a nurse and brought all of his certificates with him when he fled. He was able to contact one of his many friends in Germany who knew of a specialized programme for refugees with nurse training that functioned as both a specialized language course and a recognition programme where he would receive a full salary. But the burden of supporting his family weighed heavily on him:

'My certificates from Syria are verified here but I still need six months to earn B2 and six months of work in the hospital, and another six months to study other subjects, perhaps psychology. Then I can work as a real nurse, but it will take two years and I need to support my family.' (Mohammad, Saarbrücken 2017)

Family reunification visas for refugees were only allowed for parents and spouses, so he could not have his family join him in Germany. The cost and risk of having them travel to Germany through smugglers was also not an option; this meant he would have to wait to be able to support them financially.

Undoubtedly, there is a nuanced difference between varying essentialized descriptions of Syrians, which often frame them as one of the most well-educated groups among German refugees, but such essentialized descriptions should be considered in terms of the interplay between social capital, transnational trauma and motivational capacity based on habitus. The assumption was that Syrian refugees were in a better position than other refugees to 'integrate'. However, the context of each Syrian social group should also incorporate what particular circumstances are *visible* or recognized by bureaucratic actors that may inhibit refugees from achieving the narrow aims of integration. In addition, the question of what capacity caseworkers have, more often arbitrary luck of caseworker selection, to assess each situation plays a significant role. Conversely, the question of how much agency refugees have to circumvent structures should their challenges remain *invisible* to the bureaucratic state works into the relationship.

In terms of scaling up to the broader bureaucratic standards that have indeed shaped the social understanding of who is a refugee or what rights refugees should have, the preceding nuance is not factored into the social imaginaries about refugees – the approaches in statecraft are not generally exercised in political rhetoric or policy. That is not to discount the strides that have been made to recognize formal qualifications (Westdeutscher Handwerkskammertag 2014; Aumüller 2016) and to organize career-oriented courses offered by the BA's support for German for Professional Purposes (ESF-BAMF-Programm 'Berufsbezogene Deutschförderung') (Laschet 2015), as well as family-friendly courses that offer childcare for mothers attending them (to name but a few). However, many of these programmes, like the integration courses themselves, had a limited impact in terms of reaching refugees.

Syrians negotiate the space between the need to send money back to family and their ability to access structural boundaries, including the particularity of the German labour system. Most obviously, habitus and social capital were two of the most immediate factors that determined the quality and speed of access to finding work in Germany. In other words, to understand how Syrian refugees applied capital to access work in Germany, an analysis of the transnational relationship refugees had with Syria and how the relationship was embodied by them at the time, had accumulated throughout their journey and continued to evolve as they arrived and settled, is necessary . Not only were most Syrians informally trained for positions that require certification in Germany, and lacked the relevant documentation to support and validate such training, but extensive resources were also being distributed to specialized programmes that few refugees were aware of or utilizing (Brücker et al 2019). For this group of young male Syrian collaborators, only one collaborator used programmes recommended by the Job Centre to find training programmes or work. The majority relied on their personal relationships to find work, but the ability or decision to actually start working was heavily influenced by locality and external influences like trauma, family relationships, and educational background. More often, the Job Centre presented bureaucratic barriers that inhibited their access to explore the options available to them through these networks.

Racism and democracy

Certainly, the social construction of race and racism has been present throughout most of this book, either discreetly influencing factors of navigation or directly referenced in the refugee experience. Addressing the issue of race in only one section and in the final chapter of this book seems negligent. However, the way in which I have approached race in this text has to do with race as a central hindrance to 'belonging'. In other words, it confronts head-on the ways in which racism directly influences collaborators' ability to envision a future in Germany and thus often discourages the more symbolic orientation of active citizenship. Ethnographic research is framed in conditions of inclusion, which are highly racialized, but cannot be solely framed as a racism problem. However, the racialization of refugees and their ability to sustainably be included in German society often revolved around their subjectification in the public imaginary.

In earlier work, Ong (1996) considered *cultural citizenship* as a form of subjectification and more recently reconsidered the role of race in citizen making (Ong 2003). Framed in a capital list mode of immigration, Ong's argument is fundamentally that transnational citizenship produces various forms of citizenship that 'are the passports to wealth production as well as to the power to rule over others' (Ong 2003, 228). This contention is framed in postcolonial imaginary of White histories that base the subject making of 'good citizens' in the European histories that reassert power over unprivileged migrants. The lack of citizenship also limits the symbolic security that has allowed my collaborators to invest in perceived *fairness* in the European democratic welfare state.

Race and democracy set the stage for some the most consequential decisions that collaborators had made and potentially will make as they develop Germany as a central piece of their identity: it will shape how and if they or their children hold a dualism of being both Syrian and German or permanent outsiders; perhaps becoming Syrians *living* in Germany – something that perhaps speaks to a sentiment of diaspora. Additionally, it has and will dictate how they apply their capital, investment and trust in German institutions, and their general acceptance in the European welfare state.

Discrimination seems to be where collaborators first seek a rationale in the face of conflict with members of the German public, who consider themselves perhaps more *German* than a Syrian refugee. Whether it was Rasha when she first arrived, living in that shipping container with her family only to have landlords reject them without reason for a rental, or Mohammad's first encounter with border guards as he crossed from Austria, and later people shouting insults from passing cars as he awaited an asylum decision in the north of Germany, these early experiences were framed in discrimination. Later, when nearly all collaborators experienced conflict with German bureaucracies, from language schools to Job Centres, they again felt discriminated against. Finally, after overcoming many of the bureaucratic processes, they began to experience life as professionals and higher education students. Abdul told me in Mannheim in 2020: "I feel discriminated against. I do not have the same language skills as the others, it isn't fair." He had just been told by a professor that for the second time, he had not met the requirement to submit a term paper, so he would appeal the decision to the dean of his faculty. He said he found it unfair that he be held to the same standards as other Germans; after all, he had a much more complicated situation other than just language difficulties. I tried to explain that perhaps the professor felt the opposite was true, that the professor thought fairness lay in treating all students the same. I was, of course, not taking seriously the structural aspects of racism that favour German 'native' students. The colourblind approach that the professor had taken denied this structural aspect and also was not sensitive to the additional challenges that refugees faced in the so-called meritocracy of higher education. Later on, the issue came up again when I asked Anas about his mother. He told me that an employee at the Job Centre (a Moroccan) was giving his mother a hard time about her language course and finding work. He said they did not care that she was a widow and had never worked or had any formal training.

This theme has in many ways characterized the experience of foreigners in Germany. Integration ideology aside, the following question continually arises: *at what point does one stop being a foreigner?* For Anas, it apparently follows refugees into the next generation. He went so far as to say that he questions whether he would have children in Germany because of the complicated identity they would be burdened with: "I am Arab but I am not Muslim, so I cannot marry a Syrian. And I am Syrian and not White, so I cannot marry a German." I reflected on my own experience of being discriminated against by neo-Nazis in Southern California in the 1990s for being Black, and then to moving to Harlem, New York in the 2000s and having to convince young Black men that I *was* indeed Black in order not to be mugged.

Migration researchers like Simonsen have argued that across Europe, discrimination has had lasting effects on inclusion and that 'symbolic boundaries' are exclusionary to Muslim populations that are multigenerational (Simonsen 2016; 2018). However, it is important to consider Balibar's sentiment on the social construction of identity:

> Every individual must construct an identity for himself or herself: but he or she can only do it by accepting or rejecting the roles imposed on him or her in the framework of transferential relations that he or she must participate in, that is, by adopting the positive or negative identifications they imply. (Balibar 2009, 26)

In other words, there are imaginaries of refugees that disseminate from above and below, and the way in which refugees interpret these governmentalities formulates part of their identity. Aside from the fundamental shortcomings of perceiving all migrants as an imagined community of a binary immobile actors in light of the 'us' and 'them' discourse, the Balibar exerpt above presents the opportunity to consider the nuanced involvement in refugee social construction.

Anas explained that his experience with the state had led to a relative rejection of some of the most beneficial elements of the welfare state. He told me that after his experiences with the Job Centre and poverty in Syria, he would never claim unemployment benefits again – a sort of 'any job is a good job' mentality.

Bureaucracies are systems of arbitrary authority that have an uneven amount of power at their disposal. The workers in these administrations are not unitary machines that operate unemotionally; instead, similar to the work they do and the clients whom they interact with, they have variable capabilities and diverse personalities. The implication is that when they fail to be empathetic, they reinforce negative experiences, which perpetuates feelings of discrimination and exclusion. A certain amount of faith in the system of governance is needed to legitimize the ideals of the integration regime, which expects refugees to 'learn' German values, ideals, norms and language in order to stay in Germany.

Back to square one

Cycles appear throughout the refugee experience: cycles of hope, cycles of despair, cycles of gains and losses, and, of course, cycles of bureaucracies. As noted previously, bureaucracies are nonlinear forms of time, and they circulate back to the original point through procedure (Hoag 2014). Refugees attempted to escape bureaucracies only to be pulled back in by arbitrary paperwork.

In one of our last meetings during my fieldwork in the winter of 2020, Anas was frustrated by the endless letters from the Job Centre, although he had already been working and studying for the last seven months and had moved from the region of Saarland to Baden-Würtemberg. He should have been removed from the Job Centre's system in Saarbrücken and put in contact with the Job Centre in Mannheim, but he continued to receive letters that he should work from Saarbrücken. He was currently a full-time student, received student loans through the Federal Training Assistant Act (BAföG) and worked part time, but there was a problem with the Job Centre in Saarbrücken receiving the right documentation. He later wrote to me after I left Mannheim 'it was irrelevant to them, as long as I didn't have certificate of enrolment from the Uni and can speak German, I must go to work'.

When we talked about his family, Anas told me that his mother was still struggling with learning German and dealing with the Job Centre, which of course wanted her to work. The question was: what should an elderly widow do for work at an age when most Germans are entering retirement? In order to receive retirement benefits, residents must pay into state retirement schemes, which means Anas' mother will most likely live on long-term unemployment benefits indefinitely. Anas realizes that once he begins to work, he will have to support his mother. Welfare state benefits for refugees are intended to be temporary. However, there is no consideration for those elderly refugees, especially in the case of widows with no prior work experience and little formal education, who have to negotiate the constraints of the regime.

The majority of my collaborators, who are part of a group of well-educated, middle-class Syrian families, have the resources to move beyond the bureaucratic structures. However, there are large numbers of refugees who orientate towards repetitive cycles of misinformation and misdirection. The trajectory for integration, starting from the time of asylum applications, should take around three years to find work or start training. Taking this into account, it took Anas four years to be able to enrol in a university, Rasha four years to enrol in a pharmacist training programme, and the same amount of time for Mohammad to become recertified as a nurse. Osama and others quickly found work in lower-wage jobs quickly, but one collaborator, who was a pediatrician with a very high level of skills, was only considering how to get his experience recognized in Germany after five years of living in Germany. In other words, the return to beginning may not always be an accurate description, but a return to bureaucratic entanglements will be necessary in all forms of moving forward.

The citizenship question

Recent discourse has expanded already contested concepts of citizenship by considering citizenship in terms of space and scale (Maestri and Hughes 2017). This line of thought strengthens links between citizenship and territory, making citizenship something that is increasingly determined by a governmentality of regimes, which interplays with law and bureaucracy. The governmentality of citizenship builds on notions of what Balibar explains: 'Historically it is the democratic antinomy that forms the driving force of the transformation of citizenship as a political institution. Therefore, democratic citizenship is a problem, a stake, an enigma, an invention, a lost object or treasure to be sought and conquered again' (Balibar 2010, 2).

This in many ways merges the concept of social citizenship (Soysal 2012) and turns the pressure up on notions of *cultural citizenship* (Ong 1996) by way of a biopolitical and a governmentality approach to citizenship through both integration programmes and citizenship tests for those who meet the requirements later on. The notion that the production of labour and welfare state contributions are key markers of 'well-integrated' 'good refugees' is found throughout this book. Yet, nowhere is this notion more clear legally than in the stipulation that refugees with subsidiary protection must pay into the retirement contribution for a total of 60 months in order to apply for permanent residency (§ 26 Abs. 4 Aufenthaltsgesetz). The narrowing of refugee status has had lasting effects even years later, as does the institutional mismatch outlined in the previous chapters between BAMF and the Ausländerbehörde. For this reason, it is doubtful whether refugees would apply directly for citizenship before first acquiring a permanent residency card.

Permanent residency can be seen as a stepping stone to citizenship. However, many collaborators viewed citizenship with indifference. After Mohammad received his permanent residency, I asked him if he planned to apply for citizenship in Germany. He replied nonchalantly "sure, if they offer it to me". Since refugees prioritize the security of not being returned to Syria or a neighbouring country and the integration regime does not promote legal forms of citizenship, there is little demand from within Syrian communities to gain access to active citizenship, such as voting rights or political participation.

Anas also explained his frustration with the Ausländerbehörde because he was denied permanent residency, so there is a feeling of arbitrariness in the decision making. "In Saarland they give Niederlassungserlaubnis very easily, I know so many people that have gotten it after three years", he told me as we ate a lunch of Syrian green beans in tomato sauce in his flat in Mannheim. Yet, as of 30 June 2019, only 8 per cent of the 682,361 protected refugees held unrestricted residency permits (Bundesregierung 2019). It is too early to gain any impression of how Syrians will engage in the future now, as only a very small group of refugees from the Syrian civil war have lived in Germany long enough to apply for citizenship, but most indications point to a low number. Residents with Turkish origins, Germany's largest immigrant population, made up of just over 30,000 naturalizations between 2008 and 2015, and during this period only a few hundred Syrians were naturalized, and it is likely these were not refugees of the civil war (Destatis 2019). To that end, the integration regime, despite speaking of active democratic 'values', does not address the weak case for naturalization among refugees.

Conclusion

This chapter covered various experiences of my collaborators as they grappled with the contradictions of having fulfilled many of the integration ideals and standards, yet remained on the peripheries of social inclusion. Where the previous chapter addressed the concrete reasons that they had attempted to secure livelihood and framed the issue in part through class differences, this chapter focused on the discrimination that they encountered, and addressed how collaborators configured themselves into reconciling with the realities that they had experienced in the last stage of the integration regime. Conditional inclusion slowly produced a conditional citizenship that created forms of disillusionment and revealed how the lasting effects of racism and discrimination reduced the capacity for refugees to reach normalized middle-class social and financial indicators.

Similar to Scott's criticism of state management systems that create 'simplifications and utopian schemes', and outlining how 'the genetic formula does not and cannot supply the local knowledge that will allow … successful, nuanced, local applications' (Scott 1998, 318), a regime of integration does not produce any form of successful state management based on top-down policy and limited local knowledge of available resources. In this chapter, I have outlined how the state has failed to keep promised rewards for integration at the expense of refugee livelihood and inclusion, which presented some of the cracks in the ideological framework that would in the end produce more exclusionary effects and undermine the human rights-oriented approach to refugee programmes.

The last phase of integration presented here raises the following question: *when does one stop being a refugee and become a resident?* Officially, refugees are no longer considered as such by the bureaucracy once they gain permanent residency – in which case, they should no longer have regular interactions with the state. However, I have shown that this status is more symbolic and the real importance of residency lies in tangible security. Regardless of their status – in fact, most refugees develop an embodiment of refugee identity – they accept the notion that they will always be foreign even once they have gained citizenship and even with German-born children. These exclusions have more relevant implications than any bureaucratic taxonomy. If the integration ideologies are taken at face value, it is clear that integration is conceived from a White, heteronormative, majority society, in which only scant consideration is given to factoring in long-term effects discrimination, improving the democratic participation of migrants and removing bureaucratic barriers to citizenship. The ethnographic work presented in Chapters 5 and 6 outlines how structural social exclusion produces so-called 'parallel societies', which is not a choice made at the individual level by refugees.

Conclusion

Here and there

The 'integration' of foreigners has become a centrepiece for migration policy in many European countries and is seen as exceptional to modern Europe in comparison to immigration policies within the global north both historically and legally. While the othering of outsiders can be found throughout history, the historical exlusion of foreigners was usually an outright call for dehumanizing dominion over other groups and a complaint that those who were given equal rights would discretely pervert the mythical greatness of a homeland. Integration is built on the assumption that foreigners are intrinsically different and require mechanisms to thrive within a paradoxically homogeneous society.

Similar to Chakrabarty's (2007) notion of the magical histories and subject making of Europe, recent history shows that integration-oriented policy is the best way to support migrant populations. Scholars will return to the hundreds of thousands of Syrian refugees who gained asylum in Germany and consider how well they have integrated since arriving. *Who is employed? How are they employed? Do they speak German well? What about the second generation born after they received asylum?*

Few will ask questions regarding their ability to adapt to shifting bureaucratic expectations or how family dynamics changed over time as they gained rights or remained without certain ones. This book has attempted to avoid the gaze towards questions framed in terms of whether or not I believe there is a holistic society one can integrate into, as Schinkel frames discourse on integration (Schinkel 2017, 3). Instead, I have tried to unpack the social phenomena that works as a feedback loop for integration policy and what happened once hundreds of thousands of refugees were introduced into this feedback loop. In doing so, I engage with Schinkel's analysis of 'the phenomenon of society observing itself in terms of such integration' (Schinkel 2017, 5). Schinkel calls it the 'imagined society', but similar arguments have been made by Glick Schiller and Salazar, by way of the concept of 'national mythscapes' (Glick Schiller and Salazar 2013), and by Chakrabarty, by way of the continued exploration of Europe as subject (Spivak 1994; Chakrabarty 2007) – the latter two of the three approaches capture the more dynamic feel of the integration regime I explore here. Although my focus remains highly political with a deep presence in the bureaucratic state, I have continually attempted to return to the way in which Syrians have experienced this form of the imagined state. In many ways, this book is also about how refugees have adapted to their surroundings, in parallel to legal changes in the integration regime; in a similar manner to how Schütz's *stranger* entered his new environment (Schütz 1944) and Jackson's positioning of privilege as the narrator in relation to migrant (Jackson 2008), they have negotiated their way through the most insecure times of migration. However, although they have now blended some of their old routines with their new lives in Germany, they are layered in everyday transnationalism, fears for their family's safety and wellbeing as well as a strong nostalgia for the 'old' Syria. One hot summer day in Germany, Anas and I were remembering the scorching summer in Turkey when temperatures reached 45°C and he said "when it was that hot in Deir ez-Zor, it didn't matter. We would sit under the shade by the river and cook lunch. It was never too hot". He often recalled times that returned to a place that was not only temporarily past but also now physically destroyed. Like other Syrians, they continue to live through this everyday duality of being Syrian and German. However, symbolically and legally, he will always be a foreigner in Germany, even after gaining citizenship.

Germany has a growing foreign population, but more importantly a growing population with limited rights to participate democratically (Wiesner 2018). Their status as a person with a migrant background is a ubiquitous contradiction within the legal framework of migrant integration, which in turn makes bureaucracy ubiquitous and at the same time inconsistent. Bureaucracies in effect are only universal in that the time they cost is proportional to class, but they are in fact highly localized and, as this work has shown, even individual. As Bourdieu reminds us: 'By realizing itself in social structures and in the mental structures adapted to them, the instituted institution makes us forget that it issues out of a long series of acts of *institution* (in the active sense) and hence has all the appearances of the *natural*' (Bourdieu 1994, 4). The symbolic ability of the state to claim foreign permanence upon refugees who are no longer officially refugees but are now permanent residents or citizens adds to the difficulty for them to ever be even socially perceived as belonging. Certainly, the concept of 'always being a refugee' (Kristjánsdóttir and Skaptadóttir 2018; Sadeghi 2018) plays a significant role in the modern racialization of refugeeness. However, what I have outlined in this book are the implications that the concept of integration has to undermine the goals set forth by the state in providing a false promise of conditional inclusion.

The following will take a look back at some of the themes present throughout this text in context with the most current social and political discourses, as well as considering how this work will open up new topics of research.

The future of refugees in Germany

On 16 April 2020, I opened my weekly copy of the national newspaper *Die Zeit*. The headline read: '50 von 40.000', referring to the number of refugees who would be resettled in Germany during the COVID-19 pandemic from Greek refugee camps, despite expert calls that they were at grave risk of contracting the disease in confined areas (Lobenstein, Middelhoff and Thumann 2020). It reminded me of articles that were closer to home, one about why the victims in a terrorist attack on a shisha bar near Hanau were described by the mayor of the city as 'not foreigners, but well integrated boys from Hanau' (Latković 2020), and another in February 2020 listing the names of the 182 people killed by right-wing extremists since the German reunification in 1990 (Aisslinger et al 2020). The issue of right-wing extremism clearly has a long history in Germany, but recently more attention has been given to the mainstreaming of political parties like the AfD and their presence in the various military and policing branches. In his bestselling, recently published 1967 speech, Theodor W. Adorno gave a prescient about the rise of populism, but also understood that right-wing groups felt alienated by a threat of losing their class status and, as in the Nazi era, sought a charismatic leadership ('The Authoritarian Personality') to help show them who was to blame by taking advantage of a crisis through the use of propaganda (Adorno 2020). The migration of refugees into Europe and the related xenophobia can be seen as a common social dissonance that continues a colonial tradition. In other words, it is not only ahistorical but also indicative of an indifference in the public imaginary towards the role that the German government – weapon exports, international political deals and EU dominance – plays in the production of refugees, which raises deep questions about the continued pursuit of 'liberal democratic' values in Germany or a continued move towards populism.

Similar to the lack of political will to address the fact that the most dangerous threat to 'Germans' comes from the radical right wing, the state is not willing to commit to the broader project of solidarity in the EU by abiding by international human rights laws of asylum application review and housing as well as burden sharing, which can be linked to a populist shift in refugee policy (Chimienti 2018). Although the externalization of European borders into North Africa has not produced convincing results (Andersson 2014) or the internalization (temporality) of borders for that matter (Mezzadra and Neilson 2013), this policy on migration controls continues to expand and militarize the policing agency Frontex, actions that receive billions of dollars of finding by Germany every year.

In this regime, refugees have also become political pawns through the so-called failed EU and Turkey deal in 2016 that was supposed to return one rejected asylum seeker to Turkey for one that would be resettled from Turkey, as well as recent events such as when Turkey began bussing refugees to the Greek border as political retaliation for EU criticism of the Turkish airstrikes in Idlib in early 2020 (Fallon and Boersma 2020).

It remains questionable whether the future of the German refugee regime will continue to be more political than humanitarian. However, the integration regime is seen throughout the EU as a successful approach and will no doubt become more widely applied (at least in Central and Northern European countries). The human rights perspective of asylum is only amplified by considering that if asylum seekers in Germany are granted protection, whether that protection leads to permanent resettlement or is one of conditionality within subsidiary protection, they are forced to live in precarity through threats of loss of protection based on criminality and deepening focus on neoliberal integration indicators such as contributions to federal retirement schemes, language learning and heteronormative familial relationships. Such conditionality is contagious. It not only spreads through levels of protection, but, as I have outlined throughout this text, it is also pervasive within conditions of inclusion which cross lines of democratic participation, social and cultural norms and double for exclusiveness based on race, ethnicity, and gender identity/ sexual orientation.

From good refugee to good citizen

Who is a good refugee? In 2019, Germany faced a new 'crisis': the COVID-19 pandemic. Workers were described as 'non-essential' or 'essential'. Under this rubric, three of the Syrians I knew were at the frontline of these essential jobs. While most Germans were forced to stay at home and avoid going outside for several months, Anas and Osama experienced increased workloads as well as heightened stress levels. Both were working for large supermarket chains during a time of food hoarding and an overall increase in consumer demand due to the shift to home cooking. Additionally, Mohammad became an accredited male nurse, which meant that he was working at a hospital tending to the sick and in turn putting himself at risk of potential infection.

The social tendency in Germany to couple ethnic minorities with migrants, whether they are refugee residents or citizens, is a qualifying label that is at odds with the norms within the social imaginary. There was no conditional inclusion or coercive measure that motivated these former refugees to become part of a needed group of the citizenry. There is more nuance within the groups of citizens and refugees and therefore a need for researchers to assume a position of 'naming' by overcoming research frames that reflect certain binaries of social citizens or refugees. Otherwise, there will always be a tendency to consider 'the refugee' in terms of national borders and host societies.

The state of integration law

In some sense, this book should have analysed immigration law from the refugee perspective, but I instead chose to frame my research in an integration regime. I outlined my reasons for this in the Introduction and returned to the subject throughout the book. However, I did fail to centre my focus on one simple point of discussion: beyond international agreements, governmentality of refugee law and an argument against the reification of the state, integration law in Germany is a regime that functions across legal status and social imaginaries. The integration regime begins with asylum law, travels through residency law and continues long after a refugee actually feels German or is one legally.

In the public sphere, refugees – and for that matter regular migrants from the Global South – are discussed in terms of those who are well integrated into German society, although they are now German citizens and have children who were born in Germany. Like the concept of *Migrationshintergrund*, being a foreigner is something inherited in Germany. Countries like France, the UK and the USA have colonial and imperial histories that made the presence of foreigners an issue of *race*, although this was often defined by country of origin. Conversely, foreigners in Germany, according to the media, politicians and the law, are either part of this larger group or not.

When a refugee commits a crime or fails to meet economic standards, there is often a reflective public discussion that asks the following question: *how has society failed to integrate this person?* The false framing of this notion that there is a society into which to integrate is not the point here, but rather the need to locate blame within a society at large or the immigrant community.

The most recent integration project supported by BAMF and many other government figures continues to argue that language is key. Future immigration law, although something that operates at a local level, is driven by this federal framework, which means that for the foreseeable future, immigration law is at its core integration law. However, as Scott reminds us, state planners have outlined integration programmes in the image of 'standardized citizens', which, if history is any indication, leads to disappointing if not disastrous results (Scott 1998, 346).

The best place to be a refugee

There was a time early on in my research when Mohammad asked me if I thought Germany was a good place to live. He had considered trying to move to Canada. A few years later, he said: "Two years ago I thought, I have no work, I can't support my family. I don't understand the language 100 per cent. I won't stay. But now I can support myself and my family. Why shouldn't I stay here?". At the beginning, many of my collaborators asked me about the USA and were considering not staying in Germany – the language was too difficult, the people were unfriendly or they missed their families. Germany has a well-financed return programme to encourage refugees to go back to safe third countries or their home countries. One day at the Job Centre, one of the caseworkers said there were some people that he would refer to the return programme, but only a few would participate.

After being on the move for so long and their expectations not being met, refugees considered moving on. Similar to the way in which Vigh (2010) pulls together the work of so many theories that all discuss the way that people have to envision moving forward (*smooth space* [Deleuze and Guattari 1987], *horizon* [Schutz and Luckmann 1973], *walking* [de Certeau 1984], *protention* [Husserl 1964] and *illusio, future in the making* [Bourdieu 1998]), the idea that they had arrived at a place where they could no longer cope with the failures of the embodiment of past, present and future caused many to question their current path. They continued and muddled through, but many returned to Turkey or Syria, or moved on to other countries to try and start again there – a not uncommon reaction for migrants on the move (Treiber 2016). Those who end up disillusioned, falling into criminality, or those who failed in their claim for asylum are often forced into the system of forced returns in Germany.

Forced returns

Few works have properly addressed the subject of forced return from Germany (Oulios 2015). However, this remains one of the major issues championed by asylum advocacy groups. Along with the major legal reforms that have been at the centre of the integration regime, the designation of 'safe return country' has become one of the most controversial, most notably returns to Afghanistan once it added to the list of safe return countries. I have recently heard prominent refugee researchers support the notion of country-based asylum allocation. However, the case in Germany makes this determination unfeasible for several reasons.

From an international law perspective, country-based determination goes directly against the UN 1951 Refugee Convention because although it concerns country nationals, a major focus of the Convention was the persecution of minority groups. Taking Afghanistan as an example, there may be security in some areas, but the rural persecution of the Hazara people dates back decades and will certainly continue. However, from a less contested perspective, the 'black box' of forced returns is against basic humanitarian principles. The blurry legal ability for the German state to remove refugee protection because of criminal behaviour and thus the potential for forced removal in combination with the inability to follow the outcomes of returned people exacerbate this point. Further inquiry into the subject of returns has long been an integral part of the global refugee regime, but has only recently taken new perspectives into account (Couldrey and Peebles 2019). More research is needed in Germany to understand the social circumstances that cause criminality among refugees, the court proceedings leading to their removal and, more importantly the human rights issues that follow their deportation.

Germany's redefining of refugees

As noted previously, around 20 per cent of German residents have a migrant background distinction, but around ten per cent of those also have no access to active democratic involvement (Wiesner 2018, 81). As Germany comes up with increasingly complex definitions for those with a foreign status, we see a byproduct of moral confusion in terms of how to consider modern migrants (Crawley and Skleparis 2018; Faist 2018). More concretely, the ramifications of legal status are not something that can be overcome lightly and this has turned into an issue of class. Who can afford to pay smugglers to arrive in Europe and who must appeal to the UNHCR and wait in a camp for asylum? Who can raise the money for a lawyer to appeal to the court against their asylum decision?

Refugees as migrants

Have refugees in Germany essentially become privileged migrants? A neoliberal approach to refugee integration would suggest so. I have continued to return to the subject of security in several chapters in this book because it is something that is raised so often by Syrians, in Germany and throughout Europe. The impermanence of gaining 'refugee protection' should raise some eyebrows.

Migrants in Germany face a series of bureaucratic hurdles in order to remain there. Residency in a foreign country has become something of luck and class. However, when refugees face the same rewards-based system of residency and citizenship, it goes beyond a question of the taxonomy in bureaucracy and returns to the question of human rights and asylum. When the imaginary operates on a perception of who is a well-integrated refugee based on income alone, it speaks to the broader issues of social inequality that the accumulation of capital has produced, which leaves little hope that this will be overcome in the near future.

Notes on migration research

In the Introduction I discussed not only the complexity of doing research in relation to the phenomenon of forced migration, but also the recent discourse criticizing research on crisis (Cabot 2019) and the use of integration as a research framework (Schinkel 2018). My work certainly focuses on what Ortner (2016) calls 'dark anthropology', yet I have attempted to position myself within the complex framework of my subject as someone who has a personal connection to the work, which raises several questions. First, the extreme positivist would thinly claim notions of bias, yet I make it clear that I am actively involved in supporting refugees through solidarity and volunteer work that is not necessarily part of my research. Second, I have been drawn towards the issue of an extreme situation because it will have the most lasting social impact on both the imaginary in Europe and potential outcomes on the social welfare state. I think a call to be cautious towards focusing on crisis, and, in turn, alienation of the subjects of research is valid; however, I am unsure if this is applicable to most anthropologists. In many instances my interlocutors have shown that they do not take surveys seriously; they just fill questionnaires out quickly without putting much thought into it. They have been given surveys since they arrived in Germany and many had been given surveys before they arrived and on their journey. The same can be said for engagement with aid organizations. There are certain groups that seek support from organizations often, which makes them a more viable group of refugees among surveys and statistics, just as the research collaborators I have come to know belong to a particular middle class of refugees with above-average education backgrounds. Finally, being a part of the research nexus, my work may be used to add to the imaginary about Syrian refugees.

In my position as someone who claims to hold knowledge of refugees, and in that sense authority in naming – that is, the continuation of the taxonomy of refugees – I feel I must be conscious of my limitations. I have tried at the core of this book to address the ephemeral relationship between Syrian refugees and the German integration regime as they travel together, changing and developing new strategies to influence each other, but I lack the ability to definitively articulate this relationship either theoretically or practically. The question of how to imagine and articulate what it means when two separate but unequal groups carry with them symbolic meaning and at the same time produce strong emotional responses in subjectification (*the refugee* and *the state*) eludes me. There is something different at play here than the social theories presented throughout this book can express. I am unsure if a new vocabulary is necessary to describe this phenomenon, yet it is something I hope to develop and expand upon.

Lastly, the issue of racism is something that I have only tacitly addressed. Another way to look at integration would be to ask the following question: how do the racist foundations of integration shape refugee experiences? Treiber (2016) discusses practices that are something learned in the process of migration, so the experience of discrimination throughout the integration process also informs refugees about the social conditions of a host country. A book on integration framed through a lens of experiences with racism would indeed reveal important national narratives in Germany and unpack many exploratory discourses on integration as a continuation of colonial violence found throughout European societies. It would, however, tell an incomplete story. Nonetheless, I would have wished to more explicitly explore how the damage of racism has longitudinal effects on refugee navigation of the refugee regime. This book has provided a range of theoretical and methodological points of departure for future inquiry into the refugee/racism nexus in Europe. I only ask that such research be carried out not to 'measure' again where and to what degree racism exists (I don't believe it pushes discourse further to reinforce what we already know), but to instead consider the implications of structural and institutional racisms for refugees attempting to meet the demands placed upon them by a majority society.

Notes

Introduction

[1] The Islamic State of Iraq and the Levant (ISIL) has also been known as the Islamic State of Iraq and Syria (ISIS), Islamic State (IS) or in the Arabic world Daesh, but will be referred to as ISIL throughout most of this book.

[2] On 15 January 2016, Turkey implemented the Regulation on Work Permits of Refuges under Temporary Protection to allow Syrians access to labour. However, labour market access and education continue to be major problems for refugees in Turkey. For more on this, see UNHCR (2016).

[3] One example of this that comes to mind is the German implementation of the Residency Obligation for asylum seekers that limited movement and conflicted with EU law. German lawmakers circumvented this constraint by arguing that it could be used as a tool for integration. For a deeper analysis of this, see Chapter 2 of this book and El-Kayed and Hamann (2018).

[4] There are extensive works that detail much of what is written about in this section from a European integration perspective. For a more nuanced historical analysis, see Favell (2001) and Schierup, Hansen and Castles (2006).

[5] For a comprehensive history of the German social state, see Steinmetz (1993).

[6] In the following chapters I address this term more thoroughly, but I do not wish to diverge here to specify my approach. Yet, in order for the reader to have a more general picture, I am thinking of a more Foucauldian 'truth discourse' (Rabinow and Rose 2006; Lorenzini and Tazzioli 2018), which goes beyond interrogating subjects, media and public voices.

Chapter 1

[1] Up until this point I have not distinguished between the legal and the self-identified differences in refugee labelling. In the rest of the book I will attempt to distinguish between those who have been recognized by Germany as refugees or related protection, those in the asylum application process and those who would self-identify as refugees, but also at times as a catch-all for both groups regardless of legal distinction. When I make the point of legal status, it is in reference to the elusion and exclusion of different groups.

[2] Here I use the word *privileged* reluctantly and only to relate the rhetoric of refugees in the public imaginary and how different refugee groups are constructed and reconstructed. At the time of writing, there are certain country nationals seeking asylum in Germany who have been prioritized by policy and who are seen as an economic opportunity (Karakayali 2018). For more on how refugees and migrants were being discussed at this period, see Crawley and Skleparis (2018).

[3] An exhaustive account of asylum is available in German from Bogumil, Hafner and Kastilan (2017), but work in English by Schneider (2019) is also relevant, providing an inside perspective on policy in action. The most relevant ethnographic work in this

area to date is Eule (2014). Alternatively, Laubenthal (2019) presents the asylum policy development from a political perspective, and EU-sponsored work by Bonewit (2016) and Konle-Seidl (2018) are both helpful general overviews.

[4]   I comment here on the image of Alan Kurdi, a Syrian boy who drowned in the Mediterranean Sea on 2 September 2015 trying to reach the Greek island of Kos. This image was used to bring light to drownings as sea and refugees at large as well as critical commentary on the use of such images (Kingsley and Timur 2015).

[5]   There should be some irony here because of the historical nature of barracks used for refugee shelters in Germany following the Second World War (Malkki 1995).

[6]   She was referring to the well-known case in Germany of Franco A., who is now a convicted right-wing extremist and was living a double life as a refugee and as an officer in the German military (Bundeswehr). In 2022, he was found guilty and sentenced to five years in prison for his planned attack against prominent left-wing figures in Germany (DW 2022).

Chapter 2

[1]   Gupta uses the term 'structural violence' that was originally developed by peace researcher Johan Galtung who differentiated between three forms of violence: direct (violence that directly harms), structural (forms of exploitation, such as marginalizing an ethnic group causing famine) and cultural (the cultural legitimization of the other forms, or the form that makes violence look and even feel right) as well as negative peace and positive peace. For further reading on this subject, see Galtung (1969; 1990; 2010).

[2]   For more on the discourse on 'power-over' and 'power-to', see Dean (2013).

[3]   It should also be noted here that asylum applicants can appeal a rejected claim before a judge. Cases appealing decisions increased dramatically after 2015. Up until 2017, as much as 91 per cent of decisions had been appealed. Of those that have appealed in court from Syria and Afghanistan, 60 per cent have had their decisions overturned (Kastner 2018).

[4]   Both independent research and BAMF documentation show that because of the overwhelming number of asylum applications and the growing backlog since 2013, BAMF shifted policy in many ways to predetermine asylum cases based on previous similar cases, in effect removing the individual from decisions and applying tactics like 'case-constellations'. For a detailed account of administrative practices at BAMF and the most in-depth study of the institution available, see Schneider (2019).

[5]   After federal elections in 2017 and a highly publicized political debate, the grand coalition of the CDU/CSU and the SPD voted in favour of reducing the number of family reunifications for refugees with subsidiary protection to 1,000 per month, which came into effect in August 2018 (Anzlinger 2018). This action further reduced the rights of those with subsidiary protection; in many ways they are 'second-class refugees' because of the temporality of the status. The law also placed German law at odds with EU law (Thym 2018).

[6]   The Residency Obligation was only implemented by seven out of 17 German Länder (Nordrhein-Westfalen, Baden-Württemberg, Bayern, Saarland, Sachsen, Sachsen-Anhalt and Hessen), including every region where my collaborators were living save one (Leubecher 2019). This rule is up to the local governments themselves to decide to implement or not. However, its use in Bavaria plays a significant role in what came out of fieldwork in these areas.

Part II

[1]   Unaccompanied minors are a huge group and a very important subcategory of refugees who receive a very different kind of state support from the two groups I focus on here.

Indeed, they are part of the integration regime, but they are not included in the very specific bureaucratic structure of the empirical work presented.

Chapter 3

1. In late 2018, the administrative centre of Lebach initiated a pilot programme for a so-called *Ankerzentrum* (which translates as 'Anchor Centre', but is actually a play on words that abbreviates *Ankunft, Entscheidung und Rückführung*: arrival, decision and return). The centres have already faced controversy in the states of Bavaria and Sachsen, and tactics were immediately labelled by the police union as posing 'constitutional concerns' (Ernst 2018).
2. *Fehlbeleger* is not a word that the average German would recognize, but is framed in a rather pejorative context that produces negative images of refugees.
3. This is an official designation that follows the Common European Framework of Reference for Languages (CEFR) system of language certification.
4. As noted elsewhere, these reduction fines were deemed unconstitutional by the highest court in Germany and there are plans to reform the entire system and replace it with a so-called citizen income (Bürgergeld) (Rhein 2022).
5. See Röder (2016) for a deeper explanation of the legal changes in the 2016 law.

Chapter 4

1. For an extensive explanation of this programmes as well as the actors involved in such programmes, see Aumüller (2016).

Chapter 5

1. Here the term used by several publications is used. However, the framing of the word's meaning borders on pejorative; I translate this to mean 'wrong occupiers', which would indicate that the occupier is to blame for this position. As is carefully outlined here, there are numerous reasons why people have continued residence in temporary shelter. Additionally, there has been well-founded criticism with regard to how such housing has been financed and conceived (see news reporting from Pro Asyl (2017), Stukenberg (2017) and Bathke (2019).
2. I have returned to the issue of housing here that has been addressed in several chapters because it is one of the key things for which the Job Centre provides support; more exhaustive examples can be found in previous chapters.
3. This number excludes the refugees that participate in programs funded by the SGB III section of jobless coverage.
4. The unlimited application of sanctions was taken up in 2019 by Germany's highest court (Bundesverfassungsgericht) and was found to be unconstitutional.
5. Here I refer to the official names of the social support programmes. I give a more detailed explanation of this in Chapter 2, so I will not return to the issue here when this information has been given elsewhere.
6. I find it would be redundant to present references here to work that has been mentioned in several other chapters of this book. It can be assumed that if the agents themselves are unaware of this (although none of the agents featured here are), then the central agencies are cognisant of the interplay between secure housing and language acquisition.
7. This law was actually initiated in 2016 (Pro Asyl 2016), but I would like to stay true to my recorded conversation here, in which I wanted to engage with her experience with the multiple iterations of the legal standard. The more recent changes, again presented in brief by Pro Asyl (2019), cover legal changes we did not discuss to this extent, namely the legal change that extends the timeline for BAMF to review asylum decisions up to five years instead of what is described here as three years.

8   There is more than enough literature elsewhere critiquing citizenship tests, so I do not think it necessary to cover the discourse here. See the critique in Löwenheim and Gazit (2009) and a longitudinal analysis in Joppke (2017).

Chapter 6

1   The Bavarian government also attempted to pass legislation that formulated a version of Leitkultur within its integration law, which was summarily rejected by the regional constitutional court in 2019 on the grounds that it went against freedom of expression protection (Mittler 2019).

2   Working in Germany is regulated by employment contracts, with the exception of the so-called 'mini-job', which is allowed at a maximum rate of €450 per month and is tax-free. All other work is carried out under work contracts that are limited (*befristet*) or unlimited (*unbefristet*). Limited contracts can be from a few months to a few years.

3   The subject of racism against Muslim women has a long research history in Europe and beyond. I do not think it is helpful to justify Rasha's fears by presenting the breadth of quantitative data showing how women wearing a headscarf have a lower chance of finding employment. For more on headscarf discrimination in relation to integration, see the excellent article by Korteweg (2017).

4   The potential for having informal labour experience (such as driving a truck or raising livestock) recognized is possible through a growing number of programmes. For more on these potentials, see Döring and Kreider's work on the recognition of informal training (Döring and Kreider 2017).

References

Abadi, David, Leen d'Haenens, Keith Roe and Joyce Koeman. 2016. '*Leitkultur* and Discourse Hegemonies: German Mainstream Media Coverage on the Integration Debate between 2009 and 2014'. *International Communication Gazette* 78(6): 557–84. https://doi.org/10.1177/17480 48516640214

Abdelilah, Alexander, Kai Biermann, Astrid Geisler, Henrik Merker, Karsten Polke-Majewski and Sascha Venohr. 2019. 'Refugees in Germany: How Well Have They Integrated?' *Die Zeit*, 20 June. https://www.zeit.de/entdec ken/2019-06/refugees-germany-integration-english.

Adam, Francesca, Stefanie Föbker, Daniela Imani, Carmella Pfaffenbach, Günther Weiss and Claus-C. Wiegandt. 2019. '"Lost in Transition"? Integration of Refugees into the Local Housing Market in Germany'. *Journal of Urban Affairs* 43(6): 831–50. https://doi.org/10.1080/07352 166.2018.1562302

Adorno, Theodor W. 2020. *Aspects of the New Right-Wing Extremism*. Translated by Wieland Hoban. Medford: Polity.

AFP. 2015. 'Germany on Course to Accept One Million Refugees in 2015'. *The Guardian*, 8 December . http://www.theguardian.com/world/2015/ dec/08/germany-on-course-to-accept-one-million-refugees-in-2015

Aisslinger, Moritz, Christian Fuchs, Astrid Geisler, Malte Henk, Paul Middelhoff, Daniel Müller, Yassin Musharbash et al. 2020. 'Rechtsterrorismus: Die lange Blutspur des rechten Terrors'. *Die Zeit*, 26 February . https://www.zeit.de/2020/10/rechtsterrorismus-rechtsextremis mus-gewalt-deutschland

Aktionskreis Kindergeld und Sozialhilfe Saar. 2019. *Merkblätter zu 'Hartz IV' Arbeitskamer des Saarlands*. Saarbrücken: Aktionskreis Kindergeld und Sozialhilfe Saar.

Al-Baalbaky, Rudayna, and Ahmad Mhidi. 2018. *Tribes and the Rule of the 'Islamic State': The Case of the Syrian City of Deir Ez-Zor*. Beirut: Issam Fares Institute for Public Policy and International Affairs at the American University of Beirut.

Alba, Richard. 2017. 'Continuities in Assimilation'. *Ethnic and Racial Studies* 40(9): 1430–37. https://doi.org/10.1080/01419870.2017.1308526

Amelina, Anna, and Thomas Faist. 2012. 'De-naturalizing the National in Research Methodologies: Key Concepts of Transnational Studies in Migration'. *Ethnic and Racial Studies* 35(10): 1707–24. https://doi.org/10.1080/01419870.2012.659273

Amit, Vered (ed). 2000. *Constructing the Field: Ethnographic Fieldwork in the Contemporary World*. London: Routledge.

Amit, Vered, and Caroline Knowles. 2017. 'Improvising and Navigating Mobilities: Tacking in Everyday Life'. *Theory, Culture & Society* 34(7–8): 165–79. https://doi.org/10.1177/0263276417724876

Anderson, Bridget. 2013. *Us and Them? The Dangerous Politics of Immigration Control*. Oxford: Oxford University Press.

Andersson, Ruben. 2014. *Illegality, Inc.: Clandestine Migration and the Business of Bordering Europe*. Oakland: University of California Press.

Antidiskriminierungsstelle des Bundes. 2020. *Rassistische Diskriminierung auf dem Wohnungsmarkt: Ergebnisse einer repräsentativen Umfrage*. Berlin: Antidiskriminierungsstelle des Bundes. https://www.antidiskrim inierungsstelle.de/SharedDocs/Downloads/DE/publikationen/Umfra gen/umfrage_rass_diskr_auf_dem_wohnungsmarkt.pdf?__blob=publicat ionFile&v=10

Associated Press. 2014. 'Syria Refugees "Shot and Killed by Turkey Border Guards"'. *The Telegraph*, 20 November. https://www.telegraph.co.uk/news/worldnews/europe/turkey/11242919/Syria-refugees-shot-and-kil led-by-Turkey-border-guards.html

Aumüller, Jutta. 2016. *Arbeitsmarktintegration von Flüchtlingen: Bestehende Praxisansätze und Weiterführende Empfehlungen*. Gütersloh: Bertelsmann Stiftung.

Aybek, Can M. 2012. 'Politics, Symbolics and Facts: Migration Policies and Family Migration from Turkey to Germany'. *Perceptions: Journal of International Affairs* 17(2): 61–84.

Anzlinger, Jana. 2018. 'Bundestag stimmt für Kompromiss beim Familiennachzug'. *sueddeutsche.de*, 1 February. https://www.sueddeutsche.de/politik/familiennachzug-bundestag-kompromiss-union-spd-1.3849435

Baier, Andreea, and Manuel Siegert. 2018. '*Die Wohnsituation Geflüchteter*'. Nuremberg: Bundesamt für Migration und Flüchtlinge (BAMF).

Bakewell, Oliver. 2010. 'Some Reflections on Structure and Agency in Migration Theory'. *Journal of Ethnic and Migration Studies* 36(10): 1689–708. https://doi.org/10.1080/1369183X.2010.489382

Balibar, Étienne. 2009. *We, the People of Europe? Reflections on Transnational Citizenship*. Princeton: Princeton University Press.

Balibar, Étienne. 2010. 'Antinomies of Citizenship'. *Journal of Romance Studies* 10(2): 1–20.

Balibar, Étienne. 2012. 'The "Impossible" Community of the Citizens: Past and Present Problems'. *Environment and Planning D: Society and Space* 30(3): 437–49. https://doi.org/10.1068/d19310

Balibar, Etienne, Sandro Mezzadra and Ranabir Samaddar. 2012. *The Borders of Justice*. Philadelphia: Temple University Press.

Bartsch, Matthias, Markus Deggerich, Horand Knaup, Ann-Katrin Müller, Conny Neumann, Barbara Schmid, Fidelius Schmid, Wolf Wiedmann-Schmidt and Steffen Winter. 2015. 'Close Quarters: Asylum Shelters in Germany Struggle with Violence'. *Spiegel Online*, 6 October. http://www.spiegel.de/international/germany/asylum-shelters-in-germany-struggle-with-refugee-violence-a-1056393.html

BAMF. 2015. *Konzept für einen bundesweiten Integrationskurs*. Nuremberg: BAMF.

BAMF. 2016. *Minas: Atlas Über Migration, Integration Und Asyl*. Nuremberg: BAMF.

BAMF. 2018. *Aktuelle Zahlen Zu Asyl*. Nuremberg: BAMF.

BAMF. 2019a. *Aktuelle Zahlen: April 2019*. Nuremberg: BAMF.

BAMF. 2019b. *Bericht zur Integrationskursgeschäftsstatistik für das Jahr 2018*. Nuremberg: BAMF.

Bangel, Christian, and Frida Thurm. 2016. 'Refugees in Germany: "We Treat Women Almost Exactly as They Are Treated in Europe"'. *Die Zeit*, 21 January. https://www.zeit.de/gesellschaft/zeitgeschehen/2016-01/refugees-germany-interview-women

Bathke, Benjamin. 2019. 'Refugees with Own Income Pay up to €930 Rental Fees in Shared Accommodation in Germany'. *InfoMigrants*, 15 August. https://www.infomigrants.net/en/post/18824/refugees-with-own-income-pay-up-to-930-rental-fees-in-shared-accommodation-in-germany.

BBSR. 2017. *Integration von Flüchtlingen in den regulären Wohnungsmarkt*. Bonn: Bundesinstitut für Bau-, Stadt- und Raumforschung (BBSR).

Bauböck, Rainer (ed). 2006. *Migration and Citizenship: Legal Status, Rights and Political Participation*. Amsterdam: Amsterdam University Press.

BBC. 2015. 'Merkel Criticised over Crying Refugee'. *BBC News*, 17 July. https://www.bbc.com/news/world-europe-33555619

Betts, Alexander. 2009. 'Institutional Proliferation and the Global Refugee Regime'. *Perspectives on Politics* 7(1): 53–58. https://doi.org/10.1017/S1537592709090082

Benček, David, and Julia Strasheim. 2016. 'Refugees Welcome? A Dataset on Anti-refugee Violence in Germany'. *Research & Politics* 3(4): 205316801667959. https://doi.org/10.1177/2053168016679590

Bershidsky, Leonid. 2018. 'Germany Must Come to Terms With Refugee Crime'. Bloomberg.Com, 3 January. https://www.bloomberg.com/opinion/articles/2018-01-03/germany-must-come-to-terms-with-refugee-crime

Bhimji, Fazila. 2016a. 'Collaborations and Performative Agency in Refugee Theater in Germany'. *Journal of Immigrant and Refugee Studies* 14(1): 83–103. https://doi.org/10.1080/15562948.2015.1024813

Bhimji, Fazila. 2016b. 'Contesting the Dublin Regulation: Refugees' and Migrants' Claims to Personhood and Rights in Germany'. *Intersections* 2(4). https://doi.org/10.17356/ieejsp.v2i4.214

Bittner, Jochen, Andrea Böhm, Marc Brost, Peter Dausend, Bastian Hosan, Martin Klingst, Matthias Krupa et al. 2015. 'Refugees: Welcome! And Now What?' *Die Zeit*, 11 September. https://www.zeit.de/politik/2015-09/refugees-asylum-europe-future

BMAS. 2018. *Ein Leitfaden zu Arbeitsmarktzugang und -förderung Flüchtlinge Kundinnen und Kunden der Arbeitsagenturen und Jobcenter.* Bonn: Bundesministerium für Arbeit und Soziales.

Boccagni, Paolo. 2016. 'From the Multi-sited to the In-between: Ethnography as a Way of Delving into Migrants' Transnational Relationships'. *International Journal of Social Research Methodology* 19(1): 1–16. https://doi.org/10.1080/13645579.2014.932107

Bock, Jan-Jonathan. 2018. 'Migrants in the Mountains: Shifting Borders and Contested Crisis Experiences in Rural Germany'. *Sociology* 52(3): 569–86. https://doi.org/10.1177/0038038518759459

Bock, Jozefien de. 2018. *Parallel Lives Revisited: Mediterranean Guest Workers and Their Families at Work in the Neighbourhood, 1960–1980.* New York: Berghahn Books.

Boese, Martina, Anthony Moran and Mark Mallman. 2018. 'Multi-local Settlement Mobilities'. *Journal of Ethnic and Migration Studies* 46(15): 3277–95. https://doi.org/10.1080/1369183X.2018.1549981

Boersma, Sanne, and Willem Schinkel. 2015. 'Imagining Society: Logics of Visualization in Images of Immigrant Integration'. *Environment and Planning D: Society and Space* 33(6): 1043–62. https://doi.org/10.1177/0263775815598153

Bogumil, Jörg, Jonas Hafner and André Kastilan. 2017. *Städte und Gemeinden in der Flüchtlingspolitik. Welche Probleme Gibt es – und wie kann man sie lösen?* Essen: Stiftung Mercator/Ruhr Universitat Bochum.

Bogumil, Jörg, Sabine Kuhlmann and Isabella Proeller (eds). 2019. *Verwaltungshandeln in der Flüchtlingskrise.* Nomos Verlagsgesellschaft mbH & Co. KG.

Bogumil, Jörg, Martin Burgi, Sabine Kuhlmann, Jonas Hafner, Moritz Heuberger and Christoph Krönke. 2018. *Bessere Verwaltung in der Migrations- und Integrationspolitik: Handlungsempfehlungen für Verwaltungen und Gesetzgebung im föderalen System.* Nomos Verlagsgesellschaft mbH & Co. KG.

Bojadžijev, Manuela. 2016. 'Is There a Post-racism? On David Theo Goldberg's Conjunctural Analysis of the Post-racial'. *Ethnic and Racial Studies* 39(13): 2235–40. https://doi.org/10.1080/01419870.2016.1202433

Bojadžijev, Manuela. 2018. 'Migration as Social Seismograph: An Analysis of Germany's "Refugee Crisis" Controversy'. *International Journal of Politics, Culture, and Society* 31(4): 335–56. https://doi.org/10.1007/s10767-018-9286-x

Bommes, Michael. 2018. 'Die Rolle der Kommunen in der bundesdeutschen Migrations- und Integrationspolitik', in Frank Gesemann and Roland Roth (eds) *Handbuch Lokale Integrationspolitik*. Wiesbaden: Springer Fachmedien Wiesbaden, pp 99–123.

Bonewit, Anne. 2016. 'Reception of Female Refugees and Asylum Seekers in the EU – Case Study Germany'. Directorate General for Internal Policies Policy Department C: Citizens' Rights and Constitutional Affairs. Women's Rights & Gender Equality. Brussels: European Parliament.

Boockmann, Bernhard, and Tobias Scheu. 2018. *Integration Der Geflüchteten in den Arbeitsmarkt: Ziele, Strategien und Hemmnisse aus Sicht der Jobcenter.* Tübingen: Institut für Angewandte Wirtschaftsforschung e.V.

Borneman, John, and Parvis Ghassem-Fachandi. 2017. 'The Concept of Stimmung: From Indifference to Xenophobia in Germany's Refugee Crisis'. *Hau: Journal of Ethnographic Theory* 7(3). http://dx.doi.org/10.14318/hau7.3.006

Boswell, Christina, Andrew Geddes and Peter Scholten. 2011. 'The Role of Narratives in Migration Policy-Making: A Research Framework'. *The British Journal of Politics and International Relations* 13(1): 1–11. https://doi.org/10.1111/j.1467-856X.2010.00435.x

Bourdieu, Pierre. 1985. 'The Social Space and the Genesis of Groups'. *Social Science Information* 24(2): 195–220.

Bourdieu, Pierre. 1992. *The Logic of Practice*. Translated by Richard Nice. Stanford: Stanford University Press.

Bourdieu, Pierre. 1993. *The Field of Cultural Production: Essays on Art and Literature*. Edited by Randal Johnson. New York: Columbia University Press.

Bourdieu, Pierre. 1994. 'Rethinking the State: Genesis and Structure of the Bureaucratic Field'. Translated by Loic J.D. Wacquant and Samar Farage. *Sociological Theory* 12(1): 1–18. https://doi.org/10.2307/202032

Bourdieu, Pierre. 1998. *Practical Reason: On the Theory of Action*. Stanford: Stanford University Press.

Bourdieu, Pierre. 2000. *Pascalian Meditations*. Translated by Richard Nice. Stanford: Stanford University Press.

Bourdieu, Pierre. 2009. *Language and Symbolic Power*. Translated by Gino Raymond and Matthew Adamson. Reprint. Cambridge: Polity Press.

Bourdieu, Pierre. 2014. *On the State: Lectures at the Collège de France, 1989–1992*. Edited by Patrick Champagne, Remi Lenoir, Franck Poupeau, and Marie-Christine Rivière. Translated by David Fernbach. Cambridge: Polity.

Böhle, Thomas. 2018. *Schriftliche Anfrage gemäß § 68 GeschO*. Munich: Landeshaupstadt München Kreisverwaltungsreferat.

Böhne, Karsten (ed). 2017. *Wohnungsnot ausgenutzt: Vermieter ziehen Flüchtlinge über den Tisch*. Munich: Bayerischer Rundfunk.

Börner, Stefanie, Diana Linder, André Stiegler and Jörg Oberthür. 2017. *'Autonomiespielräume als prekäre institutionelle Funktionsvoraussetzung des Fallmanagements'*, in Frank Sowa and Ronald Staples (eds) *Beratung und Vermittlung im Wohlfahrtsstaat*. Baden-Baden: Nomos Verlag, pp 211–36.

Braun, Katherine. 2017. 'Decolonial Perspectives on Charitable Spaces of 'Welcome Culture' in Germany'. *Social Inclusion* 5(3). https://doi.org/ 10.17645/si.v5i3.1025

Brekke, Jan-Paul, and Grete Brochmann. 2015. 'Stuck in Transit: Secondary Migration of Asylum Seekers in Europe, National Differences, and the Dublin Regulation'. *Journal of Refugee Studies* 28(2): 145–62. https://doi. org/10.1093/jrs/feu028

Brettell, Caroline B., and Carolyn F. Sargent. 2006. 'Migration, Identity, and Citizenship: Anthropological Perspectives'. *American Behavioral Scientist* 50(1): 3–8. https://doi.org/10.1177/0002764206289666.

Brockling, Ulrich, Susanne Krasmann and Thomas Lemke (eds). 2011. *Governmentality: Current Issues and Future Challenges*. Abingdon: Routledge.

Bourdieu, Pierre. 1985. 'The Social Space and the Genesis of Groups'. *Social Science Information* 24(2): 195–220.

Bröse, Johanna, Stefan Faas and Barbara Stauber (eds). 2018. *Flucht: Herausforderungen für Soziale Arbeit*. Wiesbaden: Springer VS.

Brown, Wendy. 2017. *Walled States, Waning Sovereignty* (2nd edn). New York: Zone Books.

Brücker, Herbert, Johannes Croisier, Yuliya Kosyakova, Hannes Kröger, Giuseppe Pietrantuono, Nina Rother and Jürgen Schupp. 2019. 'Language Skills and Employment Rate of Refugees in Germany Improving with Time'. *DIW Weekly Report*. https://doi.org/10.18723/diw_dwr:2019-4-1

Brubaker, Rogers. 1994. *Citizenship and Nationhood in France and Germany* (new edn). Cambridge, MA: Harvard University Press.

Brubaker, Rogers. 2001. 'The Return of Assimilation? Changing Perspectives on Immigration and Its Sequels in France, Germany, and the United States'. *Ethnic and Racial Studies* 24(4): 531–48. https://doi.org/ 10.1080/0141987012004977 0.

Buhlmann, Rosemarie, Karin Ende, Susan Kaufmann, Angela Kilimann and Helen Schmitz. 2016. *Rahmencurriculum Für Integrationskurse Deutsch Als Zweitsprache*. München: Bundesministerium des Innern, Bundesamt für Migration und Flüchtlinge & Goethe Institue.

Bundesregierung. 2016. *'Gesetzentwurf der Bundesregierung'*. Entwurf eines Integrationsgesetzes. https://dserver.bundestag.de/btd/18/088/1808 829.pdf

Bundesregierung. 2019. *Antwort der Bundesregierung auf die kleine Anfrage der Abgeordneten Ulla Jelpke, Dr. Andre Hahn, Gökay Akbulut, Weiterer Abgeordneter und der Fraktion die Linke*. Berlin: Deutscher Bundestag mit Schreiben des Bundesministeriums des Innern, für Bau und Heimat.

Büchsel, Teresa, and Jan Schneider. 2016. *Ankommen und Bleiben – Wohnsitzauflagen als Integrationsfördernde Maßnahme?* Berlin: Forschungsbereich beim Sachverständigenrat deutscher Stiftungen für Integration und Migration (SVR).

Busemeyer, Marius R., and Raphaela Schlicht-Schmälzle. 2014. 'Partisan Power, Economic Coordination and Variations in Vocational Training Systems in Europe'. *European Journal of Industrial Relations* 20(1): 55–71. https://doi.org/10.1177/0959680113512731

Butler, Judith. 2009. 'Performativity, Precariety and Sexual Politics'. *AIBR Revista de Anthropologia Iberoamericana* 4(3): i–xiii.

Cabot, Heath. 2013. 'The Social Aesthetics of Eligibility: NGO Aid and Indeterminacy in the Greek Asylum Process: The Social Aesthetics of Eligibility'. *American Ethnologist* 40(3): 452–66. https://doi.org/10.1111/amet.12032

Cabot, Heath. 2014. *On the Doorstep of Europe: Asylum and Citizenship in Greece.* Philadelphia: University of Pennsylvania Press.

Cabot, Heath. 2017. '*Philia* and *Phagia*: Thinking with *Stimmungswechsel* through the Refugee Crisis in Greece'. *HAU: Journal of Ethnographic Theory* 7(3): 141–46. https://doi.org/10.14318/hau7.3.008

Cabot, Heath. 2019. 'The Business of Anthropology and the European Refugee Regime'. *American Ethnologist* 46(3): 261–75. https://doi.org/10.1111/amet.12791

Cambridge University Press (ed). 2009. *Cambridge Academic Content Dictionary.* New York: Cambridge University Press.

Carr, Matthew. 2016. *Fortress Europe: Dispatches from a Gated Continent.* New York: The New Press.

Cass, Noel, Elizabeth Shove and John Urry. 2005. 'Social Exclusion, Mobility and Access'. *Sociological Review* 53(3): 539–55.

Castles, Stephen. 2000. 'Citizenship and the Other in the Age of Migration', in *Ethnicity and Globalization: From Migrant Worker to Transnational Citizen.* London: SAGE Publications, pp 187–202.

Chakrabarty, Dipesh. 2007. *Provincializing Europe: Postcolonial Thought and Historical Difference – New Edition.* Princeton: Princeton University Press.

Charmaz, Kathy. 2014. *Constructing Grounded Theory* (2nd edn). Los Angeles: SAGE Publications.

Chatty, Dawn. 2017. 'The Syrian Humanitarian Disaster: Understanding Perceptions and Aspirations in Jordan, Lebanon and Turkey'. *Global Policy* 8: 25–32. https://doi.org/10.1111/1758-5899.12390

Chemin, J. Eduardo, Sabine Hess, Alexander K. Nagel, Bernd Kasparek, Valeria Hänsel and Mathias Jakubowski. 2018. 'Global Migration: Consequences and Responses'. Legal & Policy Framework of Migration Governance. Germany – Country Report: Horizon 2020 – RESPOND. Georg-August Universität Göttingen.

Cheung, Sin Yi, and Jenny Phillimore. 2014. 'Refugees, Social Capital, and Labour Market Integration in the UK'. *Sociology* 48(3): 518–36. https://doi.org/10.1177/0038038513491467

Chimienti, Milena. 2018. 'The Failure of Global Migration Governance'. *Ethnic and Racial Studies* 41(3): 424–30. https://doi.org/10.1080/01419870.2018.1388424

Collins, Francis L. 2018. 'Desire as a Theory for Migration Studies: Temporality, Assemblage and Becoming in the Narratives of Migrants'. *Journal of Ethnic and Migration Studies* 44(6): 964–80. https://doi.org/10.1080/1369183X.2017.1384147

Couldrey, Marion, and Jenny Peebles (eds). 2019. *Return: Voluntary, Safe, Dignified and Durable?* Oxford: Forced Migration Review.

Crawley, Heaven, Franck Duvell, Katharine Jones, Simon McMahon and Nando Sigona (eds). 2018. *Unravelling Europe's 'Migration Crisis': Journeys over Land and Sea.* Bristol: Polity Press.

Crawley, Heaven, and Dimitris Skleparis. 2018. 'Refugees, Migrants, Neither, Both: Categorical Fetishism and the Politics of Bounding in Europe's "Migration Crisis"'. *Journal of Ethnic and Migration Studies* 44(1): 48–64. https://doi.org/10.1080/1369183X.2017.1348224

Crul, Maurice. 2016. 'Strangers No More: Debunking Major Theoretical Assumptions'. *Ethnic and Racial Studies* 39(13): 2325–31. https://doi.org/10.1080/01419870.2016.1203444

Crul, Maurice, Jens Schneider and Lelie Frans (eds). 2012. *The European Second Generation Compared: Does the Integration Context Matter?* Amsterdam: Amsterdam University Press.

Cyrus, Norbert, and Dita Vogel. 2003. 'Work-Permit Decisions in the German Labour Administration: An Exploration of the Implementation Process'. *Journal of Ethnic and Migration Studies* 29(2): 225–55. https://doi.org/10.1080/1369183032000079602

Dagg, Jennifer, and Mark Haugaard. 2016. 'The Performance of Subject Positions, Power, and Identity: A Case of Refugee Recognition'. *European Journal of Cultural and Political Sociology* 3(4): 392–425. https://doi.org/10.1080/23254823.2016.1202524

Dahinden, Janine. 2016. 'A Plea for the "De-migranticization" of Research on Migration and Integration'. *Ethnic and Racial Studies* 39(13): 2207–25. https://doi.org/10.1080/01419870.2015.1124129

Dahinden, Janine, Carolin Fischer and Joanna Menet. 2020. 'Knowledge Production, Reflexivity, and the Use of Categories in Migration Studies: Tackling Challenges in the Field'. *Ethnic and Racial Studies*, 4(4): 535–44. https://doi.org/10.1080/01419870.2020.1752926

Dahlvik, Julia. 2018. *Inside Asylum Bureaucracy: Organizing Refugee Status Determination in Austria.* Cham: Springer International Publishing. https://doi.org/10.1007/978-3-319-63306-0

Danielak, Silvia. 2019. 'Einwanderungsland? Germany's Asylum Dilemma in Policy and Design'. *Journal of International Migration and Integration* 20(1): 1–13. https://doi.org/10.1007/s12134-018-0585-x

Darling, Jonathan. 2017. 'Acts, Ambiguities, and the Labour of Contesting Citizenship'. *Citizenship Studies* 21(6): 727–36. https://doi.org/10.1080/13621025.2017.1341658

Dean, Isabel. 2020. *Bildung – Heterogenität – Sprache: Rassistische Differenz- und Diskriminierungsverhältnisse in Kita und Grundschule.* Wiesbaden: Springer Fachmedien Wiesbaden. https://doi.org/10.1007/978-3-658-30856-8

Dean, Mitchell. 2013. *The Signature of Power: Sovereignty, Governmentality and Biopolitics.* London: SAGE Publications.

De Certeau, Michel. 1984. *The Practice of Everyday Life.* Translated by Steven Rendall. Berkeley: University of California Press.

Degler, Eva, and Thomas Liebig. 2017. 'Finding Their Way: Labour Market Integration of Refugees in Germany'. Directorate for Employment, Labour and Social Affairs, International Migration Division, OECD. https://www.oecd.org/els/mig/Finding-their-Way-Germany.pdf

Deleuze, Gilles, and Felix Guattari. 1987. *A Thousand Plateaus: Capitalism and Schizophrenia* (2nd edn). Minneapolis: University of Minnesota Press.

Della Puppa, Francesco. 2018. 'Ambivalent Mobilities and Survival Strategies of Moroccan and Bangladeshi Families in Italy in Times of Crisis'. *Sociology* 52(3): 464–79. https://doi.org/10.1177/0038038518764622

Dettling, Daniel, and Christian Rauch. 2016. *Vom Willkommen zum Ankommen: Die Wohnsitzauflage vor dem Hintergrund globaler Migration und ihrer Folgen für Kommunen in Deutschland.* Gütersloh: Bertelsmann Stiftung.

Deutsche Welle. 2018. 'Bremen Migration Officer Investigated for Allegedly Granting Asylum in Exchange for Bribes'. https://www.dw.com/en/bremen-migration-officer-investigated-for-allegedly-granting-asylum-in-exchange-for-bribes/a-43471724

Destatis. 2019. '*Bevölkerung und Erwerbstätigkeit: Einbürgerungen*'. Fachserie 1 Reihe 2.1. Statistisches Bundesamt (Destatis).

Deuchar, Ross. 2011. '"People Look at Us, the Way We Dress, and They Think We're Gangsters": Bonds, Bridges, Gangs and Refugees: A Qualitative Study of Inter-Cultural Social Capital in Glasgow'. *Journal of Refugee Studies* 24(4): 672–89. https://doi.org/10.1093/jrs/fer032

Deutscher Bundestag. 2019. *Bundesregierung – 2019 – Antwort der Bundesregierung auf die kleine Anfrage: Zahlen in der Bundesrepublik Deutschland lebender Flüchtlinge Zum Stand 30. Juni 2019.* Bundesregierung.

Döring, Ottmar, and Irina Kreider. 2017. 'Erkennung non-formal und informell erworbener Kompetenzen'. Hochschultage Berufliche Bildung an der Universität zu Köln. https://www.berufsbildung.nrw.de/cms/upload/hochschultage-bk/2017beitraege/WS_07_Erkennung_non-formal_und_informell_erworbener_Kompetenzen_Dring_Kreider.pdf

Droste, Christiane, Thomas Knorr-Siedow, Janina Dobrusskin and Valentin Domann. 2017. *Diskriminierung auf dem Wohnungsmarkt: Interventionsmöglichkeiten in Berlin--Gutachten im Auftrag der Landesstelle für Gleichbehandlung gegen Diskriminierung lm Land Berin.* Berlin: Senatsverwaltung für Justiz, Verbraucherschutz und Antidiskriminierung.

DW (Deutsche Welle). 2022. 'Franco A.: A German Far-Right Soldier's Double Life'. *DW.COM.* https://www.dw.com/en/germany-far-right-terrorism-refugee/a-43540639

Eggenhofer-Rehart, Petra M., Markus Latzke, Katharina Pernkopf, Dominik Zellhofer, Wolfgang Mayrhofer and Johannes Steyrer. 2018. 'Refugees' Career Capital Welcome? Afghan and Syrian Refugee Job Seekers in Austria'. *Journal of Vocational Behavior Behaviour* 105: 31–45. https://doi.org/10.1016/j.jvb.2018.01.004

Ehlich, Konrad, Elke Montanari and Anna Hila. 2007. *Recherche Und Dokumentation Hinsichtlich Der Sprach: Bedarfe von Teilnehmenden an Integrationskursen DaZ. Erstellung eines Rahmencurriculums für Integrationskurse.* Munich: Goethe Institut.

Ehret, Rebekka. 2002. 'Diskriminierung auf dem Wohnungsmarkt: Verquickung von Stadtentwicklungs- und Integrationspolitik am Beispiel Basels'. https://doi.org/10.5169/seals-80379

El Arab, Rebie, and Mette Sagbakken. 2019. 'Child Marriage of Female Syrian Refugees in Jordan and Lebanon: A Literature Review'. *Global Health Action* 12(1): 1585709. https://doi.org/10.1080/16549716.2019.1585709

El-Kayed, Nihad, and Ulrike Hamann. 2018. 'Refugees' Access to Housing and Residency in German Cities: Internal Border Regimes and Their Local Variations'. *Social Inclusion* 6(1): 135–146. https://doi.org/10.17645/si.v6i1.1334

Ellermann, Antje. 2006. 'Street-Level Democracy: How Immigration Bureaucrats Manage Public Opposition'. *West European Politics* 29(2): 293–309. https://doi.org/10.1080/01402380500512627

Elrick, Jennifer, and Luisa Farah Schwartzman. 2015. 'From Statistical Category to Social Category: Organized Politics and Official Categorizations of "Persons with a Migration Background" in Germany'. *Ethnic and Racial Studies* 38(9): 1539–56. https://doi.org/10.1080/01419870.2014.996240

Erel, Umut. 2010. 'Migrating Cultural Capital: Bourdieu in Migration Studies'. *Sociology* 44(4): 642–60. https://doi.org/10.2307/42857433

Ernst, Nora. 2018. 'Landesaufnahmestelle für Flüchtlinge: Ankerzentrum in Lebach geht an den Start'. *Saarbrücker Zeitung*, 28 September. https://www.saarbruecker-zeitung.de/saarland/ankerzentrum-in-lebach-geht-an-den-start_aid-33375919

Ersanilli, Evelyn, and Ruud Koopmans. 2010. 'Rewarding Integration? Citizenship Regulations and the Socio-cultural Integration of Immigrants in the Netherlands, France and Germany'. *Journal of Ethnic and Migration Studies* 36(5): 773–91. https://doi.org/10.1080/13691831003764318

Etzel, Morgan. 2020 'New Models of the "Good Refugee": Bureaucratic Expectations of Syrian Refugees in Germany'. *Ethnic and Racial Studies* 45(6): 1115–34. https://doi.org/10.1080/01419870.2021.1954679

Etzold, Benjamin. 2017. 'Capitalising on Asylum: The Reconfiguration of Refugees' Access to Local Fields of Labour in Germany'. *Refugee Review* 3: 82–102.

Eule, Tobias. 2014. *Inside Immigration Law: Migration Management and Policy Application in Germany.* Farnham: Routledge.

Eule, Tobias. 2018. 'The (Surprising?) Nonchalance of Migration Control Agents'. *Journal of Ethnic and Migration Studies* 44(16): 2780–95. https://doi.org/10.1080/1369183X.2017.1401516

Eule, Tobias, David Loher and Anna Wyss. 2018. 'Contested Control at the Margins of the State'. *Journal of Ethnic and Migration Studies* 44(16): 2717–29. https://doi.org/10.1080/1369183X.2017.1401511

Eule, Tobias, Lisa Marie Borrelli, Annika Lindberg and Anna Wyss (eds). 2019. *Migrants before the Law: Contested Migration Control in Europe.* Cham: Palgrave Macmillan.

Faist, Thomas. 1995. 'Ethnicizatlon and Racialization of Welfare-state Politics in Germany and the USA'. *Ethnic and Racial Studies* 18(2): 219–50. https://doi.org/10.1080/01419870.1995.9993862

Faist, Thomas. 2018. 'The Moral Polity of Forced Migration'. *Ethnic and Racial Studies* 41(3): 412–23. https://doi.org/10.1080/01419 870.2017.1324170

Fallon, Katy, and Ans Boersma. 2020. '"There Is No Future": The Refugees Who Became Pawns in Erdoğan's Game'. *The Guardian*, 8 May. https://www.theguardian.com/global-development/2020/may/08/erdogan-turkey-refugees-pawns-game

Fassin, Didier. 2011. 'Policing Borders, Producing Boundaries: The Governmentality of Immigration in Dark Times'. *Annual Review of Anthropology* 40(1): 213–26. https://doi.org/10.1146/annurev-anthro-081309-145847

Fassin, Didier, and Richard Rechtman. 2009. *The Empire of Trauma: An Inquiry into the Condition of Victimhood.* Translated by Rachel Gomme. Princeton: Princeton University Press.

Fassin, Didier, Yasmine Bouagga, Isabelle Coutant, Jean-Sébastien Eideliman, Fabrice Fernandez, Nicolas Fischer, Carolina Kobelinsky, Chowra Makaremi, Sarah Mazouz and Sébastien Roux. 2015. *At the Heart of the State: The Moral World of Institutions.* Translated by Patrick Brown and Didier Fassin. London: Pluto Press.

Favell, Adrian. 2001. *Philosophies of Integration, Second Edition: Immigration and the Idea of Citizenship in France and Britain*. Basingstoke: Palgrave Macmillan.

Favell, Adrian. 2013 'The Changing Face of "Integration" in a Mobile Europe'. *Council For European Studies Newsletter* 43(1): 53–58.

Favell, Adrian. 2016. 'Just like the USA? Critical Notes on Alba and Foner's Cross-Atlantic Research Agenda'. *Ethnic and Racial Studies* 39(13): 2352–60. https://doi.org/10.1080/01419870.2016.1203447.

Favell, Adrian. 2019. 'Integration: Twelve Propositions after Schinkel'. *Comparative Migration Studies* 7(21). https://doi.org/10.1186/s40 878-019-0125-7

Ferguson, James, and Akhil Gupta. 2002. 'Spatializing States: Toward an Ethnography of Neoliberal Governmentality'. *American Ethnologist* 29(4): 981–1002.

Foucault, Michel. 1988. *Politics, Philosophy, Culture: Interviews and Other Writings, 1977–1984*. Translated by Lawrence D. Kritzman. New York: Routledge.

Foucault, Michel. 1991. *The Foucault Effect: Studies in Governmentality: With Two Lectures by and an Interview with Michel Foucault*. Edited by Graham Burchell, Colin Gordon and Peter Miller. Chicago: University of Chicago Press.

Foucault, Michel. 2011. *The Courage of Truth: The Government of Self and Others II: Lectures at the Collège de France 1983–1984*. Edited by Frédéric Gros, François Ewald, Alessandro Fontana and Arnold I. Davidson. Translated by Graham Burchell. New York: Palgrave Macmillan

Fleischmann, Larissa, and Elias Steinhilper. 2017. 'The Myth of Apolitical Volunteering for Refugees: German Welcome Culture and a New Dispositif of Helping'. *Social Inclusion* 5(3): 17–27. https://doi.org/10.17645/si.v5i3.945

Fourier, Katharina, Julia Kracht Araújo, Katharina Latsch, Anke Siemens, Michael Schmitz and Michael Grüttner. 2018. *Integration von Flüchtlingen an deutschen Hochschulen: Erkenntnisse aus den Hochschulprogrammen für Flüchtlinge*. Bonn: Studienvorbereitung und Übergang Ins Studium. Deutscher Akademischer Austauschdienst (DAAD).

Friedrich, Lena, and Stine Waibel. 2012. 'Local Integration Concepts in Germany – Diffusion of an Integration Model?' *IMIS-Beiträge* 41: 53–72. Osnabrück: Instituts für Migrationsforschung und Interkulturelle Studien (IMIS) der Universität Osnabrück.

Galtung, Johan. 1969. 'Violence, Peace, and Peace Research'. *Journal of Peace Research* 6(3): 167–91. https://doi.org/10.1177/002234336900600301

Galtung, Johan. 1990. 'Cultural Violence'. *Journal of Peace Research* 27(3): 291–305.

Galtung, Johan. 2010. 'Peace Studies and Conflict Resolution: The Need for Transdisciplinarity'. *Transcultural Psychiatry* 47: 20–32. https://doi.org/10.1177/1363461510362041

Geddes, Andrew, and Peter Scholten. 2016. 'Germany: A Country of Immigration after All', in *The Politics of Migration and Immigration in Europe*. London: SAGE Publications, pp 74–100.

Gibney, Matthew J. 2004. *The Ethics and Politics of Asylum: Liberal Democracy and the Response to Refugees*. Cambridge: Cambridge University Press.

Gibney, Matthew J. 2015. 'Refugees and Justice between States'. *European Journal of Political Theory* 14(4): 448–63. https://doi.org/10.1177/14748 85115585325

Gibney, Matthew J. 2018. 'The Ethics of Refugees'. *Philosophy Compass* 13(10): e12521. https://doi.org/10.1111/phc3.12521

Gill, Nick, and Anthony Good (eds). 2019. *Asylum Determination in Europe: Ethnographic Perspectives*. Cham: Springer International Publishing.

Glick Schiller, Nina, and Noel B. Salazar. 2013. 'Regimes of Mobility across the Globe'. *Journal of Ethnic and Migration Studies* 39(2): 183–200. https://doi.org/10.1080/1369183X.2013.723253

Glorius, Birgit, and Jeroen Doomernik (eds). 2020. *Geographies of Asylum in Europe and the Role of European Localities*. Cham: Springer International Publishing.

Goldberg, David Theo. 2015. *Are We All Postracial Yet?* Cambridge: Polity.

Gowayed, Heba. 2020. 'Resettled and Unsettled: Syrian Refugees and the Intersection of Race and Legal Status in the United States'. *Ethnic and Racial Studies*, 43(2): 275–93. https://doi.org/10.1080/01419870.2019.1583350

Graeber, David. 2011. *Debt: The First 5,000 Years*. Brooklyn, NY: Melville House Publishing.

Groll, Tina. 2019. 'Bundesverfassungsgericht: Kippt jetzt Hartz IV?' *Die Zeit*, 5 November. https://www.zeit.de/wirtschaft/2019-01/bundesver fassungsgericht-hartz-iv-sanktionen-strafen-verfassungswidrigkeit-faq#

Grzymala-Kazlowska, Aleksandra, and Jenny Phillimore. 2018. 'Introduction: Rethinking Integration. New Perspectives on Adaptation and Settlement in the Era of Super-Diversity'. *Journal of Ethnic and Migration Studies* 44(2): 179–96. https://doi.org/10.1080/13691 83X.2017.1341706

Gullestad, Marianne. 2006. *Plausible Prejudice*. Oslo: Universitetsforlaget.

Gupta, Akhil. 1995. 'Blurred Boundaries: The Discourse of Corruption, the Culture of Politics, and the Imagined State'. *American Ethnologist* 22(2): 375–402. https://doi.org/10.1525/ae.1995.22.2.02a00090

Gupta, Akhil. 2012. *Red Tape: Bureaucracy, Structural Violence, and Poverty in India*. Durham, NC: Duke University Press.

Gupta, Akhil. 2013. 'Messy Bureaucracies'. *HAU: Journal of Ethnographic Theory* 3(3): 435–40. https://doi.org/10.14318/hau3.3.029

Gutiérrez Rodríguez, Encarnación. 2018. 'The Coloniality of Migration and the 'Refugee Crisis': On the Asylum-Migration Nexus, the Transatlantic White European Settler Colonialism-Migration and Racial Capitalism'. *Refuge* 34(1): 16–28. https://doi.org/10.7202/1050851ar

Hadj Abdou, Leila. 2014. 'Immigrant Integration and the Economic Competitiveness Agenda: A Comparison of Dublin and Vienna'. *Journal of Ethnic and Migration Studies* 40(12): 1875–94. https://doi.org/10.1080/1369183X.2014.887462

Hadj Abdou, Leila. 2019. 'Immigrant Integration: The Governance of Ethno-cultural Differences'. *Comparative Migration Studies* 7(15). https://doi.org/10.1186/s40878-019-0124-8

Hafner, Jonas, and André Kastilan. 2017. *Verwaltungshandeln im Bereich kommunaler Integration: Vollzugsprobleme und Optimierungsvorschläge*. Ruhr Universität Bochum: Verwaltungshandeln im Bereich kommunaler Integration.

Hage, G. 2003. '"Comes a Time We Are All Enthusiasm": Understanding Palestinian Suicide Bombers in Times of Exighophobia'. *Public Culture* 15(1): 65–89. https://doi.org/10.1215/08992363-15-1-65

Hage, Ghassan. 2005. 'A Not So Multi-sited Ethnography of a Not So Imagined Community'. *Anthropological Theory* 5(4): 463–75. https://doi.org/10.1177/1463499605059232

Hage, Ghassan (ed). 2009. *Waiting*. Carlton, Vic: Melbourne University Publishing.

Hage, Ghassan. 2013. 'Eavesdropping on Bourdieu's Philosophers'. *Thesis Eleven* 114(1): 76–93. https://doi.org/10.1177/0725513612463036

Hagen, Kevin, and Peter Maxwill. 2015. 'Asylunterkünfte: Flüchtlingskrise überfordert Deutsche Behörden'. *Spiegel Online*, 11 August. http://www.spiegel.de/politik/deutschland/fluechtlinge-in-deutschland-warum-so-viel-chaos-und-leid-a-1046851.html

Hannerz, Ulf. 2003. 'Being There … and There … and There!' *Ethnography* 4(2): 201–16.

Hannerz, Ulf. 2010. 'Diversity Is Our Business'. *American Anthropologist* 112(4): 539–51. https://doi.org/10.1111/j.1548-1433.2010.01274.x

Harding, Jeremy. 2012. *Border Vigils: Keeping Migrants out of the Rich World*. New York: Verso.

Harney, Nicholas. 2013. 'Precarity, Affect and Problem Solving with Mobile Phones by Asylum Seekers, Refugees and Migrants in Naples, Italy'. *Journal of Refugee Studies* 26(4): 541–57. https://doi.org/10.1093/jrs/fet017

Heckmann, Friedrich. 2015. *Integration von Migranten*. Wiesbaden: Springer Fachmedien Wiesbaden. https://doi.org/10.1007/978-3-658-06980-3

Hermsmeier, Lukas. 2020. 'Opinion | Germany's Post-Nazi Taboo against the Far Right Has Been Shattered'. *New York Times*, 7 February. https://www.nytimes.com/2020/02/07/opinion/far-right-thuringia-germany.html

Herzfeld, Michael. 1982. 'The Etymology of Excuses: Aspects of Rhetorical Performance in Greece'. *American Ethnologist* 9(4): 644–63. https://doi.org/10.1525/ae.1982.9.4.02a00020

Herzfeld, Michael. 1992. *The Social Production of Indifference*. Chicago: University of Chicago Press.

Herzfeld, Michael. 2004. *Cultural Intimacy: Social Poetics in the Nation-State* (2nd edn). New York: Routledge.

Herzfeld, Michael. 2007. 'Global Kinship: Anthropology and the Politics of Knowing'. *Anthropological Quarterly* 80(2): 313–23. https://doi.org/10.1353/anq.2007.0026

Herzfeld, Michael. 2019. 'What Is a Polity? 2018 Lewis H. Morgan Lecture'. *HAU: Journal of Ethnographic Theory* 9(1): 23–35. https://doi.org/10.1086/703684

Heyman, Josiah McC. 1995. 'Putting Power in the Anthropology of Bureaucracy: The Immigration and Naturalization Service at the Mexico-United States Border'. *Current Anthropology* 36(2): 261–87.

Hilpold, Peter. 2017. 'Quotas as an Instrument of Burden-Sharing in International Refugee Law: The Many Facets of an Instrument Still in the Making'. *International Journal of Constitutional Law* 15(4): 1188–1205. https://doi.org/10.1093/icon/mox086

Hinger, Sophie, Philipp Schäfer and Andreas Pott. 2016. 'The Local Production of Asylum'. *Journal of Refugee Studies* 29(4): 440–63. https://doi.org/10.1093/jrs/few029

Hinger, Sophie, and Reinhard Schweitzer. 2020. *Politics of (Dis)Integration*. https://doi.org/10.1007/978-3-030-25089-8

Hinte, Holger, Ulf Rinne and Klaus F. Zimmermann. 2015. 'Flüchtlinge in Deutschland: Herausforderung und Chancen'. *Wirtschaftsdienst* 95(11): 744–51. https://doi.org/10.1007/s10273-015-1897-5

Hoag, Colin. 2014. 'Dereliction at the South African Department of Home Affairs: Time for the Anthropology of Bureaucracy'. *Critique of Anthropology* 34(4): 410–28. https://doi.org/10.1177/0308275X14543395

Horr, Andreas, Christian Hunkler and Clemens Kroneberg. 2018. 'Ethnic Discrimination in the German Housing Market'. *Zeitschrift für Soziologie* 47(2): 134–46. https://doi.org/10.1515/zfsoz-2018-1009

Horvath, Kenneth, Anna Amelina and Karin Peters. 2017. 'Re-thinking the Politics of Migration: On the Uses and Challenges of Regime Perspectives for Migration Research'. *Migration Studies* 5(3): 301–14. https://doi.org/10.1093/migration/mnx055

Hörisch, Felix. 2018. 'Asylpolitik im Bundesländervergleich: Eine fuzzy-set Qualitative Comparative Analysis'. *Zeitschrift für Vergleichende Politikwissenschaft* 12(4): 783–803. https://doi.org/10.1007/s12286-018-0399-4

Hull, Matthew S. 2012. 'Documents and Bureaucracy'. *Annual Review of Anthropology* 41(1): 251–67. https://doi.org/10.1146/annurev.anthro.012 809.104953

Hummel, Steven, Beata Krasowski, Sotiria Midelia and Juliane Wetendorf. 2017. *Rassistische Diskriminierung auf dem Sächsischen Wohnungsmarkt.* Leipzig: Antidiskriminierungsbüro Sachsen e.V.

Husserl, Edmund. 1964. *Phenomenology of Internal-Time Consciousness.* Edited by Martin Heidegger. Translated by James S. Churchill. Ann Arbor: Indiana University Press.

Ihlamur-Öner, Suna Gülfer. 2013. 'Turkey's Refugee Regime Stretched to the Limit? The Case of Iraqi and Syrian Refugee Flows'. *Perceptions* XVIII(3): 191–228.

Ilgit, Asli, and Audie Klotz. 2018. 'Refugee Rights or Refugees as Threats? Germany's New Asylum Policy'. *British Journal of Politics and International Relations* 20(3): 613–31. https://doi.org/10.1177/1369148118778958

Innes, Alexandria J. 2016. 'In Search of Security: Migrant Agency, Narrative, and Performativity'. *Geopolitics* 21(2): 263–83. https://doi.org/10.1080/14650045.2015.1107044

Jackson, Michael. 1998. *Minima Ethnographica: Intersubjectivity and the Anthropological Project.* Chicago: University of Chicago Press.

Jackson, Michael. 2005. *Existential Anthropology: Events, Exigencies, and Effects.* New York: Berghahn Books.

Jackson, Michael. 2008. 'The Shock of the New: On Migrant Imaginaries and Critical Transitions'. *Ethnos* 73(1): 57–72. https://doi.org/10.1080/00141840801927533

Jäckle, Sebastian, and Pascal D. König. 2018. 'Threatening Events and Anti-refugee Violence: An Empirical Analysis in the Wake of the Refugee Crisis during the Years 2015 and 2016 in Germany'. *European Sociological Review* 34(6): 728–43. https://doi.org/10.1093/esr/jcy038

Jobcenter München. 2019. *Arbeitsmarkt- Und Integrationsprogramm.* Munich: Jobcenter München.

Joormann, Martin. 2020. 'Social Class, Economic Capital and the Swedish, German and Danish Asylum Systems', in Dalia Abdelhady and Nina Gren (eds) *Refugees and the Violence of Welfare Bureaucracies in Northern Europe.* Manchester: Manchester University Press, pp 31–49.

Joppke, Christian. 2007. 'Transformation of Immigrant Integration: Civic Integration and Antidiscrimination in the Netherlands, France, and Germany'. *World Politics* 59(02): 243–73. https://doi.org/10.1353/wp.2007.0022

Joppke, Christian. 2017. 'Civic Integration in Western Europe: Three Debates'. *West European Politics* 40(6): 1153–76. https://doi.org/10.1080/01402382.2017.1303252

Jubany, Olga. 2011. 'Constructing Truths in a Culture of Disbelief: Understanding Asylum Screening from within'. *International Sociology* 26(1): 74–94. https://doi.org/10.1177/0268580910380978

Karakayali, Serhat. 2018. 'The *Flüchtlingskrise* in Germany: Crisis of the Refugees, by the Refugees, for the Refugees'. *Sociology* 52(3): 606–11. https://doi.org/10.1177/0038038518760224

Karakayali, Serhat, and Olaf J. Kleist. 2016. *EFA-Studie 2: Strukturen und Motive der ehrenamtlichen Flüchtlingsarbeit (EFA) in Deutschland*. Berlin: Berliner Instituts für empirische Integrations- und Migrationsforschung (BIM), Humboldt-Universität zu Berlin.

Karakayali, Serhat, Mira Wallis, Leif Jannis Höfler and Mareike Heller. 2018. *Fördermittel in der Flüchtlingshilfe. Was gebraucht Wird – Was Ankommt*. Gütersloh: Bertelsmann Stiftung.

Kastner, Bernd. 2018. 'Fast jeder zweite abgelehnte Flüchtling siegt mit Klage vor Gericht'. *sueddeutsche.de*, 23 March. https://www.sueddeutsche.de/politik/asyl-fluechtlinge-klage-gericht-1.3918139

Kingsley, Patrick, and Safak Timur. 2015. 'Stories of 2015: How Alan Kurdi's Death Changed the World'. *The Guardian*, 31 December. https://www.theguardian.com/world/2015/dec/31/alan-kurdi-death-canada-refugee-policy-syria-boy-beach-turkey-photo

Kirk, Kate, Ellen Bal and Sarah Renee Janssen. 2017. 'Migrants in Liminal Time and Space: An Exploration of the Experiences of Highly Skilled Indian Bachelors in Amsterdam'. *Journal of Ethnic and Migration Studies* 43(16): 2771–87. https://doi.org/10.1080/1369183X.2017.1314600

Kivisto, Peter. 2017. 'The Origins of "New Assimilation Theory"'. *Ethnic and Racial Studies* 40(9): 1418–29. https://doi.org/10.1080/01419870.2017.1300299

Klinger, Sabine, and Enzo Weber. 2018. 'Low Wage Growth in Germany? – Don't Blame the Migrants!' *IAB Forum*, 23 March.

Knuth, Matthias. 2016. '*Arbeitsmarktintegration von Flüchtlingen: Arbeitsmarktpolitik reformieren, Qualifikationen vermitteln*'. 21. WISO Diskurs. Friedrich-Ebert-Stiftung (FES). Bonn. https://library.fes.de/pdf-files/wiso/12914.pdf

Komaromi, Priska. 2016. 'Germany: Neo-Nazis and the Market in Asylum Reception'. *Race & Class* 58(2): 79–86. https://doi.org/10.1177/0306396816657727

Konle-Seidl, Regina. 2018. 'Integration of Refugees in Austria, Germany and Sweden: Comparative Analysis'. Directorate General for Internal Policies. Policy Department A: Economic and Scientific Policy. European Parliament's Committee on Employment and Social Affairs. IP/A/EMPL/2016-23.

Koopmans, Ruud, Susanne Veit and Ruta Yemane. 2019. 'Taste or Statistics? A Correspondence Study of Ethnic, Racial and Religious Labour Market Discrimination in Germany'. *Ethnic and Racial Studies* 42(16): 233–52. https://doi.org/10.1080/01419870.2019.1654114

Korteweg, Anna C. 2017. 'The Failures of "Immigrant Integration": The Gendered Racialized Production of Non-belonging'. *Migration Studies* 5(3): 428–44. https://doi.org/10.1093/migration/mnx025

Köttig, Michaela, and Johanna Sigl. 2020. 'Racist Mobilisation and Sexualisation in the "Refugee Debate" in Germany'. *Journal of Sociology* 56(1): 69–83. https://doi.org/10.1177/1440783319882538

Krajewski, Christian. 2015. 'Arm, sexy und immer teurer: Wohnungs-marktentwicklung und Gentrification in Berlin'. *Standort* 39(2–3): 77–85. https://doi.org/10.1007/s00548-015-0381-1

Kristjánsdóttir, Erla S., and Unnur Dís Skaptadóttir. 2018. '"I'll Always Be a Refugee": The Lived Experience of Palestinian Refugee Women of Moving to a Small Society in Iceland'. *Journal of Immigrant & Refugee Studies*, October, 1–16. https://doi.org/10.1080/15562948.2018.1499065

Kumaran, R. 2014. 'Listening as a Radical Research Act'. *SSRN Electronic Journal*. https://doi.org/10.2139/ssrn.2539437

Kymlicka, Will. 2018. 'The Rise and Fall of Multiculturalism? New Debates on Inclusion and Accommodation in Diverse Societies'. *International Social Science Journal*, 68(227–228): 133–48. https://doi.org/10.1111/issj.12188

Laschet, Armin. 2015. *Robert Bosch Expertenkommission zur Neuausrichtung der Flüchtlingspolitik*. Stuttgart: Robert Bosch Stiftung.

Latković, Marija. 2020. 'Hanau: Die anderen sind wir'. *Die Zeit*, 7 March. https://www.zeit.de/2020/11/hanau-anschlag-rassismus-morde-taeter-migrationshintergrund

Laubenthal, Barbara. 2019. 'Refugees Welcome? Reforms of German Asylum Policies between 2013 and 2017 and Germany's Transformation into an Immigration Country'. *German Politics* 28(3):, 412–25. https://doi.org/10.1080/09644008.2018.1561872

Leubecher, Marcel. 2019. 'Wohnsitzauflagen für Flüchtlinge: Dort wohnen, wo der Staat es will', *Die Welt*, 1 March. https://www.welt.de/politik/deutschland/article189592587/Wohnsitzauflagen-fuer-Fluechtlinge-Dort-wohnen-wo-der-Staat-es-will.html

Lewicki, Aleksandra. 2018. 'Race, Islamophobia and the Politics of Citizenship in Post-unification Germany'. *Patterns of Prejudice* 52(5): 496–512. https://doi.org/10.1080/0031322X.2018.1502236

Liebe, Ulf, Jürgen Meyerhoff, Maarten Kroesen, Caspar Chorus and Klaus Glenk. 2018. 'From Welcome Culture to Welcome Limits? Uncovering Preference Changes over Time for Sheltering Refugees in Germany'. *PLOS ONE* 13(8): e0199923. https://doi.org/10.1371/journal.pone.0199923

Lipsky, Michael. 2010. *Street-Level Bureaucracy: Dilemmas of the Individual in Public Services*. New York: Russell Sage Foundation.

Lobenstein, Caterina, Paul Middelhoff and Michael Thumann. 2020. 'Minderjährige Flüchtlinge: 50 von 40.000'. *Die Zeit*, 15 April. https://www.zeit.de/2020/17/minderjaehrige-fluechtlinge-griechenland-deutschland-evakuierung

Lorenzini, Daniele, and Martina Tazzioli. 2018. 'Confessional Subjects and Conducts of Non-truth: Foucault, Fanon, and the Making of the Subject'. *Theory, Culture & Society* 35(1): 71–90. https://doi.org/10.1177/0263276416678291

Löwenheim, Oded, and Orit Gazit. 2009. 'Power and Examination: A Critique of Citizenship Tests'. *Security Dialogue* 40(2): 145–67. https://doi.org/10.1177/0967010609103074

Maestri, Gaja, and Sarah M. Hughes. 2017. 'Contested Spaces of Citizenship: Camps, Borders and Urban Encounters'. *Citizenship Studies* 21(6): 625–39.

Malkki, Liisa H. 1995. 'Refugees and Exile: From "Refugee Studies" to the National Order of Things'. *Annual Review of Anthropology* 24: 495–523.

Mandic, Danilo. 2017. 'Trafficking and Syrian Refugee Smuggling: Evidence from the Balkan Route'. *Social Inclusion* 5(2): 28. https://doi.org/10.17645/si.v5i2.917

Marcus, George E. 1995. 'Ethnography in/of the World System: The Emergence of Multi-sited Ethnography'. *Annual Review of Anthropology* 24: 95–117. https://doi.org/10.1080/13621025.2017.1341657

Marx, Paul, and Elias Naumann. 2018. 'Do Right-Wing Parties Foster Welfare Chauvinistic Attitudes? A Longitudinal Study of the 2015 "Refugee Crisis" in Germany'. *Electoral Studies* 52: 111–16. https://doi.org/10.1016/j.electstud.2018.01.011

Meissner, Fran. 2018. 'Mainstreaming and Superdiversity: Beyond More Integration', in Peter Scholten and Ilona van Breugel (eds) *Mainstreaming Integration Governance*. Cham: Springer International Publishing, pp 215–33. https://doi.org/10.1007/978-3-319-59277-0_10.

Mezzadra, Sandro, and Brett Neilson. 2013. *Border as Method, or, the Multiplication of Labor*. Durham, NC: Duke University Press.

Mittler, Dietrich. 2019. 'Bayerns Integrationsgesetz zum Teil verfassungswidrig'. *Süddeutsche Zeitung*, 3 December. https://www.sueddeutsche.de/bayern/bayern-integrationsgesetz-csu-verfassungswidrig-1.4707498

Moffitt, Ursula, Linda P. Juang and Moin Syed. 2018. '"We Don't Do That in Germany!" A Critical Race Theory Examination of Turkish Heritage Young Adults' School Experiences'. *Ethnicities* July: 146879681878859. https://doi.org/10.1177/1468796818788596

Morse, Janice M. 2009. *Developing Grounded Theory*. Walnut Creek, CA: Left Coast Press.

Munif, Yasser. 2020. *The Syrian Revolution: Between the Politics of Life and the Geopolitics of Death*. London: Pluto Press.

Mushaben, Joyce Marie. 2017. '*Wir Schaffen Das!* Angela Merkel and the European Refugee Crisis'. *German Politics* 26(4): 516–33. https://doi.org/10.1080/09644008.2017.1366988

Myers, Quintin W.O., and Kyle Anne Nelson. 2018. '"I Should Not Forget!": Qualitative Evidence of Social and Cultural Transnationalism among Refugees Who Are Disconnected from Home'. *Ethnic and Racial Studies*, February, 1–18. https://doi.org/10.1080/01419870.2018.1432874

Ndhlovu, Finex. 2016. 'A Decolonial Critique of Diaspora Identity Theories and the Notion of Superdiversity'. *Diaspora Studies* 9(1): 28–40. https://doi.org/10.1080/09739572.2015.1088612

Neureiter, Marcus, Frank Oschmiansky, Sandra Popp and Peter Schoen. 2017. 'Behördenunabhängige Beratungsdienstleistungen für Erwerbslose Erwerbslosenberatungsstellen in Nordrhein-Westfalen', in Frank Sowa and Ronald Staples (eds) *Beratung und Vermittlung im Wohlfahrtsstaat*. Düsseldorf: Nomos Verlagsgesellschaft, pp 361–86.

Ong, Aihwa. 1996. 'Cultural Citizenship as Subject-Making'. *Current Anthropology* 37(5): 737–62.

Ong, Aihwa. 2003. *Buddha Is Hiding: Refugees, Citizenship, the New America*. Berkeley: University of California Press.

Ong, Aihwa. 2006. 'Mutations in Citizenship'. *Theory, Culture & Society* 23(2–3): 499–505. https://doi.org/10.1177/0263276406064831

Ong, Aihwa. 2012. 'Powers of Sovereignty'. *Focaal* 2012(64): 24–35. https://doi.org/10.3167/fcl.2012.640103

Ortner, Sherry B. 2016. 'Dark Anthropology and Its Others: Theory since the Eighties'. *HAU: Journal of Ethnographic Theory* 6(1): 47–73. https://doi.org/10.14318/hau6.1.004

Osseiran, Souad. 2020. '"Europe" from "Here": Syrian Migrants/Refugees in Istanbul and Imagined Migrations into and within "Europe"', in Nicholas de Genova (ed) *The Borders of 'Europe*. Durham, NC: Duke University Press, pp 185–209.

Ostrand, Nicole. 2015. 'The Syrian Refugee Crisis: A Comparison of Responses by Germany, Sweden, the United Kingdom, and the United States'. *Journal on Migration and Human Security* 3: 255–79.

Oulios, Miltiadis. 2015. *Blackbox Abschiebung: Geschichte, Theorie und Praxis der deutschen Migrationspolitik*. Berlin: Suhrkamp Verlag AG.

Partridge, Damani J. 2012. *Hypersexuality and Headscarves: Race, Sex, and Citizenship in the New Germany*. Bloomington: Indiana University Press.

Paulle, Bowen, and Barak Kalir. 2014. 'The Integration Matrix Reloaded: From Ethnic Fixations to Established versus Outsiders Dynamics in the Netherlands'. *Journal of Ethnic and Migration Studies* 40(9): 1354–74. https://doi.org/10.1080/1369183X.2013.847783

Paulsen, Hilko, Timo Kortsch, Simone Kauffeld, Laura Naegele, Ireen Mobach and Bernd Neumann. 2016. 'Anerkennung der beruflichen Kompetenzen von Flüchtlingen – Ein Beitrag zur Integration'. *Gruppe. Interaktion. Organisation. Zeitschrift für Angewandte Organisationspsychologie (GIO)* 47(3): 243–54. https://doi.org/10.1007/s11612-016-0338-2.

Pearlman, Wendy. 2017. 'Culture or Bureaucracy? Challenges in Syrian Refugees' Initial Settlement in Germany'. *Middle East Law and Governance* 9(3): 313–27. https://doi.org/10.1163/18763375-00903002

Pedersen, Marianne Holm. 2012. 'Going on a Class Journey: The Inclusion and Exclusion of Iraqi Refugees in Denmark'. *Journal of Ethnic and Migration Studies* 38(7): 1101–17. https://doi.org/10.1080/1369183X.2012.681453

Pielage, Patricia, Ludger Pries, Günther Schultze and Friedrich-Ebert-Stiftung (eds). 2012. *Soziale Ungleichheit in der Einwanderungsgesellschaft: Kategorien, Konzepte, Einflussfaktoren; Tagungsdokumentation im Auftrag der Abteilung Wirtschafts- und Sozialpolitik der Friedrich-Ebert-Stiftung.* Bonn: Friedrich-Ebert-Stiftung.

Pro Asyl. 2016. 'Asyl in Zahlen 2016'. https://www.proasyl.de/hintergr und/asyl-in-zahlen-2016

Pro Asyl. 2017. 'Ein Leben ohne Privatsphäre? Sammelunterbringung darf nicht zum Dauerzustand werden!'. https://www.proasyl.de/news/ein-leben-ohne-privatsphaere-sammelunterbringung-darf-nicht-zum-dauer zustand-werden/

Pro Asyl. 2018a. 'Fakten, Zahlen und Argumente'. https://www.proasyl. de/thema/fakten-zahlen-argumente

Pro Asyl. 2018b. 'Familien gehören zusammen!'. https://www.proasyl.de/ thema/familiennachzug

Pro Asyl. 2019. 'Achtung: Hau-ab-Gesetz in Kraft – Neuregelungen des 'Migrationspakets' im Überblick'. https://www.proasyl.de/news/acht ung-hau-ab-gesetz-ab-morgen-in-kraft-neuregelungen-des-migration spaktes-im-ueberblick

Rabinow, Paul, and Nikolas Rose. 2006. 'Biopower Today'. *BioSocieties* 1(2): 195–217. https://doi.org/10.1017/S1745855206040014

Reis, Claus, and Benedikt Siebenhaar. 2015. *Befähigen statt aktivieren: aktueller Reformbedarf bei Zielsetzung und Aufgabenstellung im SGB II.* WISO Diskurs. Bonn: Friedrich-Ebert-Stiftung, Abt. Wirtschafts- und Sozialpolitik.

Renner, Nona. 2018. 'Die Wohnsitzauflage als Mittel deutscher Integrationspolitik? Das Beispiel Sachsen'. Policy Paper. Dresden: Mercator Forums Migration und Demokratie (MIDEM).

Rexhepi, Piro. 2018. 'Arab Others at European Borders: Racializing Religion and Refugees along the Balkan Route'. *Ethnic and Racial Studies* 41(12): 2215–34. https://doi.org/10.1080/01419870.2017.1415455

Rhein, Jakob. 2022. 'Ersatz für Hartz IV: Wie das neue Bürgergeld aussehen soll'. *tagesschau.de* (blog), 20 July. https://www.tagesschau.de/inland/innen politik/buergergeld-101.html

Richter, Konstantin. 2016. 'Germany's Refugee Crisis Has Left It as Bitterly Divided as Donald Trump's America | Konstantin Richter'. *The Guardian*, 1 April. https://www.theguardian.com/commentisfree/2016/apr/01/germany-refugee-crisis-invited-into-my-home-welcoming-spirit-divided

Riedel, Lisa, and Gerald Schneider. 2017a. 'Dezentraler Asylvollzug diskriminiert: Anerkennungsquoten von Flüchtlingen im bundesdeutschen Vergleich, 2010-2015'. *Politische Vierteljahresschrift* 58(1): 23–50. https://doi.org/10.5771/0032-3470-2017-1-23

Riedel, Lisa, and Gerald Schneider. 2017b. 'Die föderale Asyllotterie: Anerkennungschancen für Flüchtlinge variieren stark'. *Netzwerk Fluchtforschung*. https://fluchtforschung.net/blogbeitraege/die-foderale-asyllotterie/

Röder, Sebastian. 2016. *Überblick zu den Änderungen durch das Integrationsgesetz vom 6. August 2016*. Stuttgart: Flüchtlingsrat Baden-Württemberg.

Rozakou, Katerina. 2017. 'Nonrecording the "European Refugee Crisis" in Greece'. *Focaal* 2017(77): 36–49. https://doi.org/10.3167/fcl.2017.770104

Ryan, Louise. 2011. 'Migrants' Social Networks and Weak Ties: Accessing Resources and Constructing Relationships Post-migration'. *Sociological Review* 59(4): 707–24. https://doi.org/10.1111/j.1467-954X.2011.02030.x

Ryan, Louise, Rosemary Sales, Mary Tilki and Bernadetta Siara. 2008. 'Social Networks, Social Support and Social Capital: The Experiences of Recent Polish Migrants in London'. *Sociology* 42(4): 672–90. https://doi.org/10.1177/0038038508091622

Sadeghi, Sahar. 2019 'Racial Boundaries, Stigma, and the Re-emergence of "Always Being Foreigners": Iranians and the Refugee Crisis in Germany'. *Ethnic and Racial Studies* 42(10): 1613–31. https://doi.org/10.1080/01419 870.2018.1506145

Safouane, Hamza. 2017. 'Manufacturing Striated Space for Migrants: An Ethnography of Initial Reception Centers for Asylum Seekers in Germany'. *VOLUNTAS: International Journal of Voluntary and Nonprofit Organizations* 28(5): 1922–39. https://doi.org/10.1007/s11266-016-9813-1

Scheffer, Thomas. 2001. *Asylgewährung, Eine ethnographische Verfahrensanalyse*. Berlin: De Gruyter Oldenbourg.

Scherschel, Karin. 2018. 'An den Grenzen der Demokratie – Citizenship und Flucht'. *Berliner Journal für Soziologie* 28(1–2): 123–49. https://doi.org/10.1007/s11609-018-0366-6

Schierup, Carl-Ulrik, Peo Hansen, and Stephen Castles. 2006. *Migration, Citizenship, and the European Welfare State: A European Dilemma*. Oxford: Oxford University Press.

Schinkel, Willem. 2013. 'The Imagination of "Society" in Measurements of Immigrant Integration'. *Ethnic and Racial Studies* 36(7): 1142–61. https://doi.org/10.1080/01419870.2013.783709

Schinkel, Willem. 2017. *Imagined Societies: A Critique of Immigrant Integration in Western Europe*. Cambridge: Cambridge University Press.

Schinkel, Willem. 2018. 'Against "Immigrant Integration": For an End to Neocolonial Knowledge Production'. *Comparative Migration Studies* 6(1): 31. https://doi.org/10.1186/s40878-018-0095-1

Schittenhelm, Karin, and Stephanie Schneider. 2017. 'Official Standards and Local Knowledge in Asylum Procedures: Decision-Making in Germany's Asylum System'. *Journal of Ethnic and Migration Studies* 43(10): 1696–713. https://doi.org/10.1080/1369183X.2017.1293592

Schmidt, Christin. 2017. '*Mehr als Hartz IV? Was Flüchtlinge vom Staat bekommen*'. *MAZ – Märkische Allgemeine*, 14 February. https://www.maz-online.de/Lokales/Havelland/Mehr-als-Hartz-IV-Was-Fluechtlinge-vom-Staat-bekommen

Schneider, Christine, Stefanie Joos and Kayvan Bozorgmehr. 2015. 'Disparities in Health and Access to Healthcare between Asylum Seekers and Residents in Germany: A Population-Based Cross-Sectional Feasibility Study'. *BMJ Open* 5(11): e008784. https://doi.org/10.1136/bmjopen-2015-008784

Schneider, Jan. 2007. 'Rückblick: Zuwanderungsgesetz 2005'. *Die Bundeszentrale für politische Bildung* (blog), 15 May. http://www.bpb.de/gesellschaft/migration/dossier-migration-ALT/56351/zuwanderungsges etz-2005

Schneider, Stephanie. 2019. 'Becoming a Decision-Maker, or: "Don't Turn Your Heart into a Den of Thieves and Murderers"', in Nick Gill and Anthony Good (eds) *Asylum Determination in Europe*. Cham: Springer International Publishing, pp 285–306.

Schnuck, Oliver, and Robert Schöffel. 2017. 'Diskriminierung auf dem Mietmarkt: Ausländer unerwünscht', June. https://interaktiv.br.de/hanna-und-ismail/

Schroeder, Matt. 2014. 'Fire and Forget: The Proliferation of Man-Portable Air Defence Systems in Syria'. Number 9. Issue Brief. Geneva: Small Arms Survey.

Schuler, Katharina, and Sören Götz. 2018. 'Masterplan: Bleiben noch 62 potenzielle Streitpunkte'. *Die Zeit*, 5 July. https://www.zeit.de/politik/deut schland/2018-07/masterplan-horst-seehofer-asyl-migration-fluechtlinge

Schütz, Alfred. 1944. 'The Stranger: An Essay in Social Psychology'. *American Journal of Sociology* 49(6): 499–507. https://doi.org/10.1086/219472.

Schütz, Alfred, and Thomas Luckmann. 1973. *The Structures of the Life World*. Translated by J. Tristam Engelhardt Jr and Richard M. Zaner. Evanston, IL: Northwestern University Press.

Schuller, Karin, Susanne Lochner and Nina Rother. 2011. *Das Integrationspanel: Ergebnisse einer Längsschnittstudie zur Wirksamkeit und Nachhaltigkeit von Integrationskursen*. Nuremberg: Bundesamt für Migration und Flüchtlinge (BAMF).

Scott, James C. 1998. *Seeing Like a State: How Certain Schemes to Improve the Human Condition Have Failed*. New Haven: Yale University Press.

Scott, Penelope. 2018. ' "It's Like Fighting for Survival": How Rejected Black African Asylum Seekers Experience Living Conditions in an Eastern German State'. *Journal of Immigrant & Refugee Studies* 16(4): 372–90. https://doi.org/10.1080/15562948.2017.1316534

Sigona, Nando. 2014. 'The Politics of Refugee Voices', in Elena Fiddian-Qasmiyeh, Gil Loescher, Katy Long, and Nando Sigona (eds) *The Oxford Handbook of Refugee and Forced Migration Studies*. Oxford: Oxford University Press.

Sigona, Nando. 2018. 'The Contested Politics of Naming in Europe's "Refugee Crisis"'. *Ethnic and Racial Studies* 41(3): 456–60. https://doi.org/10.1080/01419870.2018.1388423

Sim, Amanda, Mina Fazel, Lucy Bowes and Frances Gardner. 2018. 'Pathways Linking War and Displacement to Parenting and Child Adjustment: A Qualitative Study with Syrian Refugees in Lebanon'. *Social Science & Medicine* 200: 19–26. https://doi.org/10.1016/j.socscimed.2018.01.009

Simonsen, Kristina Bakkær. 2016. 'How the Host Nation's Boundary Drawing Affects Immigrants' Belonging'. *Journal of Ethnic and Migration Studies* 42(7): 1153–76. https://doi.org/10.1080/1369183X.2016.1138854

Simonsen, Kristina Bakkær. 2018. 'What It Means to (Not) Belong: A Case Study of How Boundary Perceptions Affect Second-Generation Immigrants' Attachments to the Nation'. *Sociological Forum* 33(1): 118–38. https://doi.org/10.1111/socf.12402

Söhn, Janina. 2013. 'Unequal Welcome and Unequal Life Chances: How the State Shapes Integration Opportunities of Immigrants'. *European Journal of Sociology* 54(2): 295–326. https://doi.org/10.1017/S0003975613000155

Sökefeld, Martin. 1999. 'Debating Self, Identity, and Culture in Anthropology'. *Current Anthropology* 40(4): 417–48. https://doi.org/10.1086/200042

Sökefeld, Martin. 2004. 'Das Paradigma kultureller Differenz: Zur Forschung und Diskussion über Migranten aus der Türkei in Deutschland', in Martin Sökefeld (ed) *Jenseits des Paradigmas kultureller Differenz*. Bielefeld: transcript Verlag. https://doi.org/10.14361/9783839402290-002.

Sökefeld, Martin. 2006. 'Mobilizing in Transnational Space: A Social Movement Approach to the Formation of Diaspora'. *Global Networks* 6(3): 265–84. https://doi.org/10.1111/j.1471-0374.2006.00144.x

Sökefeld, Martin (ed). 2015. *Spaces of Conflict in Everyday Life: Perspectives across Asia*. Kultur Und Soziale Praxis. Bielefeld: Transcript.

Sökefeld, Martin. 2016. *Crossroads Studies and the State: Anthropological Perspectives*. Working Papers in Social and Cultural Anthropology. Vol. 20. Crossroads Asia. LMU Munich.

Sökefeld, Martin. 2017. 'Between Humanitarian and Political Realism: Anthropological Perspective on the Refugee Crisis in Germany'. *NUST Journal of International Peace & Stabiility* 1(1): 72–85.

Sökefeld, Martin, and Sabine Strasser. 2016. 'Introduction: Under Suspicious Eyes – Surveillance States, Security Zones and Ethnographic Fieldwork'. *Zeitschrift für Ethnologie* 141: 159–76.

Sontag, Susan. 2005. *On Photography*. New York: RosettaBooks.

Soysal, Yasemin Nuhoğlu. 2012. 'Citizenship, Immigration, and the European Social Project: Rights and Obligations of Individuality'. *British Journal of Sociology* 63(1): 1–21. https://doi.org/10.1111/j.1468-4446.2011.01404.x

Sozialreferat München. 2017. *Münchner Gesamtplan zur Integration von Flüchtlingen*. Munich: Landeshauptstadt München.

Spivak, Gayatri Chakravorty. 1994. 'Can the Subaltern Speak?' In *Colonial Discourse and Post-colonial Theory: A Reader*. New York: Columbia University Press, pp 66–111.

Spivak, Gayatri Chakravorty. 2019. 'Initial Employment Pathways of Immigrants in Germany. Why Legal Contexts of Reception Matter: An Analysis of Life-Course Data'. *Transfer: European Review of Labour and Research* 25(1): 43–62. https://doi.org/10.1177/1024258918818069

Strotmann, Harald, Martin Rosemann, Sabine Dann and Christine Hamacher. 2011. 'Stärken und Schwächen integrierter und spezialisierter Modelle der Kundenbetreuung im SGB II'. *Sozialer Fortschritt* 60(9): 203–9. https://doi.org/10.3790/sfo.60.9.203

Steinmetz, George. 1993. *Regulating the Social. The Welfare State and Local Politics in Imperial Germany*. Princeton: Princeton University Press.

Stukenberg, Timo. 2017. 'Flüchtlinge: Gemeinschaftsunterkünfte Behindern Integration'. *Die Welt*, 16 October. https://www.welt.de/finanzen/imm obilien/article169666950/Fluechtlinge-sind-im-teuren-Fehlbeleger-Sta tus-gefangen.html

Süddeutsche Zeitung. 2016. 'Vom Asylbewerber zum Obdachlosen'. *Süddeutsche.de*, 4 July. https://www.sueddeutsche.de/muenchen/unterb ringung-vom-asylbewerber-zum-obdachlosen-1.3062905

SVR. 2019. *Bewegte Zeiten: Rückblick auf eie Integrations- und Migrationspolitik der letzten Jahre*. Berlin: Sachverständigenrat deutscher Stiftungen für Integration und Migration.

Szczepanikova, Alice. 2010. 'Performing Refugeeness in the Czech Republic: Gendered Depoliticisation through NGO Assistance'. *Gender, Place & Culture* 17(4): 461–77. https://doi.org/10.1080/0966369X.2010.485838

Taylor, Charles. 2004. *Modern Social Imaginaries*. Durham, NC: Duke University Press.

Tazzioli, Martina. 2018. 'The Temporal Borders of Asylum: Temporality of Control in the EU Border Regime'. *Political Geography* 64: 13–22. https://doi.org/10.1016/j.polgeo.2018.02.002

Tegeler, Hartwig. 2016. '100 hier – 1000 da – Wie die Flüchtlinge das Dorf Sumte verändert haben'. *Deutschlandfunk Kultur*, 7 October. https://www.deutschlandfunkkultur.de/100-hier-1000-da-wie-die-fluechtlinge-das-dorf-sumte.1076.de.html?dram:article_id=359662

Thränhardt, Dietrich. 2014. 'Europäische Abschottung und deutscher Asylstau: Gibt es Wege aus dem Dilemma?' *Zeitschrift für Ausländerrecht und Ausländerpolitik (ZAR)* 34(5–6): 177–212.

Thränhardt, Dietrich. 2016. 'Speed and Quality: What Germany Can Learn from Switzerland's Asylum Procedure'. Program Integration and Education. Gütersloh: Bertelsmann Stiftung.

Thränhardt, Dietrich, and Karin Weiss. 2017. 'Flüchtlingspolitik im deutschen Föderalismus'. Gute gesellschaft--Soziale Democratie. Friedrich-Ebert-Stiftung (FES).

Thym, Daniel. 2018. 'Beyond the "Welcome Culture": Projects of the New German Government on Migration, Asylum and Integration – EU Immigration and Asylum Law and Policy'. *EU Immigration and Asylum Law and Policy*, 9 March. http://eumigrationlawblog.eu/beyond-the-welcome-culture-projects-of-the-new-german-government-on-migration-asylum-and-integration

Treiber, Magnus. 2013. 'Lessons for Life: Two Migratory Portraits from Eritrea', in Alessandro Triulzi and Robert McKenzie (eds) *Long Journeys: African Migrants on the Road*. Leiden: Brill, pp 187–212.

Treiber, Magnus. 2014. 'Grasp Ing Kiflu's Fear – Informality and Existentialism in Migration from North-East Africa'. *Modern Africa: Politics, History and Society* 1(2): 111–41.

Treiber, Magnus. 2016. 'Informality and Informalization among Eritrean Refugees: Why Migration Does Not Provide a Lesson in Democracy'. In *Handbook of Research on Transitional Justice and Peace Building in Turbulent Regions*, edited by Fredy Cante and Hartmut Quehl. IGI Global, pp 158–80. https://doi.org/10.4018/978-1-4666-9675-4

Tsianos, Vassilis, and Serhat Karakayali. 2010. 'Transnational Migration and the Emergence of the European Border Regime: An Ethnographic Analysis'. *European Journal of Social Theory* 13(3): 373–87. https://doi.org/10.1177/1368431010371761

Tuckett, Anna. 2015. 'Strategies of Navigation: Migrants' Everyday Encounters with Italian Immigration Bureaucracy'. *Cambridge Journal of Anthropology* 33(1). https://doi.org/10.3167/ca.2015.330109

Tuckett, Anna. 2016. 'Moving on: Italy as a Stepping Stone in Migrants' Imaginaries'. *Focaal* 2016(76): 99–113. https://doi.org/10.3167/fcl.2016.760107

Tuckett, Anna. 2018. *Rules, Paper, Status: Migrants and Precarious Bureaucracy in Contemporary Italy.* Stanford: Stanford University Press.

UNHCR. 2016. 'Regional Refugee and Migration Response Plan for Europe: Eastern Mediterranean and Western Balkans Route'. Office of the United Nations High Commissioner for Refugees, 2016.

UNHCR. 2019. 'Desperate Journeys: Refugees and Migrants Arriving in Europe and at Europe's Borders, Janurary–December 2018'.. https://data2.unhcr.org/en/documents/download/67712#_ga=2.53697582.705708 646.1551689118-457777474.1551689118

Vertovec, Steven. 2007. 'Super-Diversity and Its Implications'. *Ethnic and Racial Studies* 30(6): 1024–54. https://doi.org/10.1080/0141987070 1599465

Vollmer, Bastian, and Serhat Karakayali. 2018. 'The Volatility of the Discourse on Refugees in Germany'. *Journal of Immigrant & Refugee Studies* 16(1–2): 118–39. https://doi.org/10.1080/15562948.2017.1288284

von Einem, Eberhard. 2017. *Wohnungen für Flüchtlinge: Aktuelle Sozial- und Integrations-politisch Herausforderung in Deutschland.* Wiesbaden: Springer.

Vigh, Henrik. 2006. *Navigating Terrains of War: Youth and Soldiering in Guinea-Bissau.* New York: Berghahn Books.

Vigh, Henrik. 2010. 'Youth Mobilisation as Social Navigation: Reflections on the Concept of Dubriagem'. *Cadernos de Estudos Africanos* 18/19: 140–64. https://doi.org/10.4000/cea.110

Wacquant, Loic J.D. 1998. 'Negative Social Capital: State Breakdown and Social Destitution in America's Urban Core'. *Netherlands Journal of Housing and the Built Environment* 13(1): 25–40.

Weaver, Matthew. 2010. 'Angela Merkel: German Multiculturalism Has "Utterly Failed"'. *The Guardian*, 17 October. https://www.theguardian.com/world/2010/oct/17/angela-merkel-german-multiculturalism-failed

Wendel, Kay. 2014. *Unterbringung von Flüchtlingen in Deutschland: Regelungen und Praxis der Bundesländer im Vergleich.* Frankfurt am Main: Pro Asyl.

Werner, Christian, and Tarek Khello. 2016. 'Das Geschäft der Schwarzmakler – Wie Flüchtlinge am Wohnungsmarkt betrogen werden'. *Deutschlandfunk*, 16 December. https://www.deutschlandfunk.de/das-geschaeft-der-schwar zmakler-wie-fluechtlinge-am.724.de.html?dram:article_id=374158

Westdeutscher Handwerkskammertag. 2014. *Die Qualifikationsanalyse – Das Verfahren zur Analyse und Festellung von Berufsqualifkationen im Rahmen von Anerkennungsverfahren.* Düsseldorf: Deutscher Handwerkskammertag.

Wiesner, Claudia. 2018. *Multi-level-Governance und lokale Demokratie.* Wiesbaden: Springer Fachmedien Wiesbaden.

Will, Anne-Kathrin. 2019. 'The German Statistical Category "Migration Background": Historical Roots, Revisions and Shortcomings'. *Ethnicities* 19(3): 535–57. https://doi.org/10.1177/1468796819833437

Will, Anne-Kathrin, and Magdalena Nowicka. 2021. *'Der "Migrationshintergrund' und seine Fallstricke wie weiter in der interkulturellen Öffnung des öffentlichen Dienstes in Deutschland?'* WiSo Direkt. Bonn: Freidrich Ebert Stiftung.

Williams, Helen. 2014. 'Changing the National Narrative: Evolution in Citizenship and Integration in Germany, 2000–10'. *Journal of Contemporary History* 49(1): 54–74. https://doi.org/10.1177/0022009413505658

Woellert, Franziska, Stephan Sievert and Nina Neubecker. 2016. *'An die Arbeit Wie lokale Initiativen zur Integration von Flüchtlingen in den Arbeitsmarkt beitragen können'.* Stiftung Berlin-Institut für Bevölkerung und Entwicklung.

Woltin, Karl-Andrew, Kai Sassenberg and Nihan Albayrak. 2018. 'Regulatory Focus, Coping Strategies and Symptoms of Anxiety and Depression: A Comparison between Syrian Refugees in Turkey and Germany'. *PLOS ONE* 13(10): e0206522. https://doi.org/10.1371/journal.pone.0206522

Worbs, Susanne, Eva Bund and Axel Böhm. 2016. *'Asyl – und Dann? Die Lebenssituation von Asylberechtigten und anerkannten Flüchtlingen in Deutschland BAMF-Flüchtlingsstudie 2014'.* Forschungsbericht 28. Bundesamt für Migration und Flüchtlinge.

Xenia, Frei, and Jan Kluge. 2016. 'Die Wohnsitzauflage als kostspielige Integrationsbremse für Flüchtlinge'. *ifo Dresden berichtet* 23(6): 30–4.

Xiang, Biao. 2013. 'Multi-Scalar Ethnography: An Approach for Critical Engagement with Migration and Social Change'. *Ethnography* 14(3): 282–99. https://doi.org/10.1177/1466138113491669

Zeit Online. 2015. 'Kassel-Calden: Viele Verletzte bei Massenschlägerei unter Flüchtlingen'. *Die Zeit,* 28 September. https://www.zeit.de/gesellschaft/zeitgeschehen/2015-09/kassel-calden-fluechtlinge-schlaegerei

Zeit Online. 2020. 'BAMF-Skandal: Landgericht Bremen prüft Anklage gegen frühere BAMF-Chefin'. *Die Zeit,* 12 January. https://www.zeit.de/politik/deutschland/2020-01/bamf-skandal-landgericht-bremen-anklage-pruefung

Zetter, Roger. 2007. 'More Labels, Fewer Refugees: Remaking the Refugee Label in an Era of Globalization'. *Journal of Refugee Studies* 20(2): 172–92. https://doi.org/10.1093/jrs/fem011

Zimmermann, Susan E. 2011. 'Reconsidering the Problem of "Bogus" Refugees with "Socio-economic Motivations" for Seeking Asylum'. *Mobilities* 6(3): 335–52. https://doi.org/10.1080/17450101.2011.590034

Zuwanderungs- und Integrationsbüro (ZIB). 2014. *Erster Integrationsbericht für Saarbrücken.* Saarbrücken: Landeshauptstadt Saarbrücken.

Index

References to endnotes show both the page number and the note number (231n3).